Praise for
Your Retirement Sketchbook

"It's been said that a picture is worth a thousand words, and in this visual 'sketchbook' Jamie and Bonnie have crafted more than a hundred (125, to be exact) images of a wide array of retirement-related topics and perspectives; visual insights that can both clarify and demystify the complexities that too often stand between 'regular' folks and a workable plan for a comfortable retirement. Both interactive and instructive, in these pages you'll find dozens of valuable touchpoints that can help you make sense of the nonsense from two of the industry's most relatable experts."

—**Nevin Adams, Former Chief Content Officer for the American Retirement Association**

"*Your Retirement Sketchbook* stands out in a sea of retirement-planning guides because it treats retirement as the beginning of the journey, not the end. I was inspired by its approach and readers will be, too."

—**Christine Benz, Director of Personal Finance and Retirement Planning, Morningstar, and Author,** *How to Retire*

"*Your Retirement Sketchbook* is aptly named—it provides a very brief, and therefore very accessible, introductory overview of everything you need to consider as you approach retirement. The book's breezy, informal style shows you the topics—giving you just enough depth to let you pursue each topic with everyone from your spouse to your financial advisor to your therapist. It's a handy, valuable tool."

—**Ric Edelman, Author,** *The Truth About College*

"Retirement isn't an equation to be solved. It's a story to be lived. This book reminds us that life after work is not an end, but rather the beginning of something deeply human. *Your Retirement Sketchbook* helps readers align their finances with their values and their time with what truly matters. Practical, thoughtful, and full of heart, it transforms retirement from a financial finish line into a meaningful new chapter."

**—Dr. Daniel Crosby, Psychologist
and Author, *The Soul of Wealth***

"*Your Retirement Sketchbook* offers readers a useful overview of the many interconnected decisions retirees face—from Social Security timing to healthcare, taxes, legacy planning, and finding your passion. For readers looking for a broad, accessible starting point on retirement planning, this book will introduce you to the key issues to explore."

**—Wade Pfau, Ph.D., CFA, RICP, Author,
*Retirement Planning Guidebook***

"This book brings the human side of retirement planning to life. Hopkins and Treichel use behavioral insight and hands-on exercises to help readers connect financial goals with personal meaning."

**—Eric Ludwig, PhD, CFP®, RICP® CEO,
Stockbridge Private Wealth Management**

YOUR RETIREMENT SKETCHBOOK

HARRIMAN HOUSE LTD
3 Viceroy Court
Bedford Road
Petersfield
Hampshire
GU32 3LJ
GREAT BRITAIN
Tel: +44 (0)1730 233870

Email: enquiries@harriman-house.com
Website: harriman.house

First published in 2026 by Harriman House, an imprint of Pan Macmillan
EU Representative: Macmillan Publishers Ireland Ltd, 1st Floor, The Liffey Trust Centre, 117-126 Sheriff Street Upper, Dublin 1, D01 YC43
Associated companies throughout the world
www.panmacmillan.com

Copyright © Jamie P. Hopkins and Bonnie Treichel 2026

The right of Jamie P. Hopkins and Bonnie Treichel to be identified as the authors has been asserted in accordance with the Copyright, Design and Patents Act 1988.

Paperback ISBN: 978-1-80409-195-1
eBook ISBN: 978-1-80409-196-8

British Library Cataloguing in Publication Data
A CIP catalogue record for this book can be obtained from the British Library.

All rights reserved. No part of this publication may be reproduced, stored in a retrieval system, or transmitted in any form or by any means (including without limitation electronic, mechanical, photocopying, recording, or otherwise) without the prior written permission of the publisher. This book is sold subject to the condition that it shall not, by way of trade or otherwise, be lent, hired out, or otherwise circulated without the publisher's prior consent. This work is reserved from text and data mining (Article 4(3) Directive (EU) 2019/790).

Harriman House does not have any control over, or any responsibility for, any author or third-party websites (including without limitation URLs, emails and QR codes) referred to in or on this book. This book is for informational purposes only. Readers are advised to consult an appropriate professional in light of their relevant circumstances and requirements before acting on any information in this book.

No responsibility or liability for loss occasioned to any person or corporate body acting or refraining to act as a result of reading material in this book can be accepted by the publisher, by the authors, or by the employers of the authors.

Cover design by Tata Wijana.

Printed and bound by CPI Group (UK) Ltd.

YOUR RETIREMENT SKETCHBOOK

125 Retirement Planning Lessons from Financial Experts

JAMIE HOPKINS &
BONNIE TREICHEL

CONTENTS

Introduction	**1**
Chapter I. Your Relationship with Money	**5**
Introduction	7
1. Rewirement	12
2. Success is Not a Straight Path	14
3. Money: A Means to an End	16
4. Understand Your Why	18
5. Money Memories	20
6. Why Spending Feels Like Loss	22
7. Behavioral Biases in Retirement Decision-Making	24
8. Get Connected with Future You	26
9. Balancing Today and Tomorrow	28
Chapter II. Saving for Retirement	**33**
Introduction	35
10. Defined Benefit Plans	38
11. Defined Contribution Plans	40
12. Matching Contributions	42
13. Retirement Plan Loans	44
14. Retirement Plan Hardships	46
15. Emergency Withdrawals from Retirement Plans	48

16. Student Loan Matching	50
17. Retirement Account Rollovers	52
18. Auto Portability	54
19. Individual Retirement Accounts	56
20. Health Savings Accounts: Triple Tax Benefits	58
21. Roth Tax Treatment	60
22. Roth Versus Traditional	62
23. Social Security Funding	64

Chapter III. Investing for Retirement — 69

Introduction	71
24. Investing in Retirement	74
25. The Power of Compound Interest	76
26. Bond Ladders	78
27. Target Date Funds	80
28. Digital Assets	82
29. Alternative Investments	84
30. Survivor Bias	86
31. Home Bias	88
32. Sustainable Investing	90
33. Annuities	92
34. Life Insurance in Retirement	94
35. LTCI and Hybrid Policies	96
36. Cash Value Life Insurance as an Income Tool	98
37. Capital Gains Strategies in Retirement	100
38. Working with an Advisor	102

Chapter IV. Getting Ready to Retire — 107

Introduction — 109
39. Envision Your Future — 112
40. Retirement Preparedness — 114
41. Retirement Confidence — 116
42. Going Beyond Goals to Aspirations — 118
43. Issue with Averages in Retirement — 120
44. Pay Yourself First — 122
45. Planning Through the Decades — 124
46. Paycheck Replacement — 126
47. The Retirement Change — 128
48. Retirement Change Management — 130
49. Part-Time Work in Retirement — 132
50. Retire To or Retire From — 134
51. Forced Retirement — 136
52. Phased Retirement — 138
53. Retirement Planning for Couples Versus Singles — 140

Chapter V. Preparing Your Retirement Income Plan — 145

Introduction — 147
54. Retirement Income Planning — 150
55. Value of Lifetime Income — 152
56. What is Retirement Income? — 154
57. Mortality Credits — 156
58. Your Retirement Income Picture — 158
59. Bucketing Approach — 160
60. Flooring Approach — 162
61. Retirement Risks — 164

62. Tax Diversification	166
63. Roth Conversions	168
64. Retirement Planning for Small Business Owners	170

Chapter VI. Managing Retirement Income — 175

Introduction	177
65. Public Policy Risk	180
66. Taxes in Retirement	182
67. Knowledge in Retirement	184
68. When to Retire?	186
69. Power of Delaying Retirement	188
70. Guardrails	190
71. Adaptive Spending	192
72. Smart Income	194
73. When to Claim Social Security	196
74. Taxation of Social Security	198
75. Power of Delaying Social Security	200
76. Rule 72(t) Penalty Taxes	202
77. Permission to Spend	204
78. Traveling in Retirement	206
79. IRMAA	208
80. RMDs	210
81. Reverse Mortgages	212
82. Tapping Home Equity in Retirement	214
83. Lines of Credit	216
84. Navigating Sequence Risk	218
85. Time Segmentation	220
86. Retirement Planning Checkups	222

Chapter VII. Living in Retirement — 227

Introduction — 229

87. Retirement is Not Binary — 232
88. Stop Saving Right Before Retirement — 234
89. Retirement Housing — 236
90. Downsizing in Retirement — 238
91. Managing Debt in Retirement — 240
92. Continuing Care Retirement Communities — 242
93. Inflation — 244
94. The Four Percent Finding — 246
95. Learn Everything You Can — 248
96. Changing Your Identity — 250
97. Silver Divorce — 252
98. Social Network in Retirement — 254
99. Changing Interest Rates — 256
100. Refilling Buckets — 258
101. Medicare — 260
102. Aging in Place — 262
103. Aging and Frailty — 264
104. Health is Wealth — 266
105. Long-Term Caregivers — 268
106. Cognitive Decline and Financial Decision-Making — 270
107. Pet Care and Planning in Retirement — 272
108. Second Careers — 274
109. Finding Meaning in Retirement — 276

Chapter VIII. When Finality Becomes Reality — 281

Introduction	283
110. Estate Planning Basics	288
111. The Digital Afterlife	290
112. Digital Estate Planning Process	292
113. Inherited Accounts	294
114. Trusts: Revocable Versus Irrevocable	296
115. Prepare for a Good End of Life	298
116. Medicaid Spend Down	300
117. Long-Term Care Delivery	302
118. Longevity	304
119. Elder Abuse	306
120. Medicaid	308
121. Leaving a Legacy	310
122. Giving Back: Charitable Giving	312
123. Qualified Charitable Distributions	314
124. Giving to Grandchildren	316
125. The G3 Summit	318

Conclusion — 323
Endnotes — 327
Acknowledgments — 337
About the Authors — 339

INTRODUCTION

Have you ever found yourself standing in a room, wondering how you got there and why you're there in the first place? Were you looking for the remote, your shoes, your keys? Maybe you went in to clean something or to ask someone a question? But now, as you stand there, you've forgotten not only why you came in but also how you ended up there. You rack your brain, trying to remember that one small detail that explains your entire current situation.

Eventually, you either remember what brought you there and accomplish your goal—or you don't, and you have to move on with a new plan.

This feeling—being lost in a familiar space—is something many Americans relate to when they enter retirement. They find themselves asking: How did I get here? What was I supposed to do? What's my purpose? What's next? Sometimes we dismiss these moments as a product of busyness, overwhelm, or forgetfulness. But, in truth, when we know our "why"—when we examine what drives us and fill our lives with purpose—we're less likely to forget why we do what we do.

Now, imagine that feeling of standing in a room and not remembering why you went there. Imagine feeling that way every day… for 30 years… for the entire duration of your retirement. That would be daunting and disorienting.

Instead, picture a time when you finished a long hike, crossed a race's finish line, finalized that beautiful painting you've been working on, or completed a meaningful journey. Think about that sense of accomplishment, of being exactly where you were meant to be.

Retirement can feel like either scenario: standing in a room with no purpose or arriving at the finish line of a joyful, fulfilling journey.

That's why we created *Your Retirement Sketchbook*—to help you envision what retirement might look like for you. Everyone's retirement is different—location, timing, length, activities, finances, health, family, and goals all vary—so no single plan can be written in stone. Even for one individual, retirement is dynamic; it evolves over time. So too should your planning.

There are no commandments or universal laws for retirement. Instead, there are rules of thumb, best practices, and helpful guides. The path is yours.

That's why thinking of retirement as a sketch is so powerful. Instead of aiming for perfection, consider it a flexible, evolving outline—something you can redraw as your desires and circumstances change. Retirement should be fun, not just a series of numbers in a rigid financial plan. It shouldn't be reduced to a spreadsheet or a Monte Carlo simulation predicting the statistical likelihood of success. Retirement is something to be lived and enjoyed.

This sketchbook will walk you through the many dynamic phases leading up to and during retirement. It will help you to explore:

- Your relationship with money
- Saving for retirement
- Investing for retirement
- Getting ready to retire
- Preparing your retirement income plan
- Managing retirement income
- Living in retirement
- When finality becomes a reality.

We take a modular approach—breaking this long span of life, from your first savings to your final days, into manageable sections. Since not every topic applies to every person, you can pick and choose which elements matter most to your unique retirement sketch. *Your Retirement*

INTRODUCTION

Sketchbook introduces 125 unique topics you may face in retirement. By exploring these one by one, you can begin to sketch what your retirement will look like. But it should stay a sketch—because the story won't truly be written until you live it.

And because retirement should be engaging and enjoyable, we've incorporated artistic elements into this book—along with space for you to draw, write, or reflect on key questions. This isn't a textbook or a lecture; it's meant to spark inspiration for your own journey.

Your retirement can follow the arc of the hero's journey. You begin with your past experiences, likely unprepared for what lies ahead. Along the way, you'll need guidance, but, eventually, you must walk your own path—overcoming challenges, celebrating victories, and finding meaning in the process. You'll face unique hurdles, but you'll also encounter moments of joy and wonder that no one else will.

This journey will be yours alone. No one else can plan it or live it for you. Map your journey with *Your Retirement Sketchbook*!

CHAPTER 1

YOUR RELATIONSHIP WITH MONEY

- Rewirement
- Success is Not a Straight Path
- Money: A Means to an End
- Understand Your Why
- Money Memories
- Why Spending Feels Like Loss
- Behavioral Biases in Retirement Decision-Making
- Get Connected with Future You
- Balancing Today and Tomorrow

CHAPTER I.
Introduction

Welcome to *Your Retirement Sketchbook*, a place where we do more than just crunch numbers. This is where we pause to reflect, explore, and sketch the life you want to live—not just the one you can afford. This journey isn't only about financial calculations; it's about transformation. It's about rewirement—a rethinking of purpose, value, and what "enough" looks like for the next chapter of your life.

You've probably heard the phrase, "Money doesn't buy happiness." But in retirement, money absolutely shapes your freedom, security, and ability to live life on your terms. The challenge is that we rarely make purely rational decisions about money. Instead, we make deeply personal ones, shaped by decades of experience, upbringing, habits, fear, hope, and emotion.

Before we can plan a purposeful and fulfilling retirement, we need to look back. Understanding your relationship with money is a critical first step to designing a future that's not only financially stable but also emotionally satisfying.

Your money story

Every person has a "money story"—a mental narrative built from childhood, early jobs, family values, culture, and past financial wins or regrets. Maybe you grew up in a home where money was tight, and every dollar was stretched. Or maybe money was never discussed—a silent, stressful subject. Maybe you received strong financial guidance early on, or maybe you've been figuring it out on your own, piece by piece.

Take a moment to reflect:

- What is your earliest memory of money?
- Was it a source of comfort or conflict?
- How did your parents talk about money (if they did at all)?
- What financial decision are you most proud of?
- Which one still keeps you up at night?

These memories don't disappear with time—they linger in our subconscious and subtly influence our financial behavior. In retirement, they can either empower or sabotage your decisions.

Why behavioral biases matter

As humans, we are wired with cognitive shortcuts—mental rules of thumb—that helped our ancestors survive. But in today's complex financial world, these behavioral biases often lead us astray.

Let's look at a few that often show up in retirement planning:

Loss Aversion: We tend to feel the pain of losing money more than the joy of gaining it. That's why some retirees hoard cash, even when it's eroded by inflation.
Present Bias: We focus on short-term gratification over long-term benefits, which can lead to overspending early in retirement or delaying saving in our working years.
Home Bias: We favor investments or financial decisions rooted in our own country or familiar environment. This bias can limit growth potential and increase risk by concentrating exposure in a single economy.
Overconfidence: We might overestimate how long we can work, how well we manage money, or how much we truly need.

Recognizing these biases is not about shame—it's about awareness. Once you know how your brain may be tricking you, you can start making more conscious, informed choices.

From fear to flexibility

A client once told me, "I'm afraid to spend any of my retirement money. I grew up poor, and I don't trust that it'll last." Despite having more than enough saved, this deep-seated fear of scarcity held her back from traveling, gifting, or even turning on the air conditioning in summer or the heat in the winter. She could never give herself permission to spend. So most of our conversations were not about taxes or investment ideas, but instead about life—about spending, about what she enjoyed, and reinforcing that she was okay financially.

Another had the opposite story: "My dad died young, so I want to live while I can." Well, this is more of my story. My dad passed away in a job-site accident when I was eight years old. This has impacted so many things in my life—my desire to be a dad, a sense I would die early, a fear of heights, and a scarcity mindset for years around money. But it also told me to prepare—have life insurance, hug my loved ones close, and make sure I live life to the fullest because it is a temporary and beautiful thing.

Both stories are valid. Both are rooted in emotion. And both required a shift—not in dollars, but in mindset. Retirement planning isn't just about managing money. It's about navigating feelings of uncertainty, abundance, legacy, and identity.

Start with grace and gratitude

In this sketchbook, you'll be invited to draw your own retirement—in goals, in values, in numbers, and in aspirations. But before any of that, we start with self-compassion. Your money journey is unique. You are not just a spreadsheet. You are a human being shaped by experience. But do not forget to give others grace when they approach life differently than you do. Think about spouses and family members not as having walked the same path as you but as travelers that saw a different road than you. Don't immediately go to judgment when they behave differently around money than you do. Instead show some grace for their beliefs and gratitude for your own.

So before we dive into planning, take a moment to sketch this:

- What are three money beliefs you currently hold?
- Which ones serve you?
- Which ones might be holding you back?
- What would financial peace look like in retirement?

Understanding who we were and our experiences allows us to better understand who we will become. Since retirement planning is about planning for the future, this is a crucial step in building out your retirement sketchbook. Make it real. Make it personal. Make it yours.

1. Rewirement

"Retirement isn't just a finish line. It's a starting line for your next great adventure."

CHAPTER 1

Welcome to rewirement: the art of flipping the switch from saving to spending, from clocking in to checking out, and from a life built around work to a life built around purpose.

Think about it: After decades of budgeting, investing, and chasing the elusive "average rate of return," now it's time to reverse the flow. This is your moment to spend smart, live large, and finally enjoy what you've worked so hard for. But be warned: Shifting from saver to spender isn't just a financial change. It requires some mental rewiring.

About 60% of retirees say they need to reinvent themselves. That's not a midlife crisis, that's a retirement awakening.

Why? Because work gave us structure. So did the kids' soccer practices and school calendars. But in retirement, the calendar flips… and suddenly, every day is a Saturday. Sounds great, right? Until it feels like every day is also a Monday. Without routine, some retirees feel lost. The solution? Create your own rhythm. It's time to travel, to volunteer, or to learn something new. You might even want to launch that llama farm you joked about for 20 years.

Retirement isn't just about what you're retiring from, it's about what you're retiring to. If you don't rediscover your passion, you might find yourself rich in time but poor in meaning. And no one wants to binge-watch their way through the next 30 years.

And don't forget the practical stuff. Your new life costs money. Whether it's downsizing, relocating, or transforming your garage into a pottery studio, these changes come with price tags. Plan for it. Budget for joy, not just bills.

 What is the biggest thing you will need to rewire in life from your working years to your retirement years?

2. Success is Not a Straight Path

"Retirement success isn't about creating a flawless journey. It's about resilience. Life's setbacks aren't roadblocks; they're stepping stones."

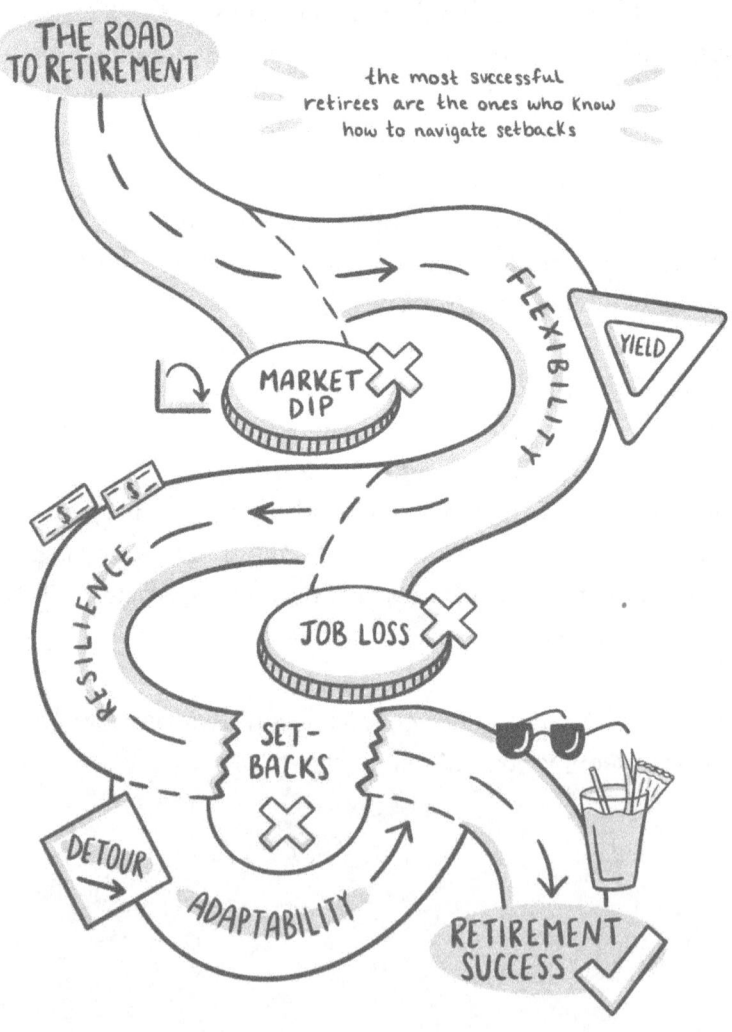

CHAPTER 1

If life came with a guarantee of smooth sailing, we'd all be retired on a beach at 40, sipping iced tea and wondering how to spend our unlimited fortune. But let's be real: More than 50% of successful retirees didn't get there without a few bumps, bruises, and extraordinarily challenging moments along the way.

Maybe you lost a job. Maybe the stock market did that fun thing where it free-falls overnight. Maybe you invested in a "sure thing" that turned out to be… not so sure (looking at you, Beanie Babies collection). Whatever the case, setbacks happen. And guess what? They don't define you—your ability to bounce back does.

Think of life like a road trip. You start off with a full tank and a plan, but sooner or later, you'll hit some unexpected detours. Retirement works the same way. The most successful retirees aren't the ones who never faced setbacks; they're the ones who knew how to navigate them. They adapted, adjusted, and kept moving forward.

When planning for retirement, think of flexibility as your financial shock absorbers. If life throws you a pothole (or three), you don't want your entire plan to fall apart. Building flexibility into your finances—whether that's having a diversified portfolio, an emergency fund, or just the ability to scale back in lean times—can keep you on track even when the unexpected happens.

Whatever the case, retirement isn't about avoiding life's challenges—it's about embracing them, learning from them, and thriving anyway. So, buckle up, stay flexible, and get ready for the next great adventure.

 How have your setbacks shaped the way you think about retirement? How will these life lessons help you navigate unforeseen challenges after you retire?

3. Money: A Means to an End

"Money is a tool, an invention, designed to enable progress. Money is a means to an end, not the end goal itself."

If money were just about numbers, we'd all be obsessing over spreadsheets and hoarding pennies like a dragon guarding the treasure. But many investors see money as so much more—it's a tool to build the life they want, create security, and make an impact. In other words, it's not about stacking cash just for the sake of it—it's about what that cash allows you to do.

So why do so many financial plans focus on some magical number you need to retire, as if hitting that jackpot suddenly makes life perfect? Spoiler alert: It doesn't. What really matters is what you're working toward, not just what's in your bank account.

Think about it: Would you rather have a million dollars with no clear purpose, or just enough money to live the life you actually want? Yes, your money can finance building mansions, but what about building memories? A purposeful, enlightened approach to retirement and spending money will allow you to invest in things you truly care about, while still taking care of all the material things you will need.

That's why the best financial strategy isn't about chasing the highest possible number—it's about making sure your money aligns with your actual goals. Want to travel more? Invest in experiences, not just stocks. Want to leave a legacy? Plan for giving, not just saving. Want peace of mind? Build security, not just wealth. More on each of these topics later in the *Sketchbook*, so start thinking about your goals.

 How does your current financial strategy support your personal and family goals? If it's not aligned, it might be time for a financial refresh—one that puts purpose before profit and meaning before money.

4. Understand Your Why

*"Retirement isn't just about saving money—
it's about saving for something."*

Imagine this: You finally retire, wake up on Day 1, and realize… your calendar is completely empty. No tasks. No schedules. No responsibilities. It all sounds amazing at first, until you eventually find yourself reorganizing the spice rack for fun and bored out of your mind.

Turns out, about 40% of retirees admit they had no clear idea of their goals when they started saving. They focused on the how (saving money) but not the why (what they actually wanted to do with it). Imagine packing for a vacation but not knowing where you are headed. No one wants to wear a swimsuit while climbing an Alaskan glacier.

If you just save money without a clear vision, you might end up in a similar scenario. You can be retired, financially stable, and completely miserable with no clear direction. Retirement is about more than just stopping work. It's about starting something new.

Figuring out what you want that "new retirement lifestyle" to include is a decision you should make long before you actually retire. Once you know where you want to go, you can begin taking the right steps to get there.

Now is a great time to really consider *why* you want to retire. Do you want adventure, travel, and new experiences? Are you dreaming of quiet mornings with a good book? Do you want to start a passion project, volunteer, or even launch a second act?

The clearer you are about your goals, the easier it is to align your financial plan with the life you actually want—not just a generic "retired person" stereotype.

 Do you have a clear idea of why you're retiring and what you'll do with your time? If not, now's the perfect moment to dream big, get specific, and make sure your savings are building a future—not just a bank balance.

5. Money Memories

"Your childhood money memories are the first financial lessons you ever learned. And some lessons were better than others."

CHILDHOOD FINANCIAL LESSONS LIKELY SHAPED HOW YOU THINK ABOUT MONEY TODAY

We can't afford that.
—OR—
treat yourself

BUT YOU CAN REWRITE THOSE OLD MONEY HABITS

CHAPTER 1

Get ready for a wild ride through the treasure trove of your childhood memories—specifically, the ones about money. If you're like most people, your personal finance habits didn't start with spreadsheets, budgeting apps, or visions of stock market success. Nope. They probably began somewhere way earlier—like when you were a kid watching your parents swipe that mysterious plastic card, or when your mom told you, "Money doesn't grow on trees!"

A whopping 80% of adults say their money habits were shaped by their parents. Your childhood money lessons are like the foundation of your financial house—and just like any foundation, it can either be rock solid or a little, well, wobbly. Whether you were raised in a house where you learned to pinch pennies until Abraham Lincoln squeaked, or one where money was treated like an endless fountain, those early money memories probably still linger in the back of your brain.

Were you the kid who heard, "We can't afford that," and internalized it like a financial mantra? Or did you grow up in a household where "Treat yourself!" was the family motto, and every day was a shopping spree? Whatever it was, it's likely shaped the way you think about money today. If you check your bank account balance and instantly reach for a shopping cart, well, that's probably a result of seeing your parents or guardians approach spending that way. On the flip side, if your parents were "savers" to the extreme, you might find yourself hesitating to spend a dime, even when it's well-deserved.

But those early money lessons are not written in stone. Your parents may have had their own financial quirks, but you don't have to inherit them. You have the power to reassess and rewrite those old money scripts. If your childhood involved seeing money as scarce or always being told to "save for a rainy day," you might find it tough to take financial risks. But what if your personal finances could be about finding the right balance between saving and enjoying life's pleasures? Maybe it's time to start seeing the money in your account as a tool for both today and tomorrow.

 What's your earliest memory of money? How did those moments shape the way you handle cash now?

6. Why Spending Feels Like Loss

"I hate losing more than I enjoy winning."

For most of our lives, we received a paycheck. Spending that paycheck was pretty easy… it's how we covered our costs of living. Buying groceries, managing a budget, purchasing basic items—these were simple, everyday tasks.

In retirement, that steady paycheck is no longer arriving every two weeks. Instead, we are often spending money from an investment account. And let's face it, taking money out of an investment account to buy milk and eggs just *feels* different. In fact, it might even make you feel guilty.

On average, people experience financial loss at a rate that is almost 2.5 times more painful than the same amount of financial gain provides pleasure.

Spending our investments or savings can feel like a financial loss as we see our balances go down. In retirement, this spending can be even more painful as our investments might be in a forever cycle of decline or spend down as we use up our financial assets throughout retirement with little hope to replenish them in the future.

Consider thinking about your spending in retirement less like a loss and more like you are paying yourself a paycheck. This simple mindset shift can move you from thinking about spending as money going out of your pocket to money coming into your pocket. Additionally, consider spending some money from your investments or savings pre-retirement to get used to seeing money come out of these accounts.

 Consider a large purchase you might need to make after you retire, like a new roof or new car. Think about how you would pay for this item. Would you spend your investments or retirement savings? Would this feel like a loss? If so, consider how you can practice resetting your mindset.

7. Behavioral Biases in Retirement Decision-Making

"Don't make your retirement planning decisions based on temporary emotions."

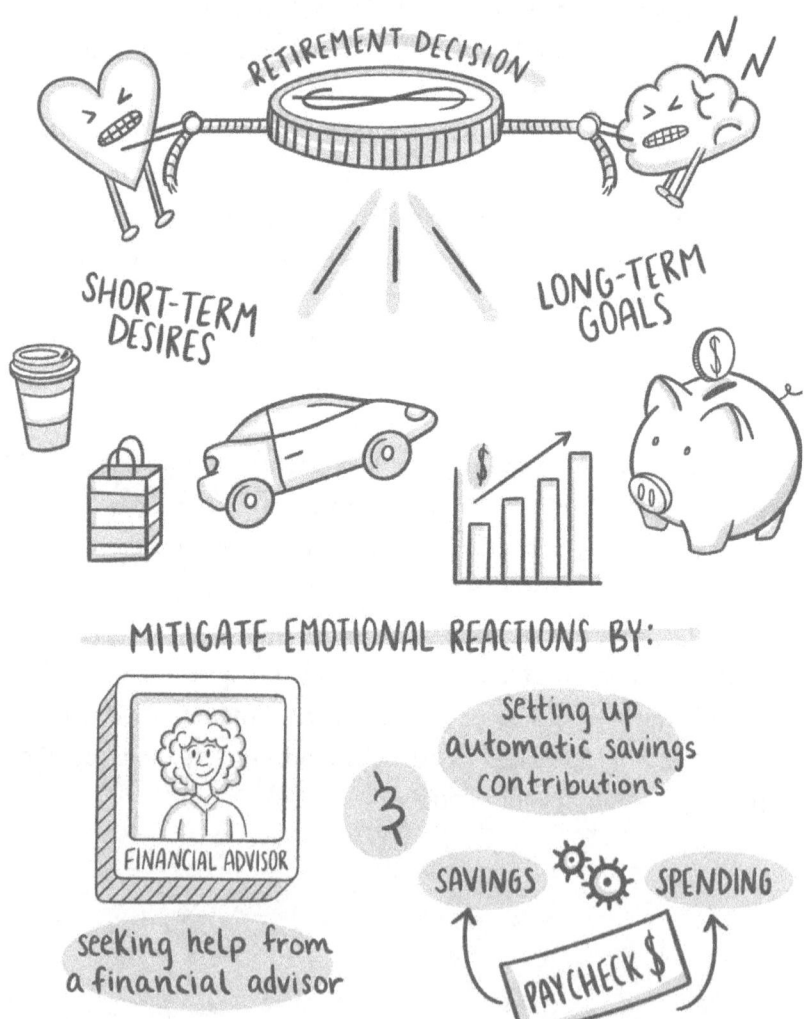

Let's talk about a shocking statistic: 85% of our financial decisions are based on emotions, with only 15% driven by logic. When you think you're making a smart, well-reasoned decision about your finances, it's more likely that you're being led by your emotions than by numbers and math.

It's a little like choosing your dinner based on the sound of the food sizzling in the pan instead of reading the nutritional facts. We often think we're being rational, but when it comes to money, our emotions take the wheel. You'd think with something as technical as money, we'd be all about logic. Instead, our brains are more focused on how we feel about the numbers.

As human beings, we've got a unique mix of emotions and experiences that shape how we make decisions. That's why we sometimes find ourselves prioritizing the now over the later, believing we're invincible (that "I've got plenty of time to save" mindset). We may take on way more risk than we should because we fear losses more than we appreciate gains. When it comes to retirement planning, these emotional decisions can have a huge impact. They can steer us off course and prevent us from making the best long-term choices. Recognizing these biases and how they shape our thinking is crucial.

So, what's the solution? The first step is getting informed and aware of how our emotions influence our financial choices. Seek help from a financial advisor. They can help you navigate the emotional rollercoaster of saving for retirement. Just having someone else provide a rational perspective can help keep you grounded. Automating decisions is another powerful way to mitigate those knee-jerk emotional reactions. Setting up automatic savings contributions, retirement plan deposits, and even bill payments to remove emotion from the equation. So, your future self gets paid first, before those impulsive decisions can sneak in.

> Can you identify a time when a behavioral bias or emotion might have negatively influenced your financial decisions? How about one that might have had a positive impact on your retirement?

8. Get Connected with Future You

"Plan wisely—your future self is counting on you."

Ever met Future You? No? Maybe it's time to officially make an introduction to your future self.

Studies show that the better you know them, the more likely you are to actually save for retirement. And trust me, Future You is going to have opinions about the financial choices Present You is making.

Research shows that people who feel more connected to their future selves are way more likely to save for retirement. In fact, these individuals who feel a strong connection with their future selves save 40% more for their future.

Think about it. Would Future You appreciate that impulse purchase of yet another gadget you don't need? Probably not. But they would appreciate a solid retirement plan that lets them kick back and live their best life (preferably somewhere warm, with an endless supply of good coffee or piña coladas).

So how do we close the gap? Start by making the future feel real. Visualize it. Imagine your 70-year-old self living their best life. Use a retirement calculator. Write a letter to yourself 10 years from now. Heck, try an app that shows you what you'll look like with gray hair and laugh lines. Give your retirement account a name like "Beach House Budget" or "Future Me's Freedom Fund." The more real they feel, the easier it is to plan for them.

It turns out that when you take the time to really picture yourself in the future, you're more likely to make decisions that benefit that version of you. So take a moment. Picture yourself decades from now. Where are you? What are you doing? What do you look like? How can Present You set up Future You for success?

 How well do you know Future You? And, more importantly, are you setting up Future You for retirement luxury?

9. Balancing Today and Tomorrow

"Saving for the future while living in the present is a tightrope walk—steady your balance with smart budgeting, mindful spending, and a little faith in Future You."

CHAPTER I

Ever feel like managing your money is like performing a high-wire act without a safety net? On one side, you've got bills, groceries, rent, and that very necessary daily caffeine fix. On the other side, there's Future You, waving politely from retirement, hoping you've saved enough to afford more than just instant oatmeal and early-bird specials.

The trick? Balance.

Too much focus on the now, and Future You is stuck working until you're 90 years old. Too much focus on retirement, and Present You is living off cereal and wondering if cell phones are technically a luxury.

So how do we find the balance we need? Focus on four financial factors: budget, mindful spending, automated savings, and planning for the future.

Sticking to a smart budget every month will pay dividends for your portfolio. Hopefully, your budget also includes room for savings. If you are also mindful with your spending, you will see your retirement portfolio grow consistently. Before any purchase, you should be deciding if it is a need, a want, or a momentary burst of impulse-buying excitement.

Additionally, the easiest way to grow your portfolio is with automated transfers. Even a small amount each month can have enormous results over time.

Most importantly… always be planning for the future. The more you focus on where you want to be in retirement and think about how you will get there, the better off you will be. Keep that vision in mind—it makes the sacrifices today feel worth it.

✻ What's the hardest part about keeping your financial balance? And are you making moves to keep both Present You and Future You happy?

Your Retirement Notes

Your Retirement Sketches

CHAPTER II
SAVING FOR RETIREMENT

- Defined Benefit Plans
- Defined Contribution Plans
- Matching Contributions
- Retirement Plan Loans
- Retirement Plan Hardships
- Emergency Withdrawals from Retirement Plans
- Student Loan Matching
- Retirement Account Rollovers
- Auto Portability
- Individual Retirement Accounts
- Health Savings Accounts: Triple Tax Benefits
- Roth Tax Treatment
- Roth versus Traditional
- Social Security Funding

CHAPTER II.
Introduction

Do you remember the first opportunity you had to start saving? The image most of us have is a piggy bank sitting on our bedroom dresser. In fact, that's exactly what I had! It was a big, pink, plastic pig, filled to the brim with loose change. My first piggy bank was adorably cute and overflowing with pennies that I thought would clearly make me rich one day.

There was only one problem: That piggy bank didn't offer compounding interest.

Growing up, my parents weren't financial experts. In fact, we followed the rules of etiquette and generally avoided speaking about money, politics, and religion. While it may be polite to avoid these topics, not discussing wealth can lead to some major setbacks. We survived and we always had just enough to get by, but never enough to enjoy life's extravagant luxuries. Those were treasures that my piggy bank could never accommodate.

I did learn that my dad had access to a pension and a 401(k) plan. Again, we didn't talk much about money, and I wasn't one of those kids that learned to start an individual retirement account (or IRA) as soon as I had my first job working at the flower shop when I turned 16. Looking back, I wish I would have, but I wasn't that forward thinking. Instead, I learned a very basic principle from my parents. If you have access to a workplace retirement savings plan—take advantage of it.

And, that's where this chapter begins. We will put a focus on workplace savings. Many of us might not have had the advantage of learning about IRAs or how to have more forward-thinking planning at a young age but that shouldn't discourage you. Workplace retirement savings still present an opportunity to save and it is never too late to start. Earlier is always better and we will talk about the power of compounding in another chapter. This chapter will dive into the difference between the pension (or defined benefit plan) that some people (but now very few people) have and the defined contribution plan (such as a 401(k) plan) that many of us have where we are responsible in large part for our own savings.

Some 401(k) plans offer a lot of flexibility and "bells and whistles" so to speak. Whether you are at a job for a long time or looking for a new job, check out the opportunities available through your workplace retirement plan to ensure you understand everything available to you so that you can take advantage of it.

And, once you leave your job, consider how to keep track of your money. Too often, people lose track of their money, and it may seem like a small amount of a few thousand dollars, but it is rolled into an IRA and consumed by fees. Even a small amount can compound over time and become a larger amount, so keeping track of your money is part of your retirement roadmap.

Now that you have thought about your *why* in retirement, let's get to sketching out your retirement savings plan with the benefits that are available to you at your workplace, which is where most of us start our savings journey. Let's jump in and get a little more technical.

10. Defined Benefit Plans

"In the old days, we used to all have access to a pension."

Over the past few decades, the landscape of retirement planning has drastically changed. Once a common benefit, defined benefit (DB) pension plans—where employers guaranteed a fixed retirement income—have become increasingly rare. This shift has placed the burden of retirement savings on individuals, requiring workers to actively participate in employer-sponsored defined contribution (DC) plans like a 401(k) plan. Other common types of DC plans include 403(b) plans and 457(b) governmental plans; these are just different code sections based on the type of entity sponsoring the plan.

In 1980, 38% of private sector workers had access to a DB plan. By 2020, only 15% of workers had access to a DB plan. Gone are the days when your employer did all the heavy lifting for your retirement. Now, it's on you to build that nest egg!

With traditional pensions becoming as rare as pink unicorns, it's more important than ever to know what retirement benefits your workplace offers. Not all industries and employers are created equal when it comes to retirement plans—some roll out the red carpet, while others hand you a piggy bank and wish you luck. If you're in a field that still offers a DB plan, choose your employer wisely—because not all retirement plans are built the same!

And don't forget to keep an eye on your current employer's benefits—pensions can change over time, and you don't want any surprises. For example, some employers "freeze" the DB plan so that it is no longer available. A quick yearly check-in could mean the difference between a cushy retirement and digging for spare change in your couch!

 What workplace retirement plans are available to you? When are you eligible to participate in the plan?

11. Defined Contribution Plans

"A 401(k) is a retirement savings plan where you contribute money and your employer probably is making a contribution as well—both of which are allowed to grow tax-deferred."

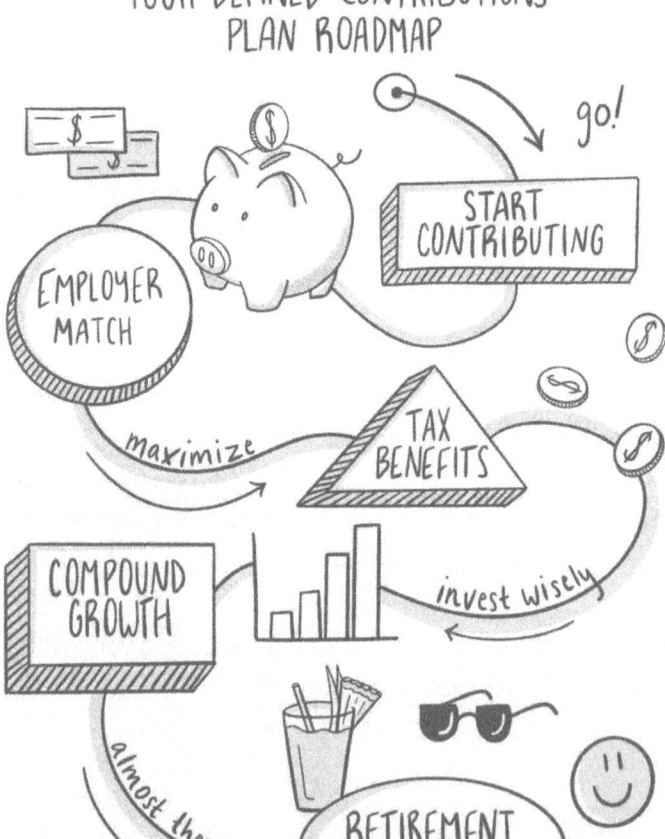

A 401(k) is a type of DC plan that lets employees save for retirement straight from their paycheck—often pre-tax (unless you're using a Roth option as discussed later in the chapter).

Some employers offer matching or other types of contributions such as a non-elective contribution (that's a contribution regardless of whether you put money into the plan), giving you free money for your future! Generally, your savings grow tax-deferred, meaning you don't pay taxes on them until retirement. But like any financial tool, there are rules—all spelled out in your plan document and Summary Plan Description (SPD). Read your SPD, know your options, and contribute enough to snag any employer match.

Access to workplace savings vehicles such as 401(k) plans increases the likelihood that an individual will save in retirement. Workers are 15 times more likely to save for retirement if they have access to a workplace retirement plan.

However, not all employees participate in their workplace plan even if they have access. Typically, only half of workers, both full- and part-time, participate in a retirement plan at work.

The sooner you start, the sooner Future You can sip piña coladas instead of stressing over dollars! Just because you haven't had a workplace savings plan before doesn't mean you're out of luck and can't start now.

If you aren't sure what's available, don't leave free savings opportunities on the table and make sure your contributions in the plan are being invested. Make sure to check in with human resources or your benefits department to find out what's available.

Future You will thank you (preferably from a beach).

 Do you have access to a 401(k) plan or other workplace retirement savings plan? If so, how can you maximize your contributions?

12. Matching Contributions

"Defined contribution plans put the savings responsibility on employees—but many employers still offer a matching contribution to sweeten the deal."

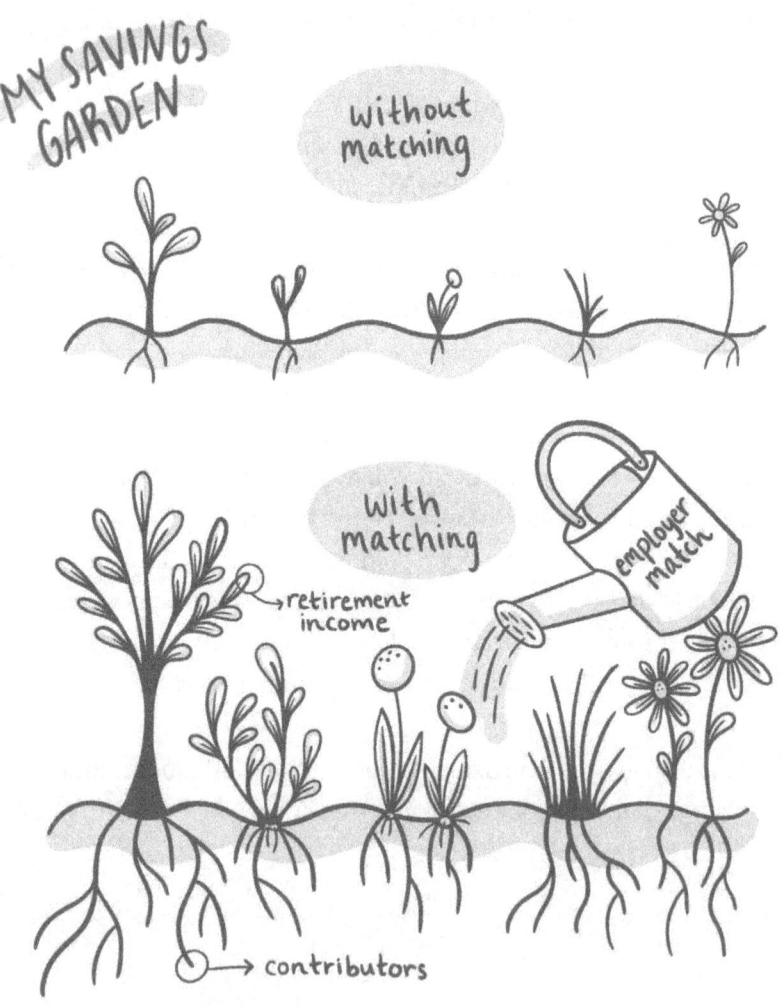

Unlike traditional pensions, DC plans require employees to fund their own retirement savings. However, if you are willing to plant the seeds, many employers will offer to water your savings garden. Employers often offer matching or non-elective contributions, giving you free money for your future if you take advantage of it.

For example, 87% of plans with more than 100 participants offer a matching contribution. Despite this, there are instances where employees don't take advantage of the matching contribution. There may be some instances where that makes sense for your own personal financial situation, but you want to make sure this is a well-thought-out decision.

Matching contributions are like workplace bonus rounds for your retirement savings, but the rules can vary. Employers can pick any matching formula they like, as long as they follow IRS rules that prevent them from playing favorites with highly paid employees. That means no "VIP-only" pension parties. To dodge those tricky rules, some employers go with "safe harbor" contributions, which follow a set formula and keep everything fair. Bottom line? If your job offers a match, find out how it works and take full advantage—because bonus money for retirement is the best kind of money!

Dig up your SPD and read it—yes, actually read it! This document spills the details on how much free money (aka matching contributions or non-elective contributions) your employer is willing to throw into your retirement fund.

Do you understand all contributions coming from my employer under the workplace retirement plan? Are you understanding any matching contributions, and if not, where can you get help?

13. Retirement Plan Loans

"Taking a loan is like borrowing from Future You—just make sure Future You isn't stuck paying for Past You's bad decisions."

Your workplace retirement plan might let you borrow from your 401(k) plan… but don't go wild just yet! Many plans allow loans (though they don't have to), letting you take out up to 50% of your vested balance or $50,000, whichever is less.

Of course, there's a catch—you'll have to pay yourself back with interest through payroll deductions, all outlined in a formal loan agreement and also provided for in your plan's SPD.

Research shows that loans are on the rise. Roughly 13% of 401(k) participants had loans against their retirement savings at the end of 2023, up from 12% in 2022.

Before you turn your retirement fund into an ATM, just remember: Future You is watching… and they'd really prefer a beach house over a quick shopping spree. Borrowing from your retirement plan is like giving yourself a low-interest loan—easy approval, no credit check, and way less paperwork! But there are risks: If you switch jobs, that loan might suddenly demand payback in full—or else the IRS slaps you with a 10% penalty for treating it like an early withdrawal (in addition to the tax consequences). If you do decide to break open your future nest egg, do so carefully, and always make sure you can put it back together.

Financial planning for retirement is like building a house: You need the right tools for the job! While a 401(k) loan might seem like a handy tool for emergencies, it's not the best wrench in the box if you're planning a job change soon. And here's a plot twist: If your company gets sold, your loan could be unexpectedly terminated, leaving you scrambling to pay it back or facing a nasty penalty. So before borrowing from your future, make sure it won't come back to hammer you later.

In formulating future "emergency" plans, be sure to review the SPD or loan policy to understand if you have access to loans (not all plans do).

 How many plan loans are available to you and what are the terms?

14. Retirement Plan Hardships

"Yes, you can break open your 401(k) piggy bank. But should you?"

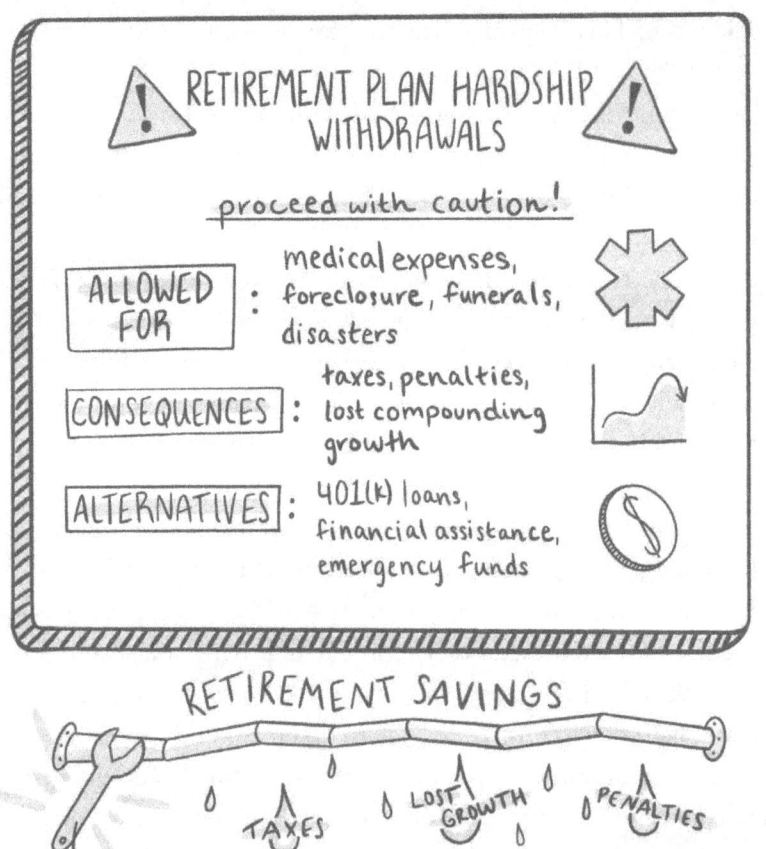

Your retirement account isn't a piggy bank, but in a real emergency, you might be able to crack it open—penalty-free! Some plans allow distributions for immediate and heavy financial needs (think medical bills, funeral costs, or other IRS-approved expenses). You'll still owe taxes, but at least you can dodge the early withdrawal penalty. And in many plans, you can now self-certify—meaning you don't have to hand over a stack of paperwork to prove your hardship. Just remember: This is a last resort, not a payday! Future You still needs those retirement dollars.

Similar to loans, hardship distributions are on the rise. Roughly 2.3% of workers took a hardship withdrawal in 2023, up from 1.8% in 2022. The top two reasons behind this uptick were avoiding foreclosure/eviction and paying medical expenses.

Loans and hardship withdrawals from your workplace retirement plan may seem similar, but they're definitely not twins! A loan is like borrowing from Future You—with no taxes or penalties as long as you pay it back on time.

A hardship withdrawal, on the other hand, is a one-way ticket out of your retirement account. There is no repayment required, but you'll owe taxes and, if you're under 59½, a 10% penalty (unless the IRS gives you a break). However, before you dip into your retirement savings, ask yourself: "Am I taking a loan or just giving Uncle Sam a bonus?"

Think of hardship withdrawals like the emergency escape hatch in your financial toolbox—helpful in a crisis, but not something you want to use unless necessary. While self-certification makes it easier to take a hardship withdrawal (no more proving your case to the IRS), the responsibility now falls on *you* to understand the rules and keep proper documentation. So, if you're tapping into your retirement fund, make sure you dot your i's, cross your t's, and don't accidentally turn an emergency fix into a future headache.

 In formulating your financial plan, have you reviewed the SPD to understand if you have access to hardship distributions from your plan in case of an emergency? This may help you get comfortable increasing contributions to your retirement plan if you know you can access money in a worst-case scenario.

15. Emergency Withdrawals from Retirement Plans

"It's tough to expect the unexpected, but we can all expect an emergency to happen sometime."

SECURE 2.0 is comprehensive bipartisan legislation for retirement plan policies introduced in 2022. Part of the SECURE 2.0 legislation provides your retirement savings with a few extra escape hatches—but use them wisely! Since 2024, you can withdraw up to $1,000 from your retirement account without penalty for emergencies. But here's the catch—your employer has to opt in to offer this feature, and taxes still apply.

Research shows that nearly two in five (37%) individuals couldn't afford an emergency expense over $400. Further, Americans have accumulated median emergency savings of just $600. Hence, these provisions from SECURE 2.0 were intended by the legislature to assist employees with saving and being able to access their money in the event of an emergency.

As part of the SECURE 2.0 withdrawals, you might be able to repay these amounts and put the money back where it belongs (double-check your SPD to be sure). Another cool option? The Pension-Linked Emergency Savings Account (PLESA) lets you sock away up to $2,500 in after-tax savings—ready to withdraw anytime, tax- and penalty-free. Even better, your employer can match it, just like a regular 401(k) match. But again, it's totally optional for employers.

Bottom line? These new features give you extra flexibility, but it's still on you to check what's available in your plan and make smart money moves!

Conventional wisdom says to build an emergency fund with three to six months of expenses—because if there's one thing you can expect, it's the unexpected. Planning ahead means you won't have to dip into your retirement savings when life throws a curveball.

 Do you have an emergency savings plan to cover at least three to six months of your expenses? Can you locate in your SPD whether your plan has any emergency savings provisions available?

16. Student Loan Matching

"There's more than one way to repay a loan."

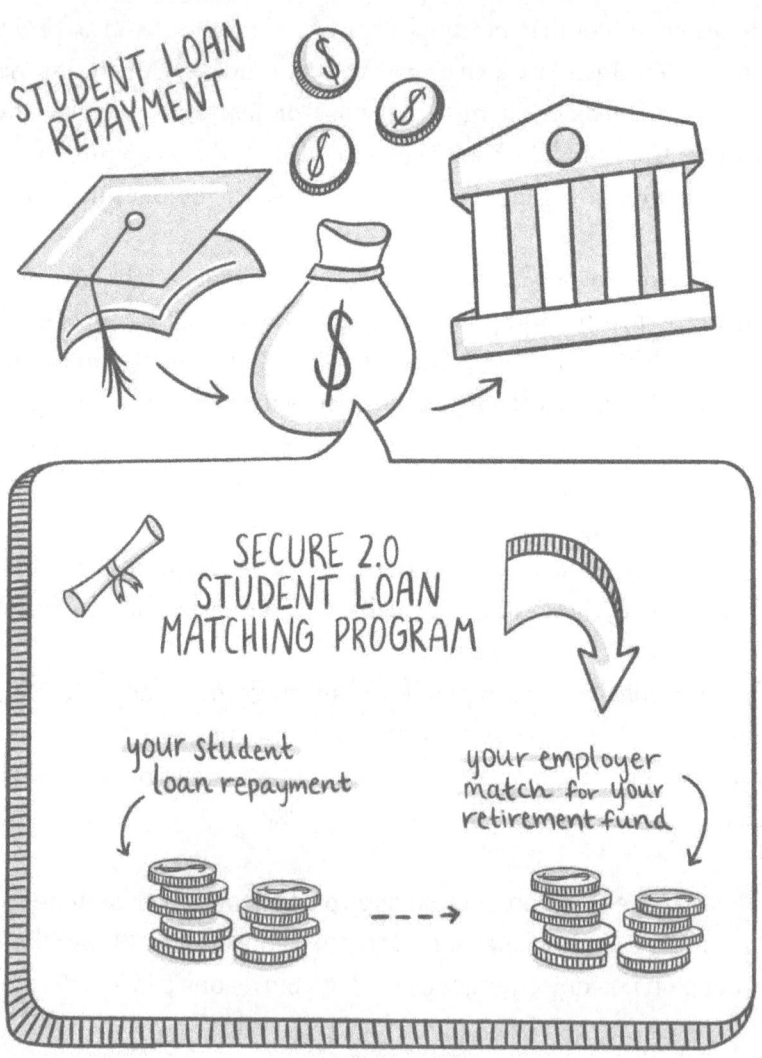

Thanks to SECURE 2.0, since 2024, employers can match your student loan payments just like they match contributions to your 401(k), 403(b), or 457 plan. That means you can tackle debt and grow your retirement savings at the same time—a win-win! The catch? This is an optional feature, so your employer isn't required to offer it. Be sure to check with the human resources or benefits department to see if this perk is available in your workplace—because who wouldn't want free money while paying off loans?

To put it into perspective, there are over 40 million Americans who carry student loan debt, totaling nearly $2 trillion.

Here's how it works: First, your employer opts into the new SECURE 2.0 student loan matching program by updating the retirement plan document. Second, they'll match your student loan payments just like they would match a 401(k) contribution. That means you pay down debt *and* build retirement savings at the same time!

To qualify, you must be repaying a qualified education loan for yourself, your spouse, or a dependent. This includes costs like tuition, fees, books, supplies, equipment, and even room and board at an eligible school. The best part? You don't have to jump through hoops—you self-certify that you're making loan payments, and your employer will match that amount into your retirement plan. Check with your human resources department to see if your company offers this free money—because getting student loan help + retirement savings = financial glow-up!

Missing out on the matching contribution from an employer is like missing out on free money. Taking advantage of new programs related to student loan repayment can accelerate repayment of loans while also maximizing participation in the workplace retirement plan. If you have student loan debt, it may no longer be an excuse to put off retirement savings. Even if your employer doesn't have this specific program set up, they may have other types of programs in place to deal with student loan debt for you or your dependents.

 Do you have any student loan debt? Do your dependents? If so, have you contacted your employer to see what programs are available?

17. Retirement Account Rollovers

"Rolling over isn't just for dogs anymore. A 'rollover' is now an important part of any retirement strategy."

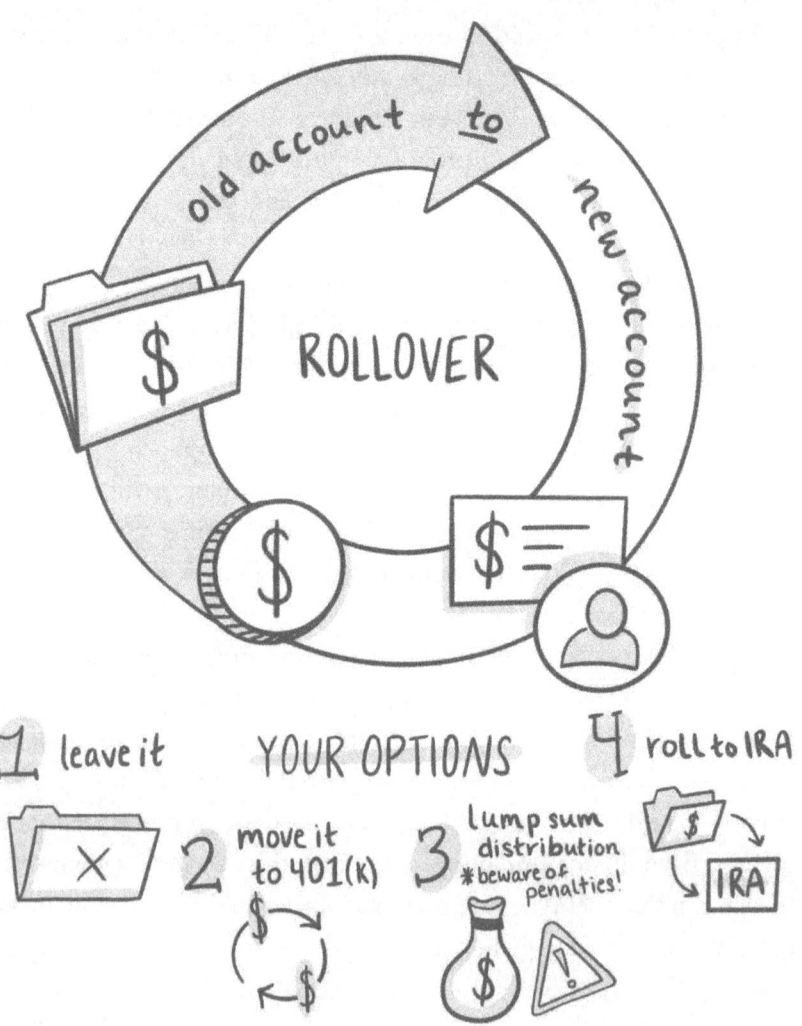

A rollover occurs when an individual withdraws their assets from one eligible retirement plan and contributes all or part of it, within 60 days, to another eligible retirement plan or IRA.

According to IRS data, about 5.7 million Americans roll over to an IRA each year. Americans held $11.0 trillion in IRAs at year-end 2019, accounting for 34% of the $32.3 trillion in dedicated retirement assets.

When you switch jobs, your employer-sponsored retirement plan doesn't just disappear. You must decide what to do with it. Here are your four main options:

1. Leave it with your old employer's plan. If allowed, you can keep your money parked there, but you'll lose the ability to contribute and may have limited investment choices.
2. Roll it into your new employer's plan. If your new job offers a retirement plan, you may be able to transfer your old savings into it, keeping everything together in one place.
3. Take a lump sum (aka cash out). Warning! This will trigger taxes and possibly a 10% early withdrawal penalty (unless you qualify for an exception). Future You will not be pleased!
4. Move it into an IRA. Rolling it into an IRA keeps your savings growing tax-advantaged while giving you more investment flexibility.

Avoid taxes and penalties by rolling over your retirement savings—either into your new employer's plan or an IRA. Future You will thank you!

Meet with a financial pro to compare your options, as investment choices, fees, and services can make a big difference in your long-term savings. Rolling to an IRA is a popular choice, but don't cash out! That triggers taxes and penalties, which no one wants to see.

If you're rolling over funds, be sure to complete the transition within 60 days to avoid tax headaches. Plan wisely, move carefully, and keep your retirement money growing.

✳ Do you have retirement plan accounts in several locations? Have you taken the opportunity to evaluate the consolidation of accounts into a single retirement plan or IRA?

18. Auto Portability

"Auto rollovers are making it easier to track accounts, but always keep track of where you are moving your precious nest eggs."

Auto portability is the automated movement of an inactive and terminated participant's (participant = you) retirement account from a former employer's retirement plan to an IRA and then their active account in a new employer's plan. In other words, auto portability is like a retirement plan GPS, automatically moving your old 401(k) from a past job into an IRA and then into your new employer's plan—without you having to lift a finger!

Leaving behind a forgotten 401(k) account has the potential to cost a single person almost $700,000 in foregone retirement savings over a lifetime.

SECURE 2.0 (this legislation did a lot as you can see!) set up the opportunity for several platforms that hold your account(s) to come together and form a consortium to transfer and roll over account balances from one plan to another across various platforms. This keeps the account balance in the retirement "system," rather than cashing it out. Instead of leaving behind "orphan" accounts or cashing out (ouch, taxes and penalties), this system keeps your savings growing and following you wherever your career takes you.

Bottom line? Auto portability helps you stay on track for retirement by making sure your hard-earned savings move with you—not get lost along the way! However, not all plans have auto portability set up.

And, auto-rollovers are great, but your retirement savings still need a CEO—and that's *you*! While SECURE 2.0 has set up a framework to help move your retirement savings when you switch jobs, don't just assume everything is handled. Keep track of all your accounts to ensure your money lands where it should—whether in your new employer's plan or an IRA.

Pro tip: Make a habit of checking your balances, updating your records, and consolidating accounts when needed—because no one cares more about your future wealth than Future You!

> ✳ Are any of your accounts in an IRA that was 'forced out' automatically from an old employer, just racking up fees without your supervision? If so, can you contact that IRA provider to initiate a distribution to consolidate your accounts?

19. Individual Retirement Accounts

"Create your IRA early in life. Future You will thank you."

An Individual Retirement Account (IRA) is your own personal retirement savings plan, separate from employer-sponsored options. IRAs come in two main flavors: Traditional IRAs, which offer tax-deferred growth, and Roth IRAs, which provide tax-free withdrawals in retirement (hold tight: discussed more shortly).

Nearly 65 million taxpayers have established an IRA of some kind, highlighting the widespread use of these retirement savings vehicles. Whether Traditional or Roth, IRAs play a crucial role in long-term financial planning, offering tax advantages that can help individuals build a more secure retirement.

When it comes to contribution limits, IRA limits are smaller but still a great place to start! Despite their lower annual limits, IRAs offer tax-advantaged growth and serve as a financial safety net for Future You.

In some states, workplace retirement savings and IRAs are becoming more intertwined, as certain states now require employers to offer IRA-based retirement plans. If you're unsure whether your workplace plan is an IRA or a 401(k), IRAs have significantly lower limits than 401(k) plans. Additionally, while funds from a 401(k) can be rolled over into an IRA, there are restrictions on transferring funds from a Roth IRA into a 401(k).

During your working years, your IRA can be a place where all your old workplace retirement plans come together under one roof. As you switch jobs, rolling over your 401(k) into an IRA can make managing your retirement funds much easier.

Additionally, assess how an IRA can supplement your workplace retirement savings, depending on your income level. If your Modified Adjusted Gross Income (MAGI) limits your ability to contribute directly to a Roth IRA or deduct Traditional IRA contributions, you may still be able to use a non-deductible Traditional IRA as part of your overall retirement strategy.

 How are you leveraging IRAs in your personal financial planning today and how might you enhance that strategy over time?

20. Health Savings Accounts: Triple Tax Benefits

"An HSA isn't just for today's doctor bills. It's a long-term investment in your future health and financial freedom."

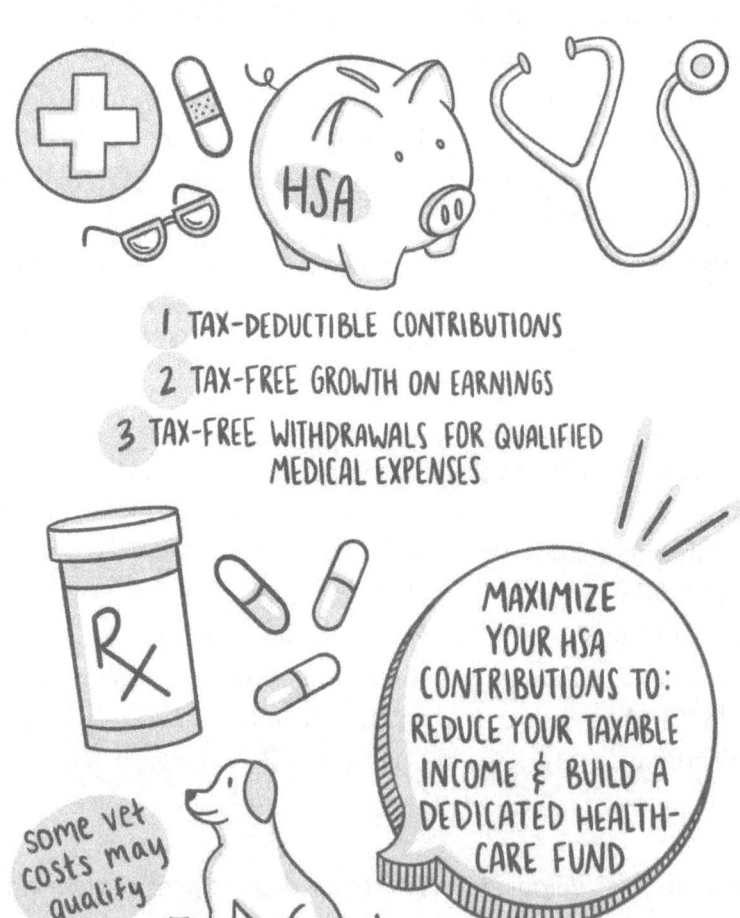

1. TAX-DEDUCTIBLE CONTRIBUTIONS
2. TAX-FREE GROWTH ON EARNINGS
3. TAX-FREE WITHDRAWALS FOR QUALIFIED MEDICAL EXPENSES

MAXIMIZE YOUR HSA CONTRIBUTIONS TO: REDUCE YOUR TAXABLE INCOME & BUILD A DEDICATED HEALTHCARE FUND

some vet costs may qualify

When it comes to healthcare and financial planning, few tools are as versatile—or as underappreciated—as the Health Savings Account (HSA). Designed for those with high-deductible health plans, an HSA offers a rare combination of tax advantages and long-term flexibility. It's not just a way to cover medical expenses today—it's a strategy for building a healthier, more financially secure tomorrow.

As of 2023, there are approximately 36 million HSAs in the US—a number that continues to grow as more people recognize the powerful benefits they offer.

If you're enrolled in a high-deductible health plan (HDHP), an HSA can be one of the smartest tools in your financial toolbox. Why? Because it's one of the few accounts that delivers a triple tax advantage:

- Tax-deductible contributions
- Tax-free growth on earnings
- Tax-free withdrawals for qualified medical expenses.

From doctor visits and prescriptions to over-the-counter meds and even certain pet care expenses (yes, really—companion animals may qualify), HSAs can help cover a surprising range of healthcare-related costs. But be careful—using funds for non-qualified expenses before age 65 comes with a 20% penalty and income tax.

Make sure you maximize your HSA contributions each year. Not only do you reduce your taxable income, but you also build a dedicated healthcare fund that can grow year after year—even into retirement.

An HSA can be more than a medical savings account—it's a powerful financial asset. With its triple tax benefits, long-term growth potential, and flexibility in retirement, it can play a key role in both your healthcare planning and overall financial strategy. Whether you're saving for next year's expenses or looking decades ahead, making the most of your HSA today can pay off in a big way tomorrow.

✵ How are you incorporating your HSA into your overall financial strategy? Could it be more than just a short-term spending account—perhaps a long-term health and wealth planning tool?

21. Roth Tax Treatment

"Choose your IRA tax treatment wisely.
The differences are in the details."

ROTH ACCOUNTS
- pay taxes upfront
- withdrawal for your retirement tax-free
- invest your money & grow it tax-free until retirement

ROTH 401(k)

growing tax-free

BALANCE YOUR CONTRIBUTIONS

ROTH — TRADITIONAL

THE DECISION ISN'T ALWAYS "EITHER/OR" BETWEEN ROTH & TRADITIONAL CONTRIBUTIONS — IN MANY CASES IT'S A BALANCE OF BOTH

A Roth account lets you pay taxes upfront when making contributions, so when it's time to retire, both your contributions and earnings can be withdrawn tax-free. This strategy offers long-term tax advantages and gives you greater financial flexibility in your retirement years. Your money grows tax-free, meaning all those years of compounding earnings won't be taxed when you withdraw them—making it one of the most powerful tools for building wealth and securing a tax-efficient retirement.

Roth tax treatment is a tool that is available in IRAs and in workplace retirement plans such as 401(k)s and 403(b)s, but only so long as your employer has made it available. While Roth accounts offer significant tax advantages, they are not as widely utilized as Traditional contributions, which provide an immediate tax benefit at the time of contribution. Approximately 23% of taxpayers hold Traditional IRAs, whereas only about 11% own Roth IRAs, highlighting the greater popularity of deferring taxes until retirement.

It's important to understand that the decision isn't always an "either/or" between Roth and Traditional contributions. In many cases, a balanced strategy can provide the best of both worlds. If your employer allows it, you may be able to split your contributions between Roth and Traditional accounts. This gives you immediate tax benefits while also securing future tax-free withdrawals.

It's also essential to distinguish Roth contributions from another workplace-plan feature—after-tax contributions. Roth contributions allow for tax-free withdrawals of both contributions and earnings in retirement, while after-tax contributions require taxes on earnings when withdrawn. Understanding these nuances can help you maximize your retirement savings strategy and create a well-structured, tax-efficient retirement plan.

Roth accounts can be a powerful tax planning tool, but their effectiveness depends on how well they fit into your overall financial strategy.

 Have you considered Roth features for your workplace retirement-plan contributions? Are you eligible for a Roth IRA?

22. Roth Versus Traditional

"A smart tax strategy will get the most out of each IRA approach."

We've all heard about Roth contributions (especially if you read the last few pages), but what about Traditional contributions? Traditional is actually the most popular choice for retirement savings. Unlike Roth contributions, which are made with after-tax dollars, Traditional contributions to workplace retirement plans and IRAs are made with pre-tax dollars—meaning they lower your taxable income for the immediate year.

The best part? Your money grows tax-deferred, so you don't pay taxes on your earnings until you withdraw them in retirement. It's like getting a tax break today in exchange for paying taxes later—hopefully, when you're in a lower tax bracket and enjoying the retirement that you sketched out!

This principle applies to both IRAs and workplace retirement-plan contributions. When it comes to IRAs, the preference for Traditional contributions is evident in account balances. According to the Tax Policy Center, the average balance in Traditional IRAs is $211,000, significantly higher than the $52,000 average balance in Roth IRAs.

Deciding between a Roth and a Traditional retirement plan can be a tough choice. Is it better to pay taxes now or pay them later? If you expect to be in a higher tax bracket in retirement, a Roth account (where you pay taxes upfront) might be the better deal.

But you don't necessarily have to pick just one! As discussed in the last section, you can contribute to a Traditional workplace retirement plan and still have a Roth IRA—as long as your income doesn't exceed the Modified Adjusted Gross Income (MAGI) limits. This strategy helps you diversify your tax treatment in retirement, giving you more flexibility when it's time to withdraw your hard-earned savings.

A diversified tax strategy can provide greater financial flexibility, allowing you to manage your withdrawals efficiently when you retire, but don't "set it and forget it." Set your initial sketch and revisit your savings strategy periodically to ensure it still aligns with your evolving goals, income, and tax outlook.

 How will your tax bracket at retirement likely compare to your current bracket, and how does this influence the decisions you make related to contributions today?

23. Social Security Funding

"Don't put all your eggs in one basket, especially not the Social Security basket."

This chapter primarily focuses on methods of saving for retirement that are within your control. An additional source of saving for retirement includes Social Security—though it is not necessarily within your control. However, relying too heavily on Social Security as your primary retirement income source may leave your financial future vulnerable. The Trustees of the Social Security and Medicare trust funds release an annual report on the financial health of these programs, and recent trends have raised concerns.

Since 2021, the Social Security trust fund has been drawing down its asset reserves to meet benefit obligations. Up to the mid-2030s, it likely will require even more redemptions. According to the Social Security Administration, for those born between the 1950s and 1990s, initial retirement benefits currently replace over one-third of pre-retirement earnings. And for disabled workers, over one-half. But that model may not hold up.

At its current trajectory, Social Security is facing a funding gap. The system is financed primarily through payroll taxes, taxes on benefits, and interest income. But with rising benefit costs and revenue growth falling behind, the long-term sustainability of full benefit payments is uncertain. This reality may impact how future retirees structure their income.

While Social Security likely will continue to exist, future benefit reductions are possible. It's wise to think of Social Security as just one piece of your retirement income puzzle. Consider building a more resilient strategy by maximizing additional income streams, such as 401(k) and IRA withdrawals, pensions, annuities, or even part-time work. As we will discuss in future chapters, delaying your Social Security claim can also boost your monthly payout.

 How much income will you need in retirement? If Social Security benefits were reduced, how would your plan be affected and what alternative sources of income are you preparing to rely on?

Your Retirement Notes

Your Retirement Sketches

CHAPTER III

INVESTING FOR RETIREMENT

- Investing in Retirement
- The Power of Compound Interest
- Bond Ladders
- Target Date Funds
- Digital Assets
- Alternative Investments
- Survivor Bias
- Home Bias
- Sustainable Investing
- Annuities
- Life Insurance in Retirement
- LTCI and Hybrid Policies
- Cash Value Life Insurance as an Income Tool
- Capital Gains Strategies in Retirement
- Working with an Advisor

CHAPTER III.
Introduction

Time in the market beats timing the market. When you are young, this is one of your most powerful tools to being wealthy and financially secure for retirement: time. Time is on your side, especially if you start investing early.

Remember that there is a big difference between saving and investing. We need to save to be able to invest, but you can't save your way to a successful retirement—you have to invest. The journey to retirement is long, and investing wisely along the way allows your money to do the heavy lifting. That's all thanks to one of the most powerful forces in finance: compound interest. Albert Einstein reportedly called it the eighth wonder of the world, and for good reason. When your investments earn returns—and then those returns start earning returns—your wealth begins to grow exponentially. The earlier you start, the more time your money has to multiply. Even modest, consistent investing can snowball into substantial wealth given enough time.

But time alone isn't enough. A successful retirement investing strategy involves aligning your portfolio with both your goals and your comfort with risk. This means balancing a mix of investments—from growth-oriented assets like stocks to income-generating tools like bonds or annuities. Fixed income products, such as treasury bonds, municipal bonds, and high-quality corporate debt, help provide stability, especially as you get closer to retirement. They generate predictable income and can act as a buffer against market volatility.

It's also important to understand the function of each one of your investments. Don't just own things to own them. Instead, invest with purpose. Many of us want to dip our toe into cryptocurrency. This does not need to be a major investment. Instead, it can be a tool to understand how to buy, hold, exchange, trade, and store a new form of currency. The entire purpose can simply be a learning experience.

One of the most common mistakes investors make is chasing a "perfect" investment—trying to outguess markets, find the next big thing, or time the perfect entry and exit. You have seen this a lot with speculative crypto investing. Unfortunately, history shows this rarely works. In fact, according to J.P. Morgan Asset Management, if you missed just the 10 best days in the stock market over the last 30 years, your overall return would have been cut in half. That's right—half. And what's even more surprising? Six of those 10 best days happened within two weeks of the 10 worst days. Markets often bounce back sharply, and if you're not invested, you miss the rebound.

Historical market data shows that it is almost impossible to consistently time the market. Leaving the market might seem wise at times, especially when a pending issue is on the horizon. However, each decision to leave the market is coupled with a second decision of when to enter back into it.

That's why staying invested—even through volatility—is one of the most powerful investing decisions you can make. Markets rise and fall, but historically they've rewarded patient, long-term investors. Investing is not about reacting emotionally to short-term noise. It's about putting a plan in place, adjusting it as life changes, and allowing your portfolio to weather the ups and downs in service of a longer-term goal: your financial freedom. Volatility is essentially the price we pay to invest. If we want long-term gains we need to be exposed to some levels of risk—in the stock market this is often volatility.

Another key strategy in retirement investing is diversification—spreading your money across different asset classes, industries, geographies, and risk levels. Diversification doesn't eliminate risk, but it helps manage it. When one part of your portfolio is struggling, another may be thriving. This balance helps reduce the chance that one bad investment derails your retirement goals. If we search for liquid and less volatile assets like fixed income government bonds, we typically give up some long-term returns for peace of mind.

In retirement, it's not just about building wealth—it's about preserving and distributing it tax-efficiently. That's where long-term capital gains come in. By holding investments for more than a year, gains are typically taxed at a lower rate than ordinary income. Leveraging this tax treatment can be a smart way to stretch your retirement dollars further, especially if you're strategic about when and how you sell assets. How the gain on an asset is taxed is crucial. *Will* it be tax free? Long-term gains or ordinary income? The taxable nature of an asset should impact our planning and investing strategy. Ultimately, if we can house our ordinary income or high-growth taxable assets inside of tax-free savings vehicles like Roth accounts, this can provide a lot of long-term flexibility.

The truth is: There is no single best investment. What works for your neighbor or coworker might not be right for you. Your goals, timeline, risk tolerance, and income needs are unique—and your portfolio should reflect that. Retirement investing is more than just picking stocks; it's about building a system that grows with you, supports your lifestyle, and helps you sleep at night.

So as you sketch your vision of retirement, remember this: Time is your greatest asset, consistency is your best friend, and staying invested may be your most important decision. Don't aim for perfection—aim for progress. Sketch out what you want from your investments and how it will help you both get to and through retirement.

24. Investing in Retirement

"When it comes to retirement, the earlier you start investing, the better your chances of building a strong financial future. But what's just as important as when you start? How you invest."

Investing might feel overwhelming if you aren't a financial pro or haven't taken the stock market up as a personal hobby. If you're feeling overwhelmed by all the choices out there, you're not alone. The good news? You don't need to be a financial expert to take smart steps. Let's look at a few common concepts associated with investing for retirement and how they can work for you:

- Stocks: these are shares of ownership in a publicly traded company, which typically can provide higher potential for long-term growth but can fluctuate widely in the short term.
- Bonds: sometimes these are referred to as fixed income and they are loans you make to a company or government in exchange for interest payments; you might want these to provide for more stability in your portfolio.
- Mutual funds: a combo made up of stocks, bonds, or both, known as a pooled investment vehicle that is managed by the finance pros.
- ETFs: similar to mutual funds but with a different fee structure and traded like stocks on an exchange.

While that's far from an exhaustive list, it gives you a few ideas to get started—some of which we will discuss in other chapters (or in this chapter). And, as we discussed in the last chapter, all of these options can be leveraged through a variety of investing vehicles such as:

- Brokerage accounts
- Employer sponsored plan like a 401(k) or 403(b)
- IRAs.

✳ Are you proficient in these terms or do you need support from a financial pro?

25. The Power of Compound Interest

"Time really is money. Especially if you structure your time correctly."

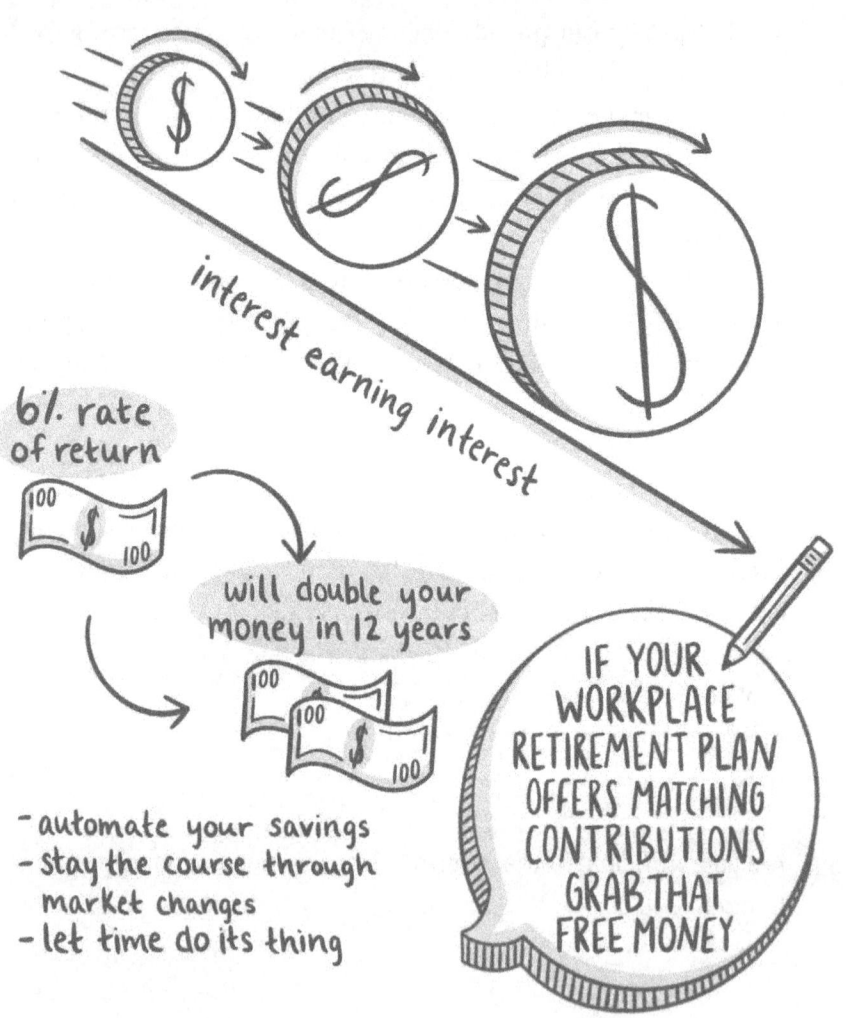

CHAPTER III

Welcome to one of the greatest financial instruments of all time: compound interest.

Think about the money you made, then that money makes more money, and then that new money makes even more money. Yeah, it's as awesome as it sounds.

Here's the deal: When you invest, your money earns interest. Then that interest earns interest. Eventually, you've got a little financial snowball rolling downhill, turning into an avalanche of wealth over time. No shovel required.

Let's break it down: Say you save just $100 a month (less than a cable bill, more than your unused gym membership). With time and a decent return, that could potentially quadruple your savings over a 30- to 50-year stretch! That's not magic. That's math. Sexy, sexy math.

Saving isn't always easy. Life throws expenses at you like it's training for dodgeball nationals: rent, kids, tacos, surprise dental work, your dog's third birthday party (you had to get the bone-shaped cake). But here's the good news: You don't have to start big. You just have to start.

And don't worry if you feel late to the party. Compound interest doesn't hold grudges. Whether you're 25 or 45, what matters is getting in the game. Even a shorter runway can lead to meaningful results if you're consistent and intentional. The trick is to automate your savings, stay the course through market ups and downs, and let time do its thing. Future You will be high-fiving Past You all the way to the bank.

Bonus tip: If your workplace retirement plan offers matching contributions, grab that free money like it's the last slice of pizza. Combine that with compounding, and you're cooking with gas (and possibly retiring on a yacht named "Interestzilla").

Start small. Start now. Stay consistent.

✱ What can you do today to unleash the awesome power of compound interest?

26. Bond Ladders

"A bond ladder is really more like a retirement step stool than a retirement ladder. It can be helpful, but likely won't get you all the way to where you want to go. But the good news is at least you won't fall too far!"

Imagine you're at a racetrack. Stocks are the flashy sports car: fast, thrilling, and capable of insane long-term wins, but with enough twists and turns to make you queasy. Bonds? They're the reliable old station wagon—slower, steadier, and far less likely to give you a heart attack.

Historically, stocks have outpaced bonds over 80% of the time annually and nearly 90% over any 10-year period.

But does that mean bonds are useless? Not at all! Enter the bond ladder, the financial equivalent of a well-planned road trip. Instead of putting all your cash into one long-haul bond, you stagger purchases so that one matures each year, giving you steady income and reinvestment opportunities. Think of it like packing 10 sandwiches for a 10-day journey—you get a fresh one each day instead of eating a decade-old mystery meat sandwich on day 10.

A bond ladder can be a great tool, especially in the first 5–10 years of retirement, providing stable cash flow without relying too much on market swings. But if you go all-in on bonds, you might end up sacrificing long-term growth—like never taking the highway because you're afraid of traffic.

That's why a mix of bonds, stocks, and maybe even annuities can help you strike the right balance. So here's the big question: Would you rather have guaranteed but potentially smaller wealth or take a chance on the market rollercoaster for a shot at greater long-term riches?

Your choice, but remember—retirement is a marathon, not a sprint (unless you're chasing grandkids, in which case, invest in good running shoes too).

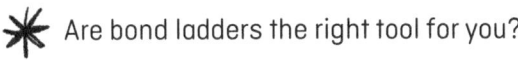 Are bond ladders the right tool for you?

27. Target Date Funds

"A target date fund is like a prepackaged meal—it's convenient, automatically adjusted, and works for most people, but it might not be seasoned to your personal taste."

A target date fund (or TDF) is a single investment option, but it is based on a mix of multiple underlying stocks and bonds that rebalance and reallocate over time based on something called your glidepath. What's a glidepath? It's your mix of stocks and bonds that are put together based on how aggressive you are in your retirement approach.

A TDF is automatically selected for you based on your date of birth and the assumed date you will retire.

Nine out of 10 individuals in workplace retirement plans say they would like access to a TDF. Employers who offer these plans set the TDF as their default option for when individuals don't otherwise make a selection.

TDFs were created in the 1990s. Congress passed a major law in 2006 that gave rise to TDFs' popularity and major growth in assets. Even though TDFs are so popular, they are developed based on limited information for investors. They offer diversification and automatic rebalancing, which makes it more ideal for someone looking to set it and forget it. On the other hand, they are created with a single data point, but often people think this single investment will take care of them for life.

TDFs may be appropriate for the right situation, but you should understand if it is right for Future You based on your actual risk tolerance and time horizon because it was set up for you likely just based on your age alone.

 How well does your current retirement investment strategy align with your risk tolerance?

28. Digital Assets

"Digital assets have reshaped how we shop, watch, play, and connect. Retirement planning won't be any different."

Cryptocurrencies and tokenized assets may define the next generation of wealth and how we plan for the future. Financial data shows that a small percentage investment (1 to 5% of your portfolio) in Bitcoin and a few other cryptocurrencies can be successful in improving returns.

Digital assets encompass a wide range of intangible items stored and accessed electronically, including emails, websites, online photos, social media accounts, cloud documents, and, increasingly, digital currencies like Bitcoin and Ethereum.

In the context of retirement planning, digital assets can represent both financial value and personal legacy. Cryptocurrencies, for example, are being used as speculative growth assets and inflation hedges, while NFTs and tokenized assets are creating new forms of ownership and wealth transfer. At the same time, non-financial digital assets—like important documents or access to accounts—need to be properly cataloged and shared to ensure continuity in estate planning.

Retirement plans must evolve to protect, manage, and pass on digital assets just like traditional ones. Ignoring them creates gaps not just in financial security but also in personal legacy and accessibility for loved ones. Investing in digital assets like cryptocurrencies and tokenized securities is becoming more common in retirement planning, especially among those seeking diversification and growth.

These assets can offer potential upside and inflation protection, but come with heightened volatility, regulatory uncertainty, and security risks. Because of this, most experts currently recommend limiting exposure to between 1 and 5% of a retirement portfolio. However, this could increase in the future if the broader adoption, institutional acceptance, and greater tokenization of traditional assets continues.

However, digital assets may not be suitable for all retirement accounts, and the tax treatment of cryptocurrencies is still evolving. In retirement, managing digital assets demands a thoughtful strategy—balancing risk, ensuring secure storage, and documenting access for fiduciaries and heirs.

> What do you think is the total value of your digital assets today? What are your most important digital assets for you to live a successful retirement?

29. Alternative Investments

"Retirement portfolios are no longer confined to stocks and bonds—they now reflect the real economy, from farmland to blockchain."

assets that fall outside of the traditional categories of stocks, bonds, & cash

alternatives can help manage risks, provide steady income, and open the door for unique growth opportunities

From farmland to infrastructure to private credit, alternatives are helping retirees create portfolios that reflect the real economy—not just the public markets.

Alternative investments are assets that fall outside the traditional categories of stocks, bonds, and cash, and includes real estate, private equity, hedge funds, infrastructure, commodities, private credit, and even collectibles or farmland.

Alternatives often offer lower correlation to public markets, providing diversification benefits and potentially smoothing returns during market downturns. They can play a crucial role in managing risk, generating steady income, and accessing unique growth opportunities that are less tied to daily market volatility.

Many alternatives are accessible to individual investors.

Be cautious of quality: The alternative investment space is less regulated, and there are many speculative or poorly structured opportunities that could harm your retirement plan if not thoroughly vetted. Therefore, access often requires guidance through advisors, platforms, or institutional channels. It's also essential to understand how each investment correlates with the rest of your portfolio. Not all alternatives reduce risk; some may actually amplify it depending on how they behave alongside your other holdings.

So, alternatives are not a one-size-fits-all solution. They can add meaningful value to a retirement plan but require thoughtful integration. Don't just add alternatives because they're trendy or because institutions are using them. Use them intentionally, as part of a well-diversified, goal-aligned portfolio that balances opportunity with risk and access with need.

 How comfortable are you with investing in assets that are less liquid but may offer higher return potential or income stability. Have you had experience with private market investments pre-retirement?

30. Survivor Bias

"Survivor bias in investing will often warp perceptions of success and risk because it only considers the companies or investments that have succeeded."

Ah, survivor bias. It sounds like something straight out of a survivor reality show, right? Except instead of getting a million-dollar prize, the losers of this show end up on the cutting room floor, while the winners get a shiny spotlight. But here's the kicker: As investors, we're the ones watching the show, and sometimes we forget that only the "winners" make it to the finale. Those companies that didn't make it are off the show… and eliminated from the data set investors often see.

Imagine you're looking at a chart that shows the stock performance of some companies over the last decade. But what if I told you that this chart conveniently forgot about all the companies that went belly-up during that time? Studies show that survivor bias could skew up to 20% of market analyses. That's a significant chunk of the data we're working with.

When you only look at the companies that succeeded, it paints a rosy picture. But in reality, it's like picking the next *American Idol* contestant by only listening to the winning tracks. The full story includes a lot of failures—some of which might have been avoidable if we'd paid closer attention.

So, what's the fix? Diversify! Don't put all your eggs in the basket of last season's winners. If you only focus on the success stories, you might miss the next big thing or, even worse, blindly follow a trend that's already on its way out.

 Are you ensuring that your investment decisions are based on comprehensive data and a holistic view of market forces?

31. Home Bias

"Sticking to domestic investments might feel safe, but home bias can turn your portfolio into a one-country show—leaving you vulnerable when the market hits a bump."

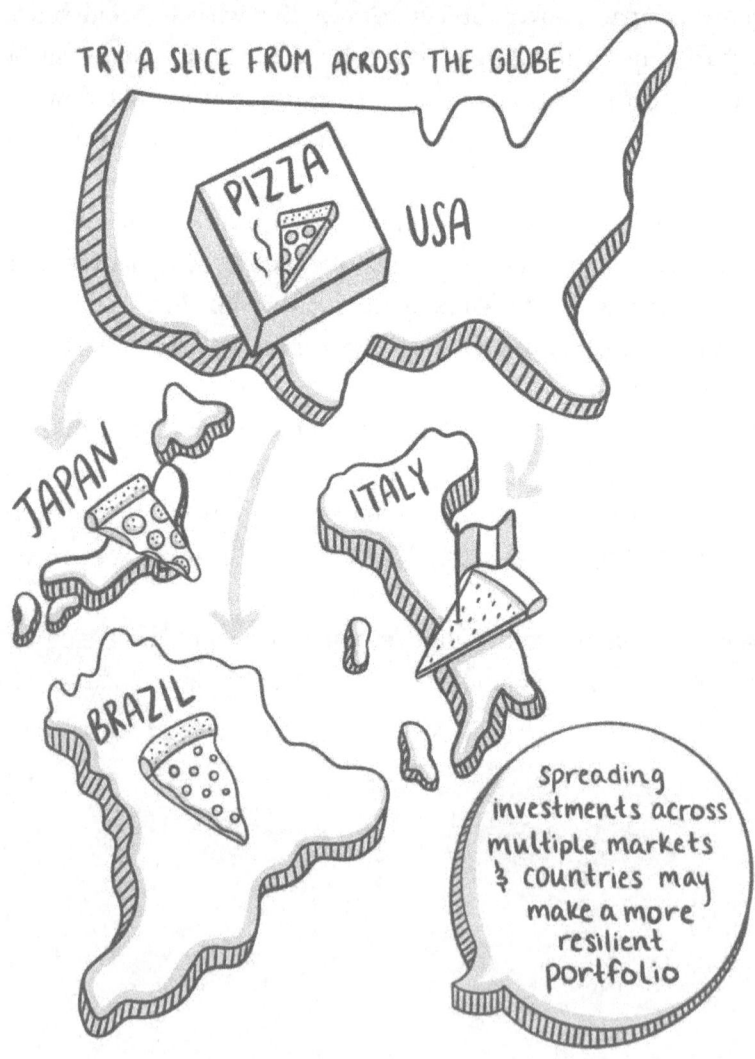

Home bias sounds harmless, but it can have a major impact on your future financial picture. Home bias is when investors tend to favor domestic investments or limit their portfolio to only markets in their own country. It's like thinking your local pizza joint is the best in the world, even though you've never tried pizza in Italy. You might be missing out on the global buffet of investment opportunities!

Here's the deal: About 70% of investors fall into the trap of home bias. It feels comfortable because, well, we know it. But just because you're familiar with your local economy doesn't mean it's immune to a little hiccup. Imagine investing only in your country's economy. That's like betting all your savings on the outcome of a single football team. What happens if your hometown team has a bad season?

Home bias sounds harmless at first, but it's like living in a bubble where you think everything outside your borders doesn't matter. When your domestic market hits a rough patch, your portfolio takes a hit. Things like a recession, political upheaval, etc., can all have a dramatic impact on finances. Meanwhile, global markets might be cruising along just fine, or even thriving.

So what should you do instead? Consider spreading your investments across multiple countries and markets to create a more resilient portfolio. Think of it like creating the ultimate international snack mix. You've got a little bit of everything: maybe some spicy stocks from Brazil, some cool tech from Japan, and a sprinkle of European bonds. That way, if one area of the world starts feeling a little unpredictable, you've got other investments keeping things balanced.

But here's the kicker: Evaluating your global exposure doesn't have to be complicated. Just ask yourself: How diversified is your investment portfolio geographically? If it's all about that local pizza place, it might be time to order a slice from somewhere else—because who knows, the best investment might just be across the globe.

> How diversified is your investment portfolio geographically? Could reducing home bias improve your financial security?

32. Sustainable Investing

"If you want your investments to reflect your values, sustainable investing lets you put your money where your morals are."

Environmental, Social and Governance (ESG) investing is about putting your money where your mouth is—or rather where your values are. There are different types of ESG—or sustainable investing—which have degrees of achieving financial benefit in addition to, or concurrent with, achieving societal benefit.

A significant majority of active managers, estimated to be around 80–90%, incorporate ESG factors into their investment decision-making process to some degree. Many actively integrate ESG considerations into their strategies when selecting investments; however, the level of integration and emphasis on ESG factors can vary widely between investment managers.

ESG investing in your workplace retirement plan (such as a 401(k)) is different from ESG investing in a brokerage account or an IRA. This is because of the rules that apply to each account type. The government gives you more leeway to decide when it's your own account like an IRA, but for workplace plans such as 401(k) plans, the rules don't allow for as much "personal preference" in the investment options available—it is focused on the financial benefit to participants (not social benefit). Keep that in mind when you deploy your personal philosophy related to ESG investing.

There is no right or wrong answer related to ESG investing, but it is important to understand the actual investment option and not be confused by what is called "greenwashing," which is like false marketing. In other words, when you go to the grocery store and something says "fat free" or "low carb" but it is not exactly fat free or low carb, you want to understand what is really inside the box. ESG investing is the same idea where you want to understand what is really included and not be misled by labels. Open up the box and understand what is inside the investment option to determine if it meets your risk tolerance, time horizon, and financial needs.

※ Do you believe that ESG investing adds financial benefit by reducing risk or increasing value to your portfolio?

33. Annuities

"Annuities could be the future financial sidekick that you need to make life easier."

a contract between you and an insurance company, a way to turn your savings into a predictable paycheck for retirement

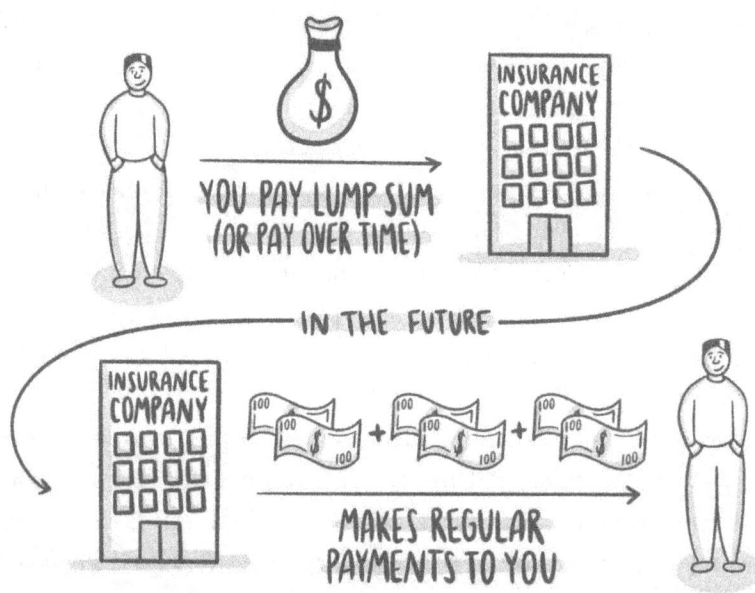

IMMEDIATE ANNUITY
payments start right away

DEFERRED ANNUITY
payments start later

Annuities are one of the most misunderstood but potentially powerful tools in retirement planning. An annuity is a contract between you and an insurance company. You give them money, either all at once or over time, and they promise to pay you a steady stream of income in the future, thereby turning your savings into a predictable paycheck for retirement.

There are several different types of annuities. A deferred annuity allows your investment to grow for a period before you begin receiving payments, making it ideal for those still a few years away from retirement. An immediate annuity starts paying out within a year, which can be useful if you're ready to start drawing income now. Fixed annuities offer a guaranteed rate of return, providing stability and predictability. Variable annuities fluctuate with the market, offering growth potential but also more risk.

If your workplace offers an in-plan annuity option, it can be a valuable part of a well-rounded retirement strategy. Otherwise, you can purchase your own.

Annuities have gained a mixed reputation, often due to the fees that can be attached to them. Some contracts do come with high costs, but when used appropriately, can be incredibly useful in retirement. They offer peace of mind by providing guaranteed income month after month and deliver protected, reliable income. Research shows that retirees who have guaranteed income tend to feel more confident and are often more comfortable spending their savings.

Key factors to evaluate when considering an annuity include what happens to the money when you pass away, whether you can access your funds in an emergency, what benefits are available to a spouse or survivor, and what fees and expenses are involved. Many annuities include optional features (called riders) that can add extra guarantees or benefits, like the ability to withdraw a set amount for life, even if the account balance goes to zero. These contract features can significantly impact your retirement income.

 Do you understand what your annuity provides? Are you confident in the protections it offers and the income it guarantees?

34. Life Insurance in Retirement

"Life insurance in retirement: Because you want to leave a legacy, and not a financial headache."

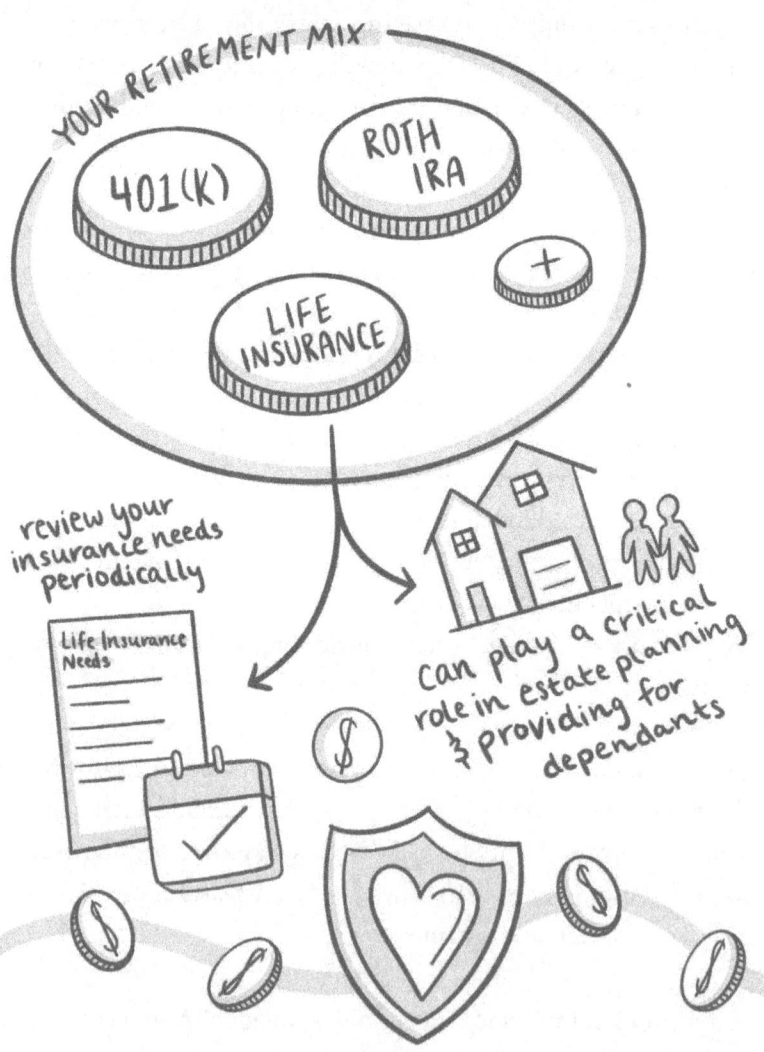

Do you think that life insurance is only for the young, mortgage-laden, or thrill-seeking skydivers? Think again. Life insurance can be the MVP of your retirement game plan.

Yes, even in retirement, life insurance plays a starring role. In fact, about 57% of retirees own life insurance policies. So even if you are already living the good life in stretchy pants and leisure suits, life insurance can play a key role.

These types of insurance policies can protect your loved ones, cover debts, and smooth out your estate plan. Best of all, they can even help you out while you're still alive and kicking.

Now, here's where things get real: If you're relying on your spouse or child to help with long-term care someday, what's the backup plan if they aren't around? Yeah… awkward pause. That's where insuring the people you depend on can be just as important as insuring yourself.

Beyond protection, life insurance can be a total financial Swiss Army knife. It can provide income replacement for a spouse that passes away. Life insurance can also cover estate taxes and help avoid probate drama. Some insurance policies can even build in a long-term care rider in case you need help down the road.

Oh, and the death benefit? Usually tax-free. Which means more peace of mind for your family and less paperwork-induced weeping.

Because when life throws curveballs—and it will—you'll be glad you had a plan. And that plan starts with the right life insurance, served with a side of foresight and a sprinkle of emotional relief.

 Is your life insurance pulling its weight, or just hanging out like that one friend who never pays for dinner? Are you covered enough to leave your family comfortable, your estate intact, and your retirement goals on track?

35. LTCI and Hybrid Policies

"Long-term care might not be a fun topic, but ignoring it can crash your retirement. Planning today with an LTC insurance or a hybrid policy means protecting your savings, your dignity, and your family's peace of mind tomorrow."

Let's talk about a financial topic that rarely gets invited to dinner parties: long-term care. It might not be flashy or fun, but it's one of the most important conversations you can have about your future.

Many people avoid long-term care insurance (LTCI) because of the "use it or lose it" reputation. But here's the reality: "Using all your savings and then some" is a much worse scenario. Years of assisted living, home care, or nursing facility costs can drain your assets faster than you think.

Only about 3.5% of adults currently have LTCI. Yet nearly 48% of us will need some form of paid long-term care after age 65. Those odds don't exactly favor your retirement nest egg.

LTCI and hybrid life insurance policies with LTC benefits are two powerful options. These policies' solutions allow you to shift some of the financial burden to an insurance provider.

LTCI can help cover the costs of home health aides, assisted living, or nursing homes—support that protects both your finances and your independence. If the "use it or lose it" concept still feels risky, hybrid policies might be the answer. These life insurance policies come with built-in long-term care coverage. If you need care, the policy pays out. If you don't, your beneficiaries receive the death benefit.

If you have an old life insurance policy you no longer need, you may be able to use a 1035 exchange—a tax-free way to convert it into a hybrid policy.

※ What can I do today to prepare for the possibility of long-term care? Would an LTCI policy be a good fit for me?

36. Cash Value Life Insurance as an Income Tool

"Cash value life insurance isn't a magic bullet—but for the right person, it can be a financial powerhouse, ready when you need it most."

NOT THE FOUNDATION OF A RETIREMENT PLAN—BUT A SMART LAYER

A lot of people compare cash value life insurance to a Swiss Army knife—versatile, compact, and useful in a variety of situations. But maybe it's more accurate to think of it as your own personal Swiss bank account in retirement—an accessible, tax-advantaged source of liquidity when you need it most.

According to research published in the Financial Services Review, using cash value life insurance as a retirement income supplement—especially when layered with an equity portfolio—can increase the sustainable withdrawal rate to between 7% and 9%.

This makes cash value life insurance a potentially powerful tool—but it is not without caveats. The cash value portion grows tax-deferred and allows for tax-free withdrawals (up to the amount of paid premiums) or tax-free policy loans, as long as they're properly managed.

It also has no contribution limits, offering a flexible option for high earners or those facing future tax concerns. And during market downturns, borrowing from your policy's cash value may help you avoid selling investments at a loss—giving your portfolio time to recover.

That said, this strategy isn't for everyone. Policies can take 10 years or more to accumulate significant value, and surrendering or lapsing a policy may trigger taxes and fees.

Those without other reliable income streams or who struggle to maintain premium payments might find the risks outweigh the benefits. And while the tax advantages are real, they may be less meaningful for retirees in lower tax brackets.

For those with long-term planning horizons, stable cash flow, and a desire for flexible, tax-efficient retirement income, cash value life insurance can be a valuable supplemental asset. It's not the foundation of a retirement plan—but it can be a smart layer on top of one.

> What ways could you see your retirement income plan benefiting from having cash value life insurance?

37. Capital Gains Strategies in Retirement

"Retirement tax planning isn't about what you owe today—it's about what you keep over a lifetime."

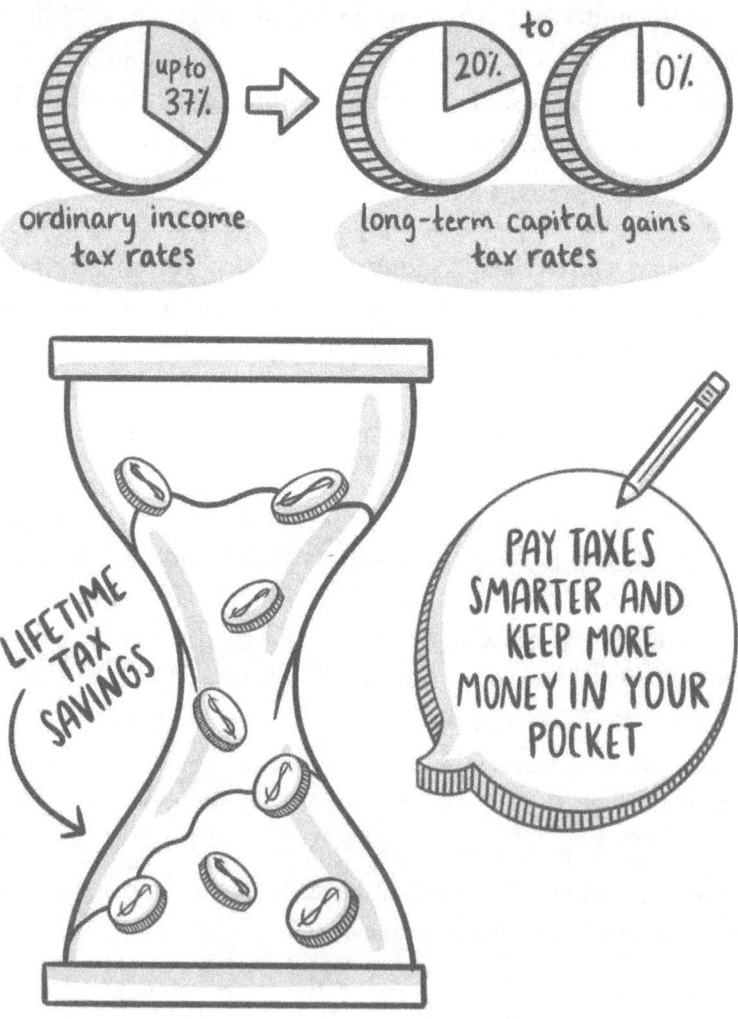

A well-crafted retirement plan doesn't dodge taxes. It navigates them. It's about knowing when to pay, how much to pay, and how to use the tax code to your advantage.

Take capital gains, for example. These taxes apply when you sell an appreciated asset like stocks, bonds, or real estate. The rate you pay depends on how long you've held the asset. If it's one year or less, you're taxed as ordinary income. If it's more than a year, you enjoy the lower long-term capital gains tax rates—0%, 15%, or 20%, depending on your income. For 2025, married couples filing jointly can realize up to $96,700 in long-term gains without owing federal tax. Gains between that and $600,050 are taxed at 15%, and gains above that are taxed at 20%.

That's a significant difference, especially when you consider that the highest ordinary income tax rate is 37%. Using capital gains strategically in retirement can help you stretch your income, reduce taxes, and avoid triggering higher Medicare premiums (discussed more later) or Net Investment Income Tax.

Long-term investing in a taxable account is often the overlooked workhorse of a retirement plan. But it can be powerful—especially when coordinated with withdrawals from Social Security, Traditional IRAs, or Roth accounts. By layering capital gains into your income plan carefully, you can smooth out taxable income and avoid tax bracket creep.

There are also tactical plays: tax-gain harvesting in low-income years to reset your cost basis; holding appreciated assets until death to give heirs a step-up in basis; and donating appreciated securities to charity to eliminate capital gains taxes while receiving a full deduction. Asset location also matters—putting growth assets in taxable accounts and interest-heavy assets in tax-deferred ones can make a difference over time.

The goal isn't just to pay less tax—it's to pay smarter. And with capital gains in your toolbox, you have more flexibility than you might think.

✳ Are you coordinating your capital gains withdrawals with other income sources like Social Security or Required Minimum Distributions (RMDs) to stay in a favorable tax bracket?

38. Working with an Advisor

"Retirement should be about living, not worrying."

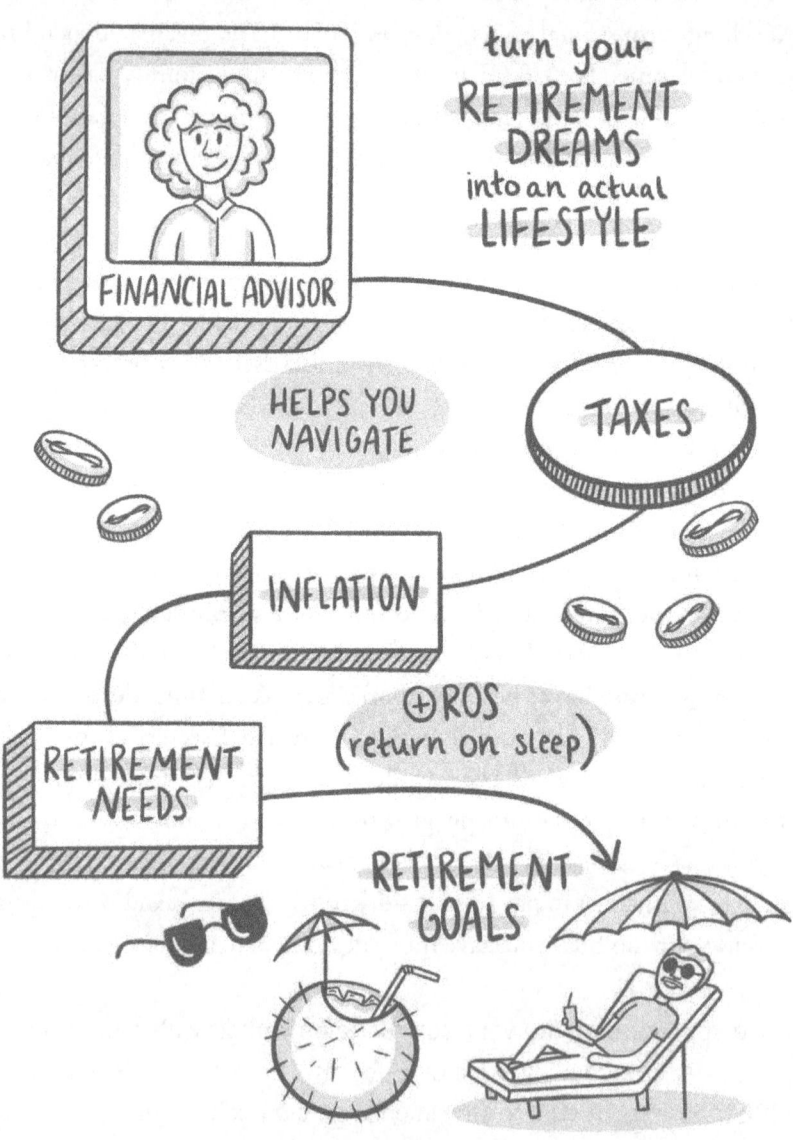

Let's be real—retirement should be about sipping something fruity out of a coconut, not stress-scrolling through your bank app at 2 am. That's where a financial advisor comes in. Not only do they help manage your money, but they also deliver something truly priceless: ROS—Return on Sleep. Because what good is a yacht if you're too anxious to enjoy the ride?

Research backs it up—Americans working with a financial advisor aren't just more confident about their financial future, they're more financially literate too (which is a fancy way of saying they know the difference between a Roth IRA and a rotten idea). In fact, about half of those with advisors feel financially secure in retirement, compared to 41% of those flying solo. Not huge math, but in retirement, every percent counts—just ask your Social Security check.

A financial advisor is like Google Maps for your money—only less annoying and way better at navigating things like taxes, inflation, and the "how much do I really need to retire comfortably?" panic spiral. They help stretch your savings, create sustainable withdrawal plans (no, not the cold-turkey-from-Netflix kind), and make sure you're not leaving a financial mess for your kids.

Think of it this way: You wouldn't go whitewater rafting without a guide, so why would you dive into retirement's wild waters without one? With the right advisor—especially one who puts your interests first (yes, that's a thing, it's called a fiduciary)—you can turn your retirement dreams into an actual lifestyle. We're talking more "fun in the sun," less "fun with spreadsheets."

So go ahead—delegate the financial stress and investing for retirement, reclaim your peace of mind, and remember: The best part of retirement isn't just the freedom, it's the naps. With a great advisor, you get to enjoy both. Yes, a financial advisor will help you invest and give you a plan (as we discuss more in later chapters). More importantly, they will give peace of mind.

 How might a financial advisor add value to your retirement planning process, and what criteria are you using to select one? What financial decisions in life do you like to delegate and which ones do you not like to delegate?

Your Retirement Notes

Your Retirement Sketches

CHAPTER IV

GETTING READY TO RETIRE

- Envision Your Future
- Retirement Preparedness
- Retirement Confidence
- Going Beyond Goals to Aspirations
- Issue with Averages in Retirement
- Pay Yourself First
- Planning Through the Decades
- Paycheck Replacement
- The Retirement Change
- Retirement Change Management
- Part-Time Work in Retirement
- Retire To or Retire From
- Forced Retirement
- Phased Retirement
- Retirement Planning for Couples versus Singles

CHAPTER IV.
Introduction

Retirement isn't just a financial event—it's a life transition. And like any major change, it requires preparation. You may have circled a date on the calendar, built up your savings, or met with a financial advisor, but are you truly ready to retire? Retirement is a fundamental shift in identity, purpose, and routine. It's a letting go of the familiar and an embrace of the unknown—which makes preparation all the more essential.

At its core, retirement is a change management process—not unlike launching a new career, relocating to a new city, or navigating a major life transition. You're moving from the structure, identity, and pace of the working world into a new chapter that's often undefined. And change, even positive change, can be uncomfortable. That's why preparing for retirement involves more than just knowing your number—it means knowing yourself.

So let's start with the big questions:

- What do you want your days to look like?
- How do you want to spend your time—and with whom?
- What gives your life meaning when work no longer does?

Too often, people jump into retirement with a list of things they want to get away from—stress, long hours, commuting. But fewer spend the time defining what they're moving toward. Retirement isn't just about freedom from work—it's about freedom to choose how you live, grow, give back, rest, and reinvent yourself.

Envisioning retirement

One of the best ways to prepare for retirement is to envision it. Not the abstract version—"I'll travel," "I'll relax," "I'll spend time with family"—but a vivid, day-in-the-life vision of what retirement will actually feel like. What time do you wake up? Do you work part-time? Volunteer? Do you pursue hobbies, start a business, move closer to your grandchildren, or finally write that novel?

Retirement isn't a finish line. It's a new beginning. And like any new chapter, you'll need to redefine your values, structure your days, and reconnect with the parts of yourself that may have been sidelined during your working years.

Try this: Draw or describe your ideal Tuesday morning five years into retirement. It's a surprisingly powerful way to ground your vision in reality.

Phasing out, not dropping out

While some people retire overnight, many benefit from phasing into retirement. That might mean reducing hours, shifting roles, or consulting part-time. This softer landing helps preserve structure, maintain income, and test-drive the emotional side of retirement. If you can gradually transition into retirement, you give yourself time to adjust and refine your plan as you go.

Think of it like warming up before a marathon or cooling down after a race—the transition phases matter. It's not just about reaching retirement, but arriving there prepared, present, and ready to thrive.

Preparing for retirement also means preparing for a shift in identity. For decades, work may have been a source of purpose, status, and social connection. Retirement can bring a surprising sense of loss—even grief—if those parts of your life aren't reimagined.

That's why it's important to ask:

- What part of my identity came from my work?
- What parts of me have I neglected that I want to bring forward now?
- What makes me feel fulfilled, challenged, or needed?

This is the emotional preparation that too often gets skipped—but it's what makes the difference between simply retiring and truly flourishing.

In the end, preparing for retirement is like preparing for any major life change: reflect, plan, communicate, and stay open to growth. Use this sketchbook to map out your vision, identify what matters most, and create your blueprint for a life that's not just long—but full.

39. Envision Your Future

"Envisioning your future helps create a strong and beneficial connection between you today and your future self that can help activate increased retirement savings and improved wellness."

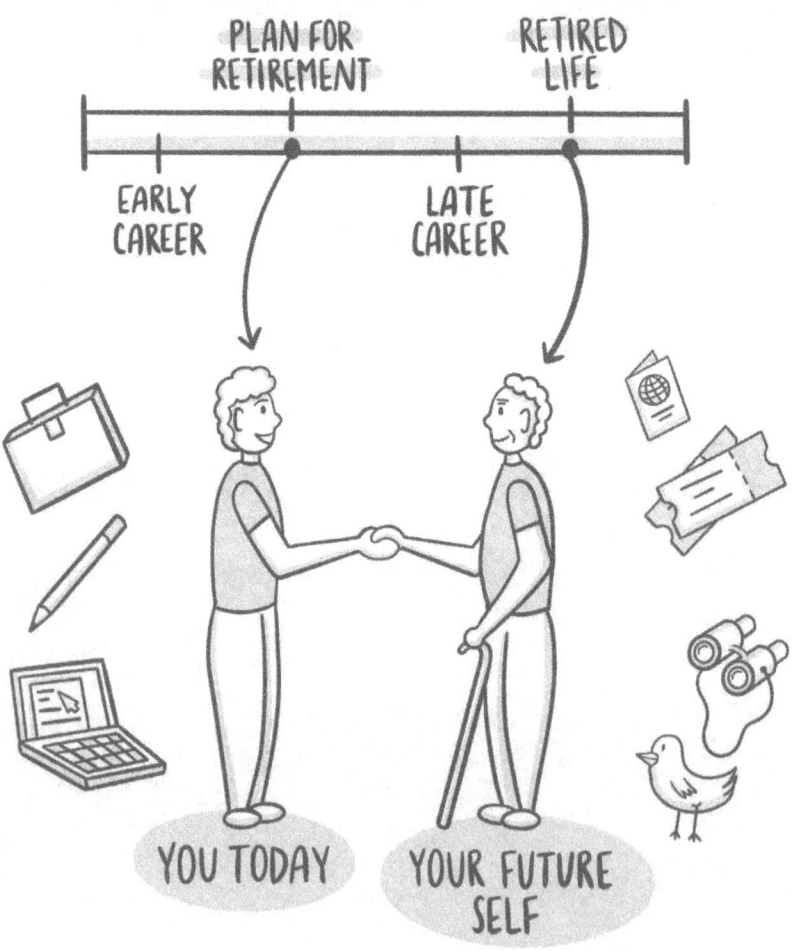

Here's something wild: Scientists analyzed over 100 brain scans (yes, with real brains!) and discovered that when we think about strangers, our brains light up in the exact same way as when we think about… our future selves.

Yep. To your brain, Future You is basically that random guy at the bus stop wearing socks with sandals. No wonder it's hard to care what happens to them.

And get this: Over half of Americans (53%, to be exact) admit they never think about life 30 years from now.

The more you actually think about your future self (yes, even the wrinkly version of you who owns a bird feeder and says "back in my day…"), the more you start making awesome choices now.

You also become more connected to your community and start feeling like you've got a real purpose, like you're the main character in your own feel-good movie montage.

So, here's your mission: Take some time to imagine your future. Not just goals, but aspirations.

A goal might be "go to Europe," whereas an aspiration is to "become a globe-trotting adventurer who collects passport stamps like Pokémon cards." Dream big. Sketch it out. Write it down. Get dramatic with it—vision boards, aged-up selfies, interpretive dance if that's your thing.

Your future self may feel like a stranger now, but with a little imagination, you can become your favorite person—and you're counting on you to get the party started.

✸ Who do you want to be? Where will you be in 30 years? What is your life aspiration? What would give you personal and life satisfaction?

40. Retirement Preparedness

"Yes, you want to have the time of your life in retirement. But getting prepared can mean a lifetime of hard work."

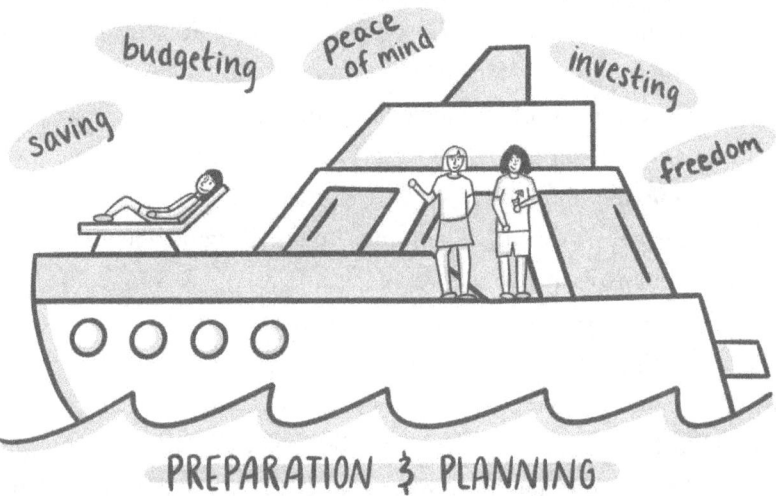

PREPARATION & PLANNING

NO PREPARATION & PLANNING

Let's be real: Retirement sounds amazing. No alarm clocks, no rush-hour traffic, just you, your hobbies, and maybe a suspiciously large collection of tropical shirts. But here's the catch: A fabulous retirement doesn't magically appear with a wish and a lucky penny. Nope, it takes some good ol' fashioned preparation and planning.

Here's the not-so-fun fact about retirement: About one-third of Americans are heading toward retirement with no real plan in place. They've got little to no savings and will have to lean heavily on government programs like Social Security, Medicare, and Medicaid... aka the financial version of a life raft made out of duct tape and hope.

But good news!

You don't have to be in that boat. You can build your own luxury yacht to retirement (okay, maybe more like a sturdy sailboat) by getting a game plan together now. That means saving, investing, and budgeting.

The earlier you start, the smoother your future cruise will be.

Wondering how much you'll need to live comfortably when you finally ditch the 9-to-5? A general rule is to aim for 70–80% of your current income.

So, if you're living large on $100,000 a year today, you'll likely need around $70,000–$80,000 per year in retirement to keep the same lifestyle—Netflix subscription, occasional fancy coffee, and all.

Bottom line: Retirement is not a mystery box you open at 65. It's something you build, little by little, one paycheck and smart decision at a time. Future You is cheering Present You on from a beach chair somewhere—piña colada in hand.

 Have you calculated how much you will need in retirement? Do you know where this money will come from? Do you have a shortfall between the two?

41. Retirement Confidence

"Confidence is a beautiful thing."

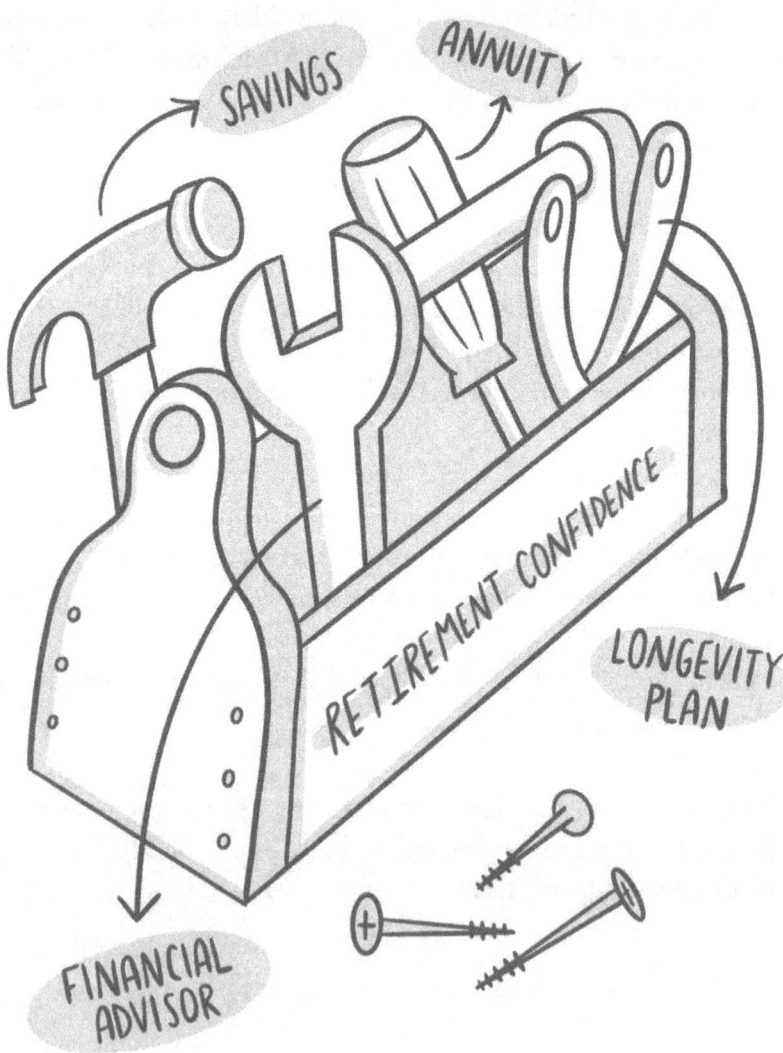

Confidence helps you walk into a room like you own it—or at least like you know where the snacks are. And when it comes to retirement, confidence is key. But here's the catch: too much confidence? That's when things go sideways. It's like trying to tightrope walk across your finances blindfolded.

Nearly two-thirds of Americans say they feel confident they'll glide through retirement just fine. But dig a little deeper and only 18% say they feel very confident. That's like saying you're "kind of sure" your parachute will open—yikes!

And then there's the other side—the Overly Confident but Unprepared Team—who think they've cracked the investment code and can outsmart the market with their gut instincts and a YouTube video.

News flash: Overconfidence in retirement can lead to big problems, like running out of money when you're 83 and suddenly searching on the internet, "how to make gourmet meals out of canned beans."

So, what's the secret to having the right kind of confidence? It's simple (but not necessarily easy): Save more. Learn more. Get a solid financial advisor. And most importantly—have a written retirement plan.

Think of your retirement plan like a GPS for your future—it keeps you on course, reroutes when life throws detours, and keeps you from accidentally driving off a financial cliff.

If you're not feeling great about your retirement outlook, don't panic. Just take action. Whether it's saving a little more, working a bit longer, or trimming back on those fancy lattes, every step helps.

Bottom line? Be confident—but be smart about it. Because in retirement, it's not just about having money. It's about making sure it lasts long enough for you to spend your golden years doing what you love.

 Where is one area of your life that you are very confident in? Why do you think this is the case? What can you apply from this area of life to your retirement confidence?

42. Going Beyond Goals to Aspirations

"Goals often reflect what we think we can achieve, whereas aspirations embody what we dream of achieving."

Let's talk goals vs. aspirations—because while goals are great, aspirations are where the magic happens.

First, a wild stat: People who wrote down their goals, included action steps, and had someone holding them accountable were 76% more likely to crush those goals. That's a whopping 33% higher than the folks who just winged it with good intentions and zero follow-through. (Turns out, "hope" is not a great financial strategy.)

We've all set goals before—New Year's resolutions, work deadlines, trying to drink more water, or actually folding laundry the same day it gets washed.

Goals are awesome because they're measurable. For example, saving $1 million? That's a clear, trackable goal.

But let's zoom out. What's beyond that goal?

That's where aspirations come in. Aspirations are the big-picture dreams. The "why" behind the goals. So yeah, saving $1 million is great—but if your aspiration is to be financially free, then that million is just a mile marker, not the destination.

The real destination? A life where you're in control of your time, your money, and your choices.

Goals are the stepping stones. Aspirations are the mountaintop. So start crafting your plan now. Write it down. Break it into steps. Add some accountability. And go make it real.

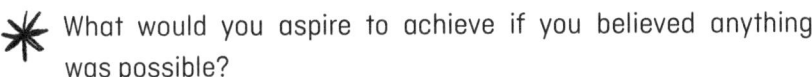 What would you aspire to achieve if you believed anything was possible?

43. Issue with Averages in Retirement

"Tracking averages is important as you plan for retirement. And making the right financial decisions will help make sure you have an above-average lifestyle."

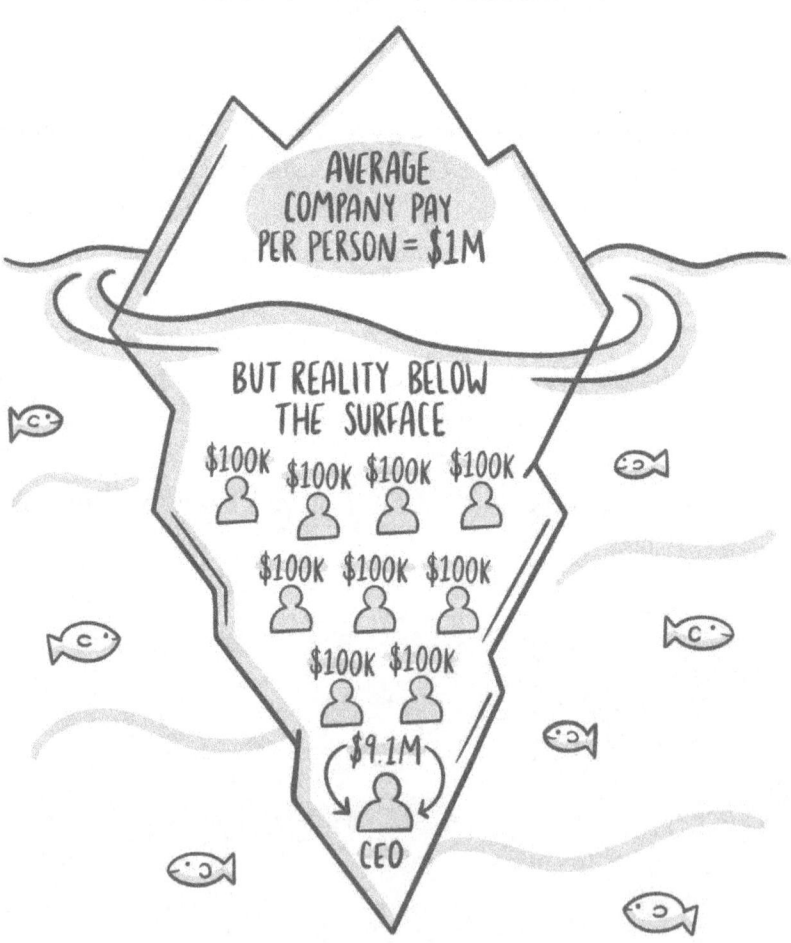

Remember learning about averages in school? It seemed simple enough. Add up some numbers, divide by how many there are, and boom, you've got a handy little statistic. But then someone told you that San Diego and Omaha have about the same average annual temperature. And you realized something important: Averages can lie.

Let's apply that to retirement.

According to recent data, Americans in their 60s have an average retirement savings balance of $1,180,022. Impressive, right? But the median, which means half have more and half have less, is only $590,777. And here's the kicker: Nearly one-third of Americans have almost nothing saved at all.

So, averages are not always helpful. They roll everyone into one number, blending millionaires with folks who are just getting by. That can give a wildly misleading view of where you stand and what you need.

Averages can also trip us up when it comes to planning life expectancy. If the average life expectancy is 82, that means half of people will live longer than that. Planning based on that number alone gives you a 50-50 shot of running out of money early.

Let's also talk about investment returns. You've probably heard that the average rate of return in the market is somewhere around 7%. That sounds great, until you learn about something called sequence of returns. If your portfolio takes a hit early in retirement, even if the average return is good, your savings might not survive the long haul.

So what do you do?

Forget about averages for a moment. Focus on you. Your lifestyle. Your health. Your goals. Use general rules like the 4% withdrawal rate or typical retirement expenses as a starting point. Then build a plan based on your actual life, not some mathematical midpoint that ignores all the details that make you unique.

 What part of your retirement do you know won't be average? Will it be your travel budget? Your healthcare needs? Your longevity?

44. Pay Yourself First

"Paying yourself first isn't selfish. In fact, it's the smartest way to make sure Future You gets the retirement you deserve."

Let's flip the script on how you think about money. Instead of saving what's left after spending, try spending what's left after saving. That's the heart of the pay yourself first philosophy.

Saving isn't about being stingy or denying yourself joy. It's about choosing lasting happiness over quick thrills. It's you making a bold statement that your future matters.

Here's the reality check. Only about 20% of Gen Z Americans consistently save for retirement, and about half aren't even sure how to prioritize their financial decisions today. That means a lot of folks are flying blind when it comes to their future.

And remember, no one is going to save for your retirement except for you.

It's tempting to want to fund your kids' or grandkids' college or help with other expenses, but if that comes at the cost of your own retirement, you might be setting yourself up for stress later on.

Think of it like this: During your working years, money is flowing in. But when you retire, that river of income turns into a trickle. That's why saving during your "times of plenty" is so important. You are storing up for the seasons ahead.

The best part? You don't have to do this manually. Automate your retirement contributions so they happen before you ever see the money in your checking account. That way, saving becomes a habit, not a chore. Through a workplace retirement account described more in an earlier chapter, this can be quite easy!

Tie your savings to something meaningful. Whether it's an emergency fund, an early retirement goal, or a dream adventure, giving your savings a name makes it easier to stick with it.

 What are you doing to make sure you are saving for retirement consistently month after month?

45. Planning Through the Decades

"Saving for retirement is like planting a tree in your 20s, nurturing it through your 30s and 40s, pruning it to grow in your 50s, and finally enjoying the shade and fruit in your 60s and later."

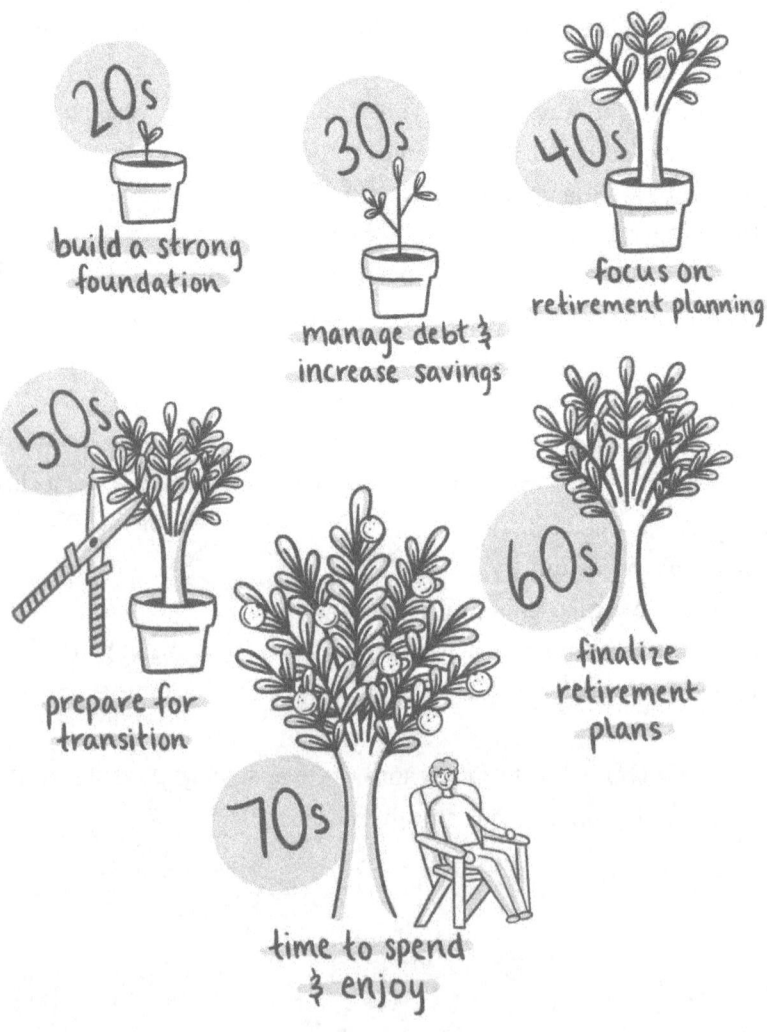

In your 20s: Build a strong foundation

Focus on investing in yourself through education or skill development. Begin saving early, even modest amounts, by contributing to employer-sponsored retirement plans or setting up an IRA.

In your 30s: Manage debt and increase savings

Start reducing your debt, including student loans and credit obligations. Aim to increase retirement contributions, targeting 15–20% of your income. Automate savings to ensure consistency.

In your 40s: Focus on retirement planning

Maximize contributions to retirement accounts like 401(k)s and IRAs. Does your asset allocation align with your risk tolerance and retirement timeline?

In your 50s: Prepare for transition

Assess your retirement savings and projected income needs. Consider working with a financial advisor to refine your retirement strategy. Explore options like catch-up contributions to retirement accounts.

In your 60s: Finalize retirement plans

Determine the optimal time to begin withdrawing from retirement accounts. Understand the implications of Social Security benefits and strategize for tax-efficiency.

In your 70s: Time to spend and enjoy

Enjoy retirement! Focus on spending your hard-earned savings and manage your taxable income by strategically withdrawing from retirement accounts to minimize tax impact.

✱ How has your retirement planning changed over the decades, and what adjustments do you anticipate needing in the future?

46. Paycheck Replacement

"Retirement isn't the end of a paycheck. It's the beginning of what Past You built for Future You."

Retirees typically need to replace approximately 70–80% of their pre-retirement income to maintain their standard of living in retirement.

One of the biggest transitions in retirement is learning how to live without your regular paycheck from work. But that doesn't mean the money stops. Your income now comes from new places. This is where paycheck replacement comes in. Think of it as crafting your own custom paycheck using all the income sources you've built up over the years.

To keep your lifestyle feeling comfortable, many experts suggest replacing about 70–80% of your pre-retirement income. That might sound like a step down, but remember, some expenses like commuting, payroll taxes, and retirement contributions often go away. On the flip side, costs like travel or healthcare might increase.

Let's say you made $80,000 a year before retiring. Aiming for $56,000 to $64,000 annually in retirement income could be a solid starting goal. This could come from Social Security, pensions, withdrawals from your 401(k) or IRA, annuities, or even part-time work. Social Security alone might cover 30–40% for many people, but the rest has to come from your personal savings and smart planning.

Why does this matter? Because without a plan, you might fall into one of two traps: spending too much too fast or holding back and not spending out of fear. Neither makes for a peaceful retirement. But with a plan in place, you gain freedom. Freedom to travel. Freedom to treat yourself. Freedom to relax without second-guessing every dollar.

No matter your age, the earlier you start planning for your retirement paycheck, the easier the shift becomes. A financial advisor can help you map it all out, showing you how much you'll need, where it can come from, and how to make it last.

 How confident are you in your current plan to replace your paycheck in retirement, and where might there be gaps?

47. The Retirement Change

"While retirement may begin on a single day, it's not a one-time event—it's a gradual journey of preparing, transitioning, and ultimately living in retirement."

Here's something not everyone talks about: Retirement can rattle you. Beyond the financial aspect we have been discussing in this chapter, there's the emotional aspect.

Studies show that new retirees are about 40% more likely to experience a dip in mental health during their first year out of the workforce, because they underestimated just how much life would shift when the job ends and the next chapter begins.

Retirement doesn't happen in one tidy step. It unfolds in phases—like acts in a play. First, you prepare. Then, you retire. And finally, you live it. The preparation stage is about dreaming, planning, and getting your ducks in a row. You imagine lazy mornings, long walks, or maybe starting that business you never had time for. You sketch out a future, crunch the numbers, and try to picture what's next.

Then… you retire. You pack up your office. You get the card. Maybe you cry. Maybe you don't. But in that moment, the familiar rhythm of life changes. That's where things get real.

Many people struggle with the identity shift. You've spent decades answering the question: What do you do? Now you're faced with a deeper one: Who are you without the job?

Here's the truth: Retiring well isn't just about having enough money. It's about having a life to step into once the job ends. That means building routines that matter, staying connected to others, and finding ways to keep your purpose alive. So how do you do it?

Start with intention. Create a plan that includes your relationships, your hobbies, your health, and your happiness.

The actual transition can feel like a celebration or a cliff dive: a long-awaited freedom, an unexpected ending, or a turning point. And once it happens, you enter a new stage: the rhythm of retired life.

 Have you built a vision you're actually excited to live in? Or are you still thinking about retirement as a finish line?

48. Retirement Change Management

"Change management in retirement means learning to manage time when every day is Saturday and changing meetings to meaning."

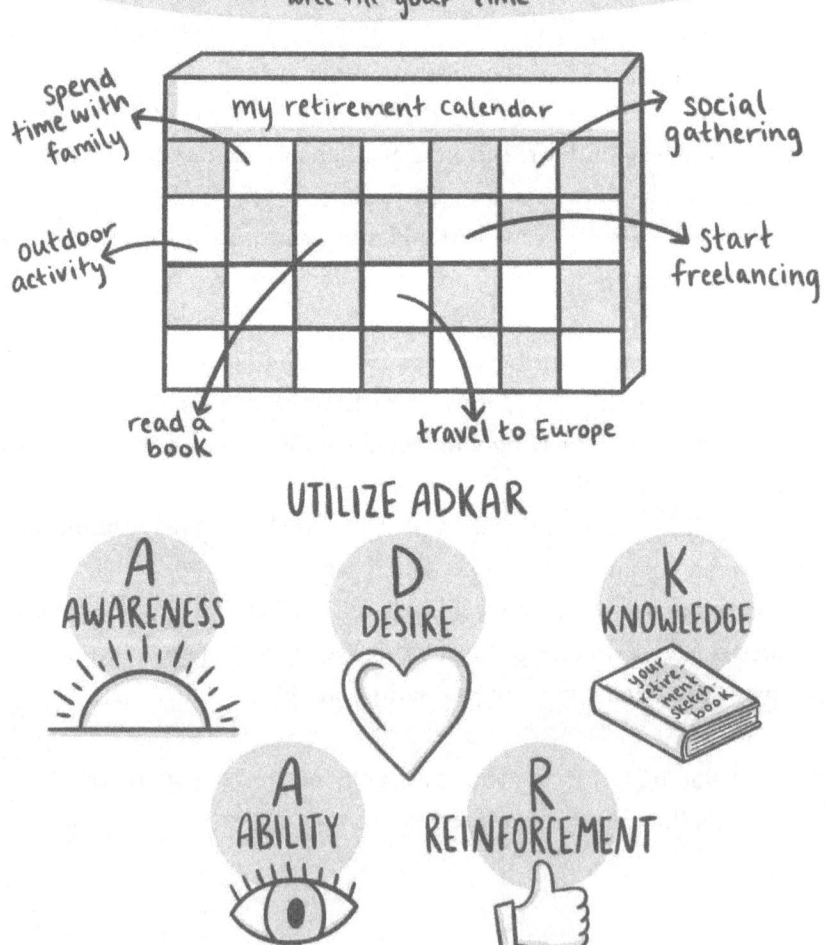

Retirement is one of the biggest changes most people will face. You're letting go of a title and structure that once defined your days, forcing you to reimagine who you are and how you spend your time. Nearly 30% of new retirees report difficulty adjusting to the lifestyle changes that retirement brings and worry about losing their connection and purpose in retirement.

Social circles may shift, making it important to build new connections and meaning outside of your job.

Prepare for the non-financial aspects of retirement, including how you will spend your time, maintain social connections, and keep mentally and physically active. Create a calendar of how you will fill your time, find meaning, and live in retirement well before you make it to retirement. You could employ change management processes like ADKAR to help with your retirement transition since retirement is one of the biggest changes we need to manage in our lives.

A—Awareness

Understand that retirement isn't just financial—it's a major life shift that impacts your identity, routine, and relationships.

D—Desire

Feel motivated to embrace the next chapter, even with its uncertainties. Do you want more freedom, fulfillment, or a healthier pace of life?

K—Knowledge

Learn what retirement actually involves—from managing finances and healthcare to building a new daily routine and sense of purpose.

A—Ability

Put plans into action—create a spending strategy, practice new habits, explore new roles (like volunteering or part-time work), and emotionally prepare for change.

R—Reinforcement

Stay engaged by celebrating small wins, revisiting your "why," and building a support system to help maintain your well-being and sense of direction.

✳ What are your plans for managing the lifestyle and psychological changes that come with retirement?

49. Part-Time Work in Retirement

"Part-time work in retirement isn't about making ends meet. It's about making life meaningful with purpose, passion, and a paycheck on your terms."

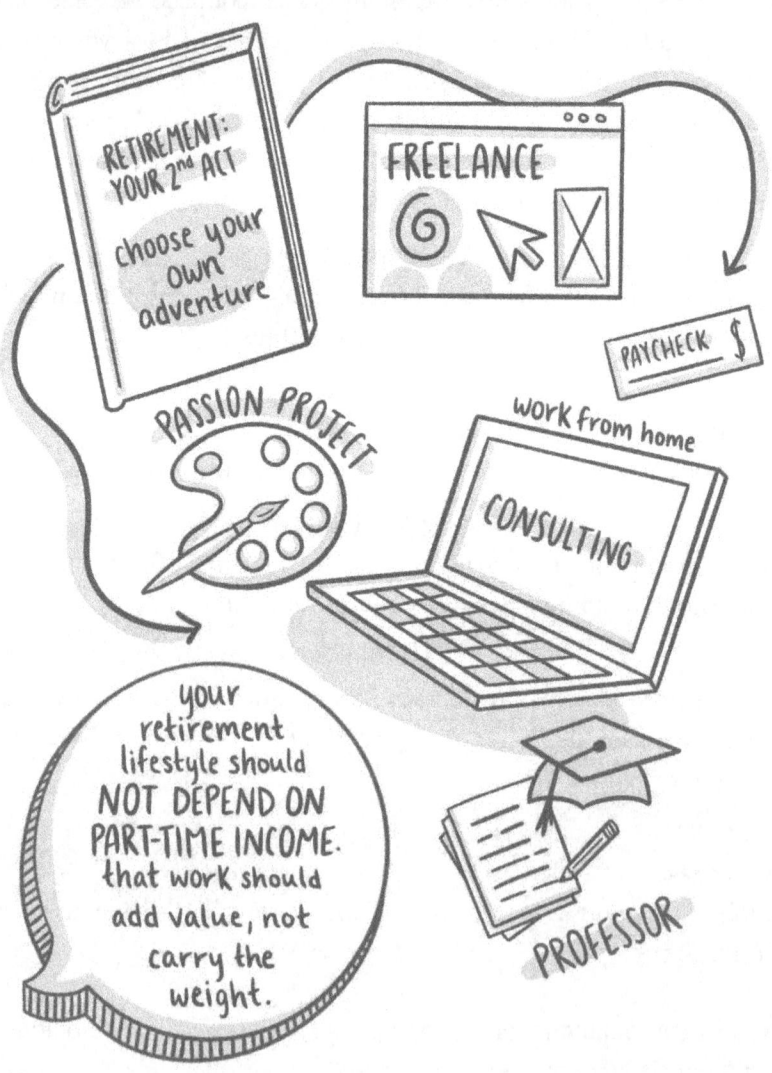

Retirement used to mean hanging up your hat and calling it a day. But in today's gig economy, it often marks the start of an exciting second act.

Here's the twist. While 70% of workers expect to work for pay during retirement, only 27% of retirees actually do. So what's going on?

For many, the idea of working in retirement isn't about the money. It's about staying sharp, staying social, and doing something that lights them up.

Whether it's turning a hobby into a side hustle, diving into freelance work, or consulting in a field they've mastered, retirees are redefining what "work" looks like.

Thanks to technology, finding part-time work is easier than ever. You can work from home, work from anywhere, or find a job that fits your schedule instead of the other way around. Flexibility is the new currency.

Most people do not keep working just for the paycheck. They keep working because they want to. They enjoy it. They find meaning in it. A second career in retirement can offer creativity, challenge, and even joy.

Still, it's important to treat part-time work as a bonus, not a backup plan. Health, energy, and priorities can change. That's why building a solid financial foundation before retirement is key. Your retirement lifestyle should not depend on part-time income. Instead, that work should add value, not carry the weight.

Think of part-time work in retirement as a choose-your-own adventure. You get to decide what it looks like, how much time you give it, and what kind of passion project it becomes.

✱ What kind of work would you want to do in retirement? What passion or talent could you finally explore with freedom and flexibility?

50. Retire To or Retire From

"Retirement is not the end of the road. It's the start of a new journey. Retire to purpose, passion, and the pursuit of what truly matters to you instead of just trying to escape the past."

Retirement is not the finish line. It's the start of a brand-new journey. If you play it right, it might just be the most exciting one yet. This chapter is about stepping boldly into a life filled with purpose, passion, and a daily schedule that actually makes you smile.

For many, retiring means "shifting focus to a new type of work or fulfilling purpose." In fact, 38% of pre-retirees already see it that way, according to the 2024 MassMutual Retirement Happiness Study.

Retirement often gets framed as a getaway car speeding away from spreadsheets, morning meetings, or that one manager who never learned to use the mute button. But the real magic of retirement doesn't come from what you leave behind—it comes from what you're heading toward.

When people retire without a plan, it's easy to feel unanchored. The routines disappear. The identity you built over decades might feel like it's fading. That's why designing your retirement matters. It's not about staying busy just to fill the hours. It's about filling your days with meaning, creativity, and connection.

So consider: What makes you feel alive? How do you want to spend your days? Who do you want by your side?

Make a retirement mood board. Talk to people who are thriving in their second act. Meet with a financial advisor who understands that your dreams need a budget too. Take your future for a test drive—volunteer, travel, or rent that cabin in the mountains for a month. And revisit your plan regularly. Retirement isn't static, and your dreams shouldn't be either.

 Are you clear on what you are retiring to, and does it give you a sense of purpose and excitement? Will you cry on your last day of work or pop a bottle of champagne?

51. Forced Retirement

"The best retirement plan isn't just one that works when everything goes right. It's one that still works in strained circumstances, even when life throws you a curveball."

Sometimes retirement doesn't knock politely. Sometimes it barges in uninvited, and you have to scramble for a plan. What happens next is still up to you.

Around 52% of retirees didn't get to choose when they retired. Health issues, company layoffs, or the need to care for a loved one often made the decision for them. That's why planning for the unexpected isn't just smart—it's essential.

Forced retirement happens when life takes a turn and cuts your working years short. If you're not ready, it can throw a wrench into your plans, your finances, and your peace of mind. But you can prepare yourself now, even if you don't know exactly what's coming.

If you're within five years of retirement, it's time to stress-test your plan. Ask yourself: What happens if I retire earlier than expected? Can I cover my expenses? Will my savings stretch far enough?

Here are a few smart moves: Build a strong emergency fund to cover 6–12 months of living expenses. Reduce debt so you have more financial freedom. Review your retirement savings regularly and make adjustments if needed. Keep your skills sharp and your network active so you're not caught off guard. Avoid big financial commitments late in your career.

It's also wise to map out two versions of your retirement plan. Create one approach where everything in your life goes according to schedule and you can retire on your terms, and another plan where retirement comes early. Because while working longer can dramatically boost your retirement plan, leaving early can just as easily strain it.

And don't forget about income. Diversify your sources: Social Security, savings, investments, and part-time work options. Flexibility is your best defense against uncertainty.

✷ How prepared are you for an unexpected early retirement? Could you manage if your plans changed tomorrow? What three steps could you take right now to be better prepared?

52. Phased Retirement

"Phased retirement is your personal on-ramp to freedom. Ease into the next chapter with purpose, flexibility, and a paycheck that helps you enjoy the ride."

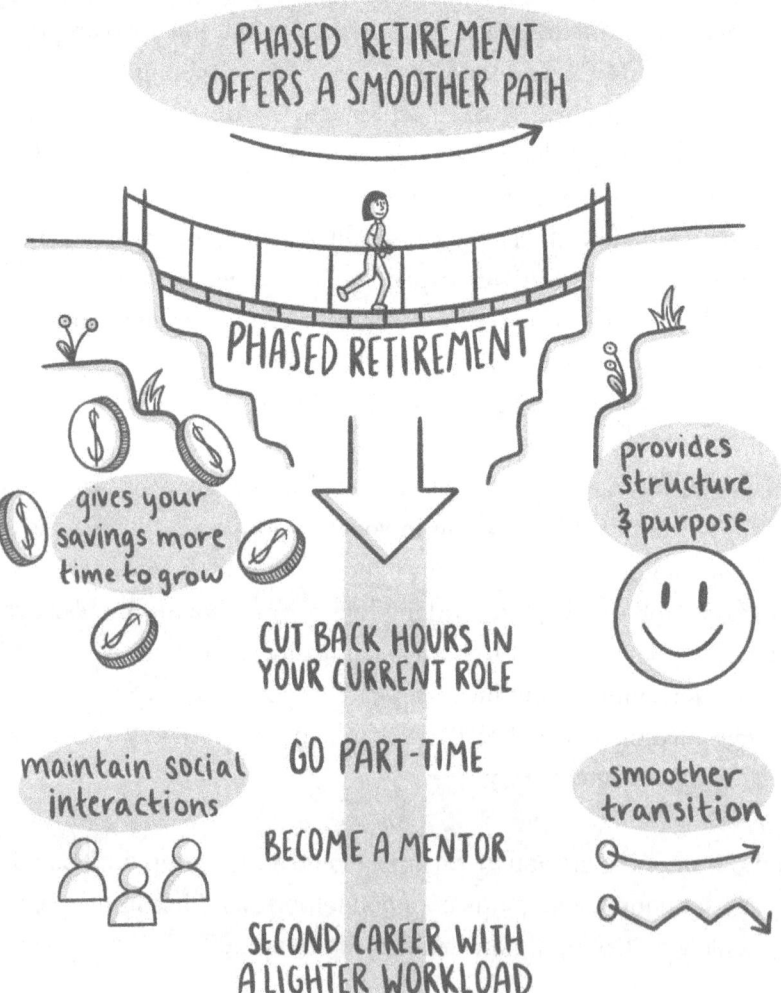

Think of phased retirement like training for a marathon. You don't just show up on race day without warming up—you ease into it, build your pace, and avoid burning out halfway through. Retiring cold turkey might work for some, but for many, it's like running that marathon with zero prep. Painful and not ideal.

Phased retirement allows you to gradually reduce your work hours or responsibilities instead of slamming the brakes on your career all at once.

The idea is catching on. Back in the 2000s, only about 10% of employers offered formal phased retirement programs. Today, that number has jumped to around 35%, as more people look for flexible ways to transition into retirement.

So what can phased retirement look like?

It might mean cutting back your hours in your current role. Or switching to part-time consulting. Some people retire, then get rehired into a new job with fewer demands. Others freelance, take on mentorship roles, or simply reduce their client load if they are self-employed.

Earning a bit longer can delay tapping into your retirement savings, giving them more time to grow. It can also provide structure, purpose, and the social interaction many retirees say they miss most. You're easing into a new lifestyle instead of diving into the deep end.

But it takes planning. Talk to your employer to see if phased retirement is even an option.

Talk to your family and a financial advisor to make sure this transition fits with your goals. Do you want to work from home? Would you be happy with less pay and fewer hours, or are you hoping to maintain the same pay with different responsibilities? What would make this second act both meaningful and manageable?

For those who can make it work, phased retirement can be the perfect bridge between the working world and the freedom of retirement.

> ✳ Would phased retirement work for you? What would your ideal arrangement look like?

53. Retirement Planning for Couples Versus Singles

"Retiring solo doesn't mean going it alone. It means creating a plan that reflects your independence, protects your future, and celebrates the life you've built on your own."

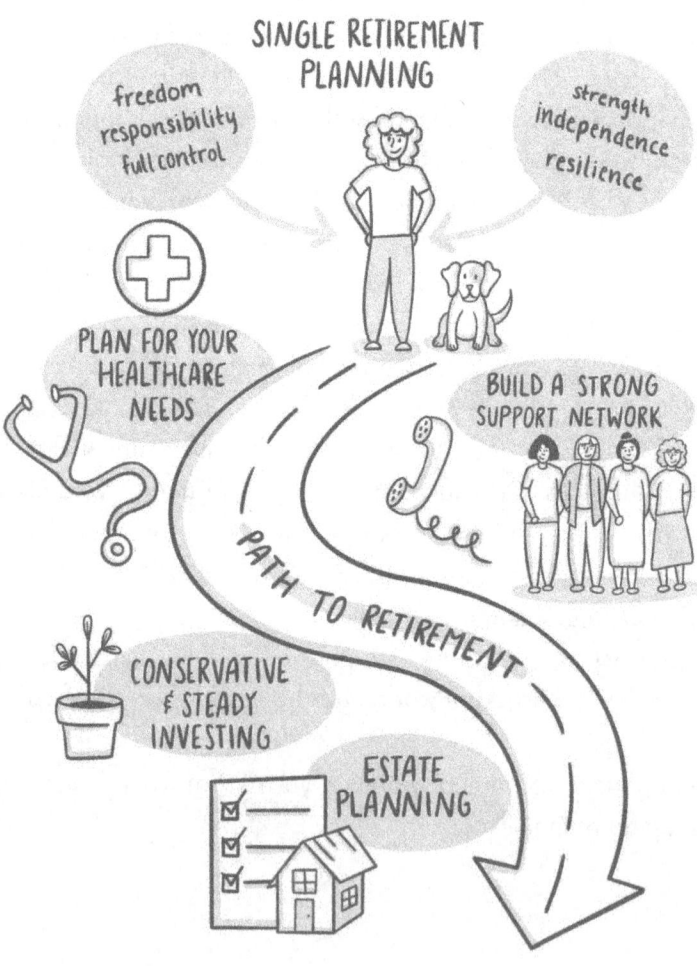

There's no shame in planning for retirement as a single person—only strength. Whether you're divorced, widowed, or never married, this stage of life brings both freedom and responsibility. Retirement planning can look different when you're on your own, but it's not something to fear. In fact, it's an opportunity to take full control of your future.

That control, however, comes with challenges. According to recent research, 46% of single people worry about running out of money in retirement, compared to just 38% of married individuals. With only one income source—one Social Security check, one retirement account, and no partner to split expenses—it's important to plan wisely.

Being single doesn't necessarily mean your expenses are half as much. Housing, utilities, and transportation don't scale down neatly. At the same time, you won't have a built-in caregiver in the home, which makes planning for healthcare and long-term care even more important. Without a spouse to lean on, a strong support network of friends, professionals, and community resources becomes essential—not just for practical help, but for emotional connection.

Your Social Security strategy may take on greater weight, too. With no spousal benefit to factor in, decisions about when to claim can have a bigger impact on your overall income. With no partner to help ride out market swings, you're more exposed to volatility and sequence of returns risk, which calls for a more conservative and steady investment approach.

Estate planning also becomes especially important. Having powers of attorney, healthcare proxies, and clear instructions in place ensures your wishes are respected if you're unable to make decisions for yourself. These are tasks many people postpone, but for singles, they're essential pieces of a well-rounded retirement plan.

Above all, this is a time for pride and preparation. Retirement as a single person is about honoring what you've built on your own and taking the steps to protect and enjoy it.

> If you're entering retirement on your own, does your plan reflect the independence and resilience that got you here? Have you set yourself up with the support—financial and personal—that will carry you forward with confidence?

Your Retirement Notes

Your Retirement Sketches

CHAPTER V

PREPARING YOUR RETIREMENT INCOME PLAN

- Retirement Income Planning
- Value of Lifetime Income
- What is Retirement Income?
- Mortality Credits
- Your Retirement Income Picture
- Bucketing Approach
- Flooring Approach
- Retirement Risks
- Tax Diversification
- Roth Conversions
- Retirement Planning for Small Business Owners

CHAPTER V.
Introduction

If saving for retirement is the uphill part of the race—consistent, disciplined, and forward-focused—then retirement income planning is the descent. And while going downhill might sound easier, it's where control, precision, and adaptability really matter.

You only get one shot at retirement, and the challenge lies in turning a lifetime of savings into a lifetime of income. When climbing Everest the ascent is not actually the dangerous part where people perish, but in the return part of the climb.

But here's the truth: Retirement income planning is not about chasing perfection. It's about building a plan that works for you—one that reflects your goals, your timeline, your values, and your fears. It's about constructing a bridge from today to the future, strong enough to hold up under pressure, yet flexible enough to bend with the winds of change.

A moving target in the wind

Think of retirement income planning like trying to hit a moving target in the wind. The target is shaped specifically for you—your spending needs, your lifestyle goals, your hopes for travel, family, and legacy. But it's constantly shifting forward and backward because we don't know how long retirement will last. You could live 15 years in retirement, you could live 35 years, or just a day.

That's a wide range to plan for—especially when you only get to retire once.

And then there's the wind: tax law changes, Social Security adjustments, healthcare costs, market volatility, inflation, and long-term care needs. These are the forces beyond your control that can throw your plan off course—unless you're prepared.

So how do you plan for something that's uncertain by nature?

You balance the certainty of today with the uncertainty of tomorrow. That's the essence of a good retirement income plan.

Planning for what we know

We start with what's known:

- Your savings and retirement accounts
- Your projected Social Security or pension income
- Your fixed expenses—housing, food, insurance
- Your short-term goals and initial retirement lifestyle.

These pieces become your "floor"—the dependable income you can count on. For some, that includes guaranteed sources like annuities or bond ladders. For others, it means building a conservative drawdown strategy that limits early withdrawals or reduces market exposure.

Planning with certainty doesn't mean locking yourself into a rigid system. It means designing for stability where it counts—covering your basic needs so you don't have to panic when markets dip or life throws a curveball.

Respecting the unknown

But we also have to respect what we don't know. No plan survives contact with reality unchanged. That's why a strong retirement income plan isn't static—it's adaptive. It flexes with new information. It includes guardrails, buckets, and strategies that allow you to make smart adjustments along the way without derailing your future.

Retirement is not binary. You don't stop working and start spending on the same day, and your needs don't stay flat year to year. Health costs might rise. Your travel desires might decline. Family needs may shift. Your plan needs to move with you—not trap you.

That's where income layers and dynamic strategies come in:

- Creating a "go-go, slow-go, no-go" spending plan
- Using tax diversification to control what you withdraw and when
- Rebalancing between growth, safety, and income as you age
- Having contingency reserves for healthcare or long-term care expenses.

The real goal: confidence

The real goal of a retirement income plan isn't just funding life—it's living life with confidence. It's knowing you've done the work, thought through the risks, and given yourself permission to enjoy retirement without being ruled by fear or scarcity.

It's waking up and deciding what to do with your time—not what to worry about with your money. And if life changes, as it surely will, your plan can change too. That's the beauty of building a thoughtful, flexible strategy.

So in this chapter, don't focus on hitting a bullseye on day one. Focus on understanding your target, gauging the wind, and crafting an approach that lets you aim with purpose and adjust with grace.

Because in retirement, just like in life, it's not about perfection—it's about progress and preparation.

54. Retirement Income Planning

"Retirement income planning is like trying to hit a moving target in the wind."

Retirement income planning can feel like trying to hit a moving target in a windstorm… while blindfolded… on roller skates. The wind? That's everything life throws at you: tax law changes, inflation, rising healthcare costs, and shifting government programs. And the moving target? That's the uncertainty of how much money you'll need and how long you'll need it. Will you live to 95? 105? Will you spend your golden years gardening or globetrotting?

That's why retirement income planning is so crucial. It's the art (and science) of preparing for the certainty that you'll need money in retirement—while navigating the uncertainty of how much, for how long, and under what circumstances.

As it turns out, only 39% of Americans have a retirement income plan in place. And while figuring out how to finance a retirement can seem challenging at first, there are some methods to ensure reliable, sustainable income.

This process of planning for the certainty of our retirement needs today but with the uncertainty of tomorrow is called retirement income planning. The process starts by figuring out our goals, adding up our income sources, figuring out our possible future expenses, then seeing if there is a gap. If there is a gap, we then set forth action items to close that shortfall by working longer, investing more aggressively, or shifting around our income sources.

A well-designed retirement income plan should change over time but keep some consistent principles in place. The plan should start with a goal in mind for both accumulation of assets and a decumulation approach. What is the retirement income philosophy that makes sense to you? Do you want to be more conservative with your money or more aggressive? Do you want to see your wealth grow or be maintained?

Generating a solid retirement plan often comes down to three main retirement income strategies: systematic withdrawals, flooring, and the bucket approach. Once you land on a retirement income planning strategy, you need to implement it and modify it as you live through retirement.

 What is one thing you can do today to put your retirement income plan in a better place?

55. Value of Lifetime Income

"Lifetime income is your forever payday. Know what it is, or risk playing financial roulette with your golden years."

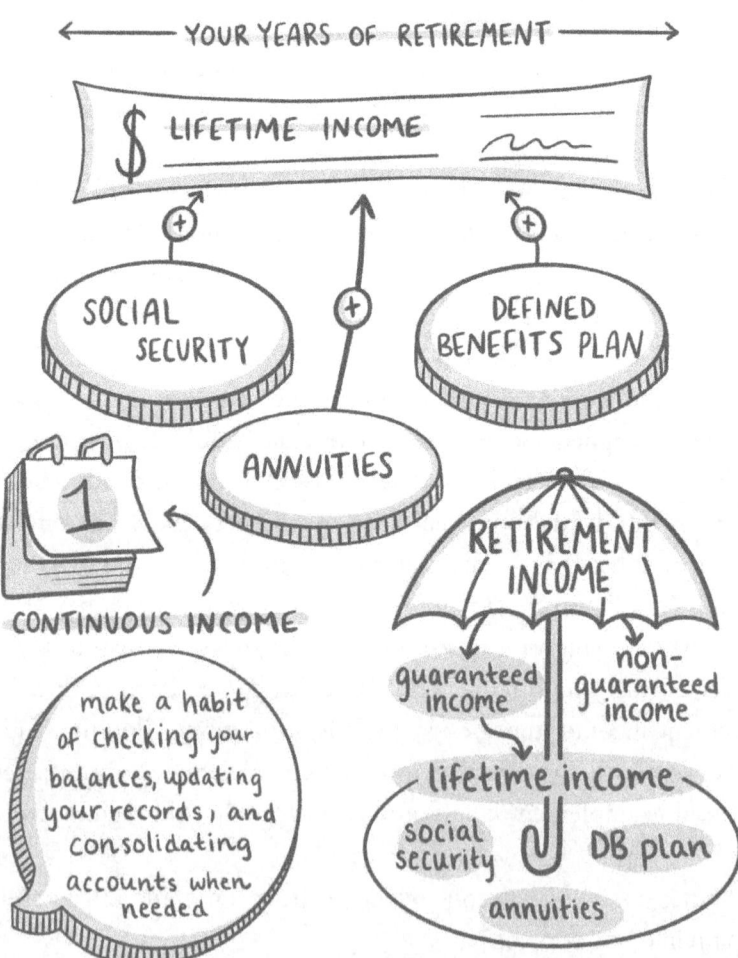

Retirement income is an umbrella term used to describe those solutions that are designed to provide you with income in retirement including both guaranteed income and non-guaranteed income. A subset of retirement income is lifetime income, which includes those options that deliver guaranteed income. In this case, the income is secured by an underlying insurer (or multiple insurers) to provide a guaranteed paycheck—or stream of income—throughout the duration of your life.

There are three main components that can make lifetime income: Social Security, annuities, and defined benefit plans that provide a guarantee. All can play important roles in retirement planning.

In our current economic climate, 2024 through 2027 is known as the "Peak 65 Zone." This is the time when more than ever before, we will see the largest surge of retiring Americans in recent history. More than 4.1 million people will hit that birthday each year through 2027, which amounts to more than 11,200 every single day.

What is your paycheck on the first day that you retire until the day before you die? That is the value of your lifetime income. Understanding your lifetime income picture and the value of your lifetime income is important because there are two types of risks when you don't: (1) overspending and not having enough for retirement, and (2) underspending and not being able to enjoy day-to-day life in the present or in retirement.

There is a perception that given all of the Americans who are now headed into retirement between 2024 and 2027, there is going to be a retirement crisis from the Peak 65 Zone. Part of the method for combating this crisis and future crises is to build in more protection for Americans through guaranteed income which helps with planning and better understanding the lifetime income picture.

Annuities are only one component of lifetime income and may not be appropriate for everyone. It is important to understand the value of your lifetime income, regardless of what method is selected for creating that lifetime income value.

 Can you determine what your paycheck will be on your first and last days of retirement?

56. What is Retirement Income?

"Before you retire, you are your income source. Once you retire, you are your debt source. Your savings become your income."

you may need roughly *70%* of your pre-retirement income to maintain your lifestyle in retirement depending on your specific needs

A well-planned retirement income strategy encompasses diverse sources to cover expenses and manage risks. Your retirement income is the money you receive from all of your financial and other resources in retirement to meet your needs.

You will need roughly 70% of your pre-retirement income as retirement income to maintain your same standard of living in retirement.

This money must last for an uncertain period of time (how long you will live in retirement) and cover an uncertain amount of money (your retirement expenses).

These two unknown variables make the sustainability of retirement income very challenging. In short, retirement income is your paycheck in retirement.

Diversify your retirement income sources to reduce dependence on any single source and to adapt to changing economic conditions. Make sure you benchmark what you might need in retirement to meet your goals and lifestyle.

Do a retirement income calculation on how much you might need and how much your current assets and income sources would provide.

Incorporating guaranteed income sources, such as Social Security or annuities, alongside investment-based income like 401(k)s or IRAs, can help strike a balance between stability and growth. Consider potential healthcare costs, inflation, taxes, and lifestyle choices when crafting your income plan. Working with a financial professional can help you create a customized strategy tailored to your timeline, risk tolerance, and long-term objectives.

 What assets or income sources will you rely on in retirement to generate your paycheck?

57. Mortality Credits

"Mortality credits reward you for living longer by turning the uncertainty of life expectancy into guaranteed income you can count on."

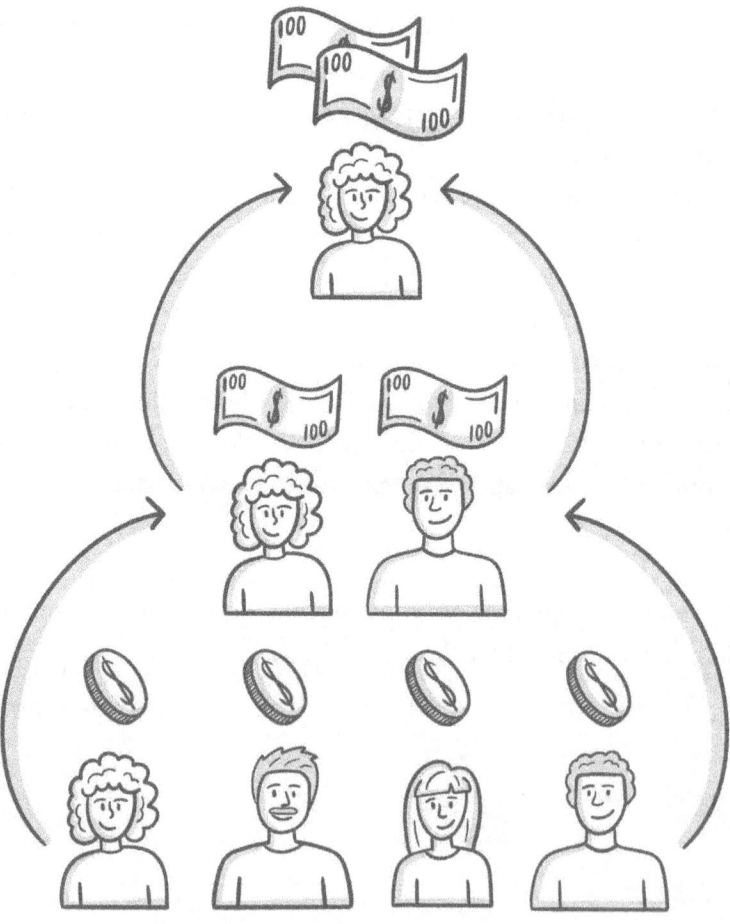

CHAPTER V

Mortality credits are a clever retirement planning tool. They are what give certain retirees that golden permission slip to spend confidently in retirement. They are a built-in benefit that rewards you for living longer than average. It's like a financial bonus round for aging well. How does it work?

Imagine you and nine other people each invest $100,000 into a lifetime income annuity. As the years go by, some in the group pass away. What happens to their unused funds? With products that include mortality credits, the insurance company doesn't send that money to their heirs. Instead, it stays in the pool and helps increase the payouts for the survivors. It's kind of like financial survivor benefits, only cooler.

This isn't the same as designating a beneficiary. When you leave money to a beneficiary, it goes to someone specific after you pass. But with mortality credits, the benefit stays in the pot and gets redistributed among those still receiving income from the annuity.

Let's look at an example: You purchase an SPIA (single premium immediate annuity) with no refund or beneficiary option. If you die early, the insurance company keeps what's left. But if you live longer than expected, you keep getting paid. Best of all, your payments are effectively boosted by the unused funds from others in the annuity pool. That's the magic of mortality credits.

These mortality credits are only found in specific types of annuities. You won't find them in annuities designed just for accumulation. That's because mortality credits are all about pooled longevity, not investment growth.

 How might mortality credits change your retirement story? Could a lifetime income stream bring you more confidence?

58. Your Retirement Income Picture

"Retirement income planning is like trying to budget for a vacation with no return date, rising costs, and surprise detours. Plan like your future depends on it… because it does."

Retirement income planning is basically the art of replacing your paycheck with... not a paycheck. You're trying to fund the rest of your life using a limited pile of money, for an undefined amount of time, while dodging financial potholes like inflation, healthcare costs, and whatever life throws at you next.

At its core, retirement income planning is about making sure you can still pay for groceries, vacations, and the occasional grandkid bribe without running out of money before you run out of birthdays.

You've probably heard of the famous 4% rule. This rule is based on the idea that if you had a 50/50 portfolio of US large-cap stocks and bonds, you could withdraw 4% a year (adjusted for inflation) and likely not run out of money for 30 years. But that's not a guarantee. It's more like a polite suggestion from history.

Why is all of this so tricky? Because you don't know how long you'll be retired (you're not psychic), how much you'll spend (hello, unexpected dentist bills and bucket list trips), or what curveballs life will throw your way (inflation, healthcare, tax surprises).

There's no perfect formula, no one-size-fits-all answer, and definitely no "undo" button. You get one shot at doing retirement right, so make it count!

 How much money do you need in retirement? What retirement risks concern you the most? What assets or income sources do you expect to rely on the most in retirement to generate your income? What risks are there to these income sources?

59. Bucketing Approach

"Bucketing is about containing something. When you can contain enough of one thing, you can control it."

When you bucket your retirement income, you give each dollar a unique purpose, a specific job to do in your life after work. In doing this, you tap into one of the strongest behavioral finance tools out there: mental accounting.

Plus, according to a 1979 study, messages are most persuasive when repeated three times. So let's say it three times for the folks in the back:

Buckets bring clarity. Buckets reduce stress. Buckets make retirement less scary.

Here's how the classic three-bucket strategy works:

Go-Go Years (Bucket 1): The early, active years of—travel, adventures, and the "I'm finally free!" lifestyle. These are your most expensive years, so your short-term money (like cash or short-term bonds) lives here.

Slow-Go Years (Bucket 2): You're slowing down a bit, maybe staying closer to home. Your mid-term assets (bonds, balanced funds) cover these over five to 10 years.

No-Go Years (Bucket 3): These are the later years, with higher healthcare needs and lower travel budgets. Your long-term investments (stocks, growth-focused assets) are here, quietly growing while you enjoy your earlier buckets.

This structure gives you two powerful advantages:

1. Income clarity: You know which dollars are for when, so you're not tempted to yank stocks in a downturn just to cover next month's groceries.
2. Emotional peace: You can sleep at night knowing your short-term needs are covered and your long-term money is marinating nicely for the future.

Buckets aren't a one-size-fits-all formula, either. They can (and should) be customized to fit your goals, your risk tolerance, and your unique retirement vision.

 How might a bucketing approach alleviate your concerns about market volatility and income stability in retirement?

60. Flooring Approach

"I've never been inside a good house that doesn't have a floor. Similarly, I haven't seen a good retirement income plan I would want without some type of income floor."

YOUR ESSENTIALS ARE FULLY COVERED

no matter what the stock market is up to

relies on guaranteed income sources like SOCIAL SECURITY, PENSIONS, or ANNUITIES to lock in coverage for must-have expenses

Only about 12% of retirees use the flooring approach—which is wild when you realize it's the retirement equivalent of making sure your parachute works before you jump out of the plane.

So what is the flooring strategy?

Think of it like this: Retirement is a lot more fun when you know your essentials—housing, healthcare, food, taxes, and maybe the occasional pizza—are fully covered, no matter what the stock market's up to. That's the beauty of flooring. It's about using guaranteed income sources like Social Security, pensions, or annuities to lock in coverage for your must-have expenses. No drama. No panic-selling stocks because lettuce costs $14.

Retirement is (usually) a one-shot deal. You don't get a do-over. So, for many people, running out of money is not an option.

That's where Life Cycle Finance Theory comes in—basically, people like steady, predictable income. We're creatures of comfort, and knowing the bills are paid gives us the freedom to enjoy the fun stuff.

Now, is flooring for everyone? Not necessarily.

If you're a market-savvy risk-taker who's okay with tightening the belt during downturns, you might prefer a systematic withdrawal strategy—riding the market rollercoaster with a flexible budget and nerves of steel.

But if you're someone who loses sleep over market dips, worries about overspending, or just doesn't want to guess whether the money will last until you're 95 (or 105), a flooring strategy might be your financial BFF.

Bonus? Guaranteed income sources like annuities become more valuable the longer you live. So if you've got great genes, a healthy lifestyle, or just plan on being really, really stubborn—this strategy has your back.

 Does having a baseline level of income that you cannot outlive appeal to you? What are you willing to trade off or pay to have this security?

61. Retirement Risks

"When you are sailing and the wind changes direction, that is what retirement risks are to a secure retirement. You either adjust, or get blown off course."

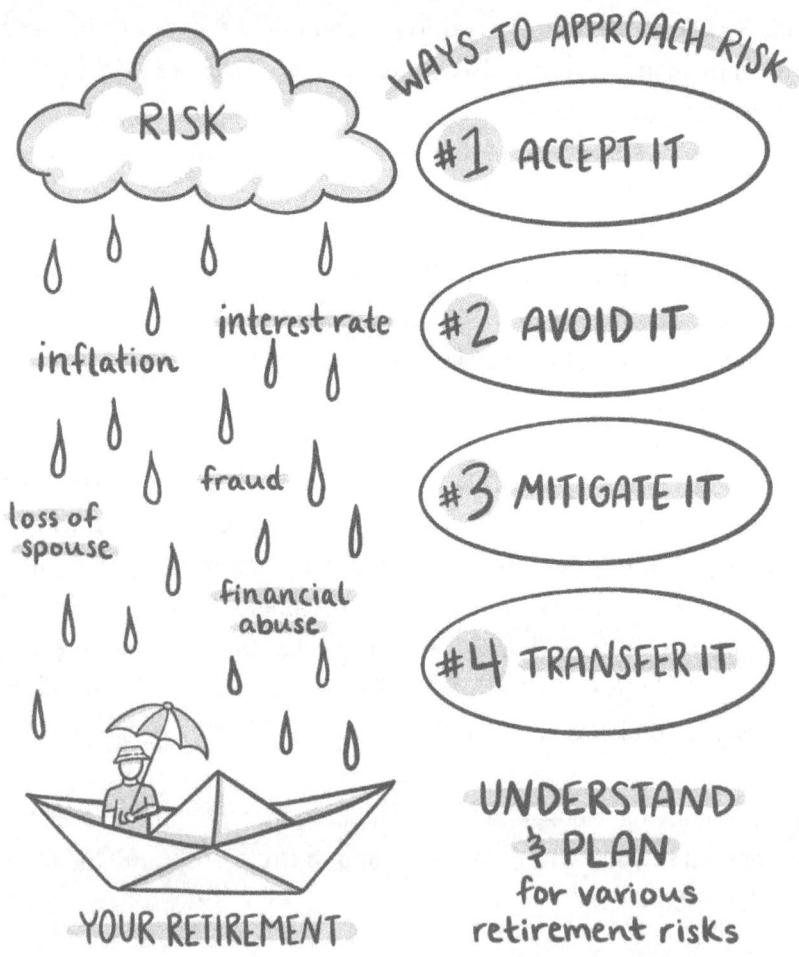

Nearly 50% of Americans are at risk of not being able to maintain their current standard of living in retirement, which highlights the importance of preparing for both expected and unexpected retirement risks. While many people are aware of common concerns—such as living longer than expected, rising healthcare costs, or inflation—it's often the lesser-known risks that can truly derail a well-thought-out retirement plan.

A wide range of risks could affect your financial security in retirement: inflation, longevity, healthcare costs, long-term care, changes in public policy, overspending, frailty, financial elder abuse, fraud, market volatility, interest rate fluctuations, liquidity limitations, sequence of returns risk, forced or early retirement, challenges with reemployment, inability to retire, employer insolvency, the death of a spouse, unexpected family financial obligations, poor timing of withdrawals, and the burden of self-insuring against major events.

Effectively managing these risks requires a strategic approach. Generally, there are four ways to deal with risk: accept it, avoid it, mitigate it, or transfer it.

To accept a risk means acknowledging it and adjusting if needed. For example, while you can't control changes in tax policy, you can accept this risk and plan to adjust your spending accordingly if tax laws shift.

To avoid a risk, you steer clear of exposure. If you distrust the solvency of insurance companies, for instance, you might avoid buying certain insurance products altogether.

To mitigate a risk, you could diversify your investment portfolio or incorporate income products like annuities, which can help soften the blow of market volatility or the risk of outliving your savings.

To transfer a risk purchase long-term care insurance or life insurance to help protect against catastrophic costs or the loss of a primary income source.

> Which retirement risks are you most concerned about, and how are you planning to accept, avoid, mitigate, or transfer them? What risk was listed that you have done no planning around today?

62. Tax Diversification

"When your mom told you not to put all your eggs in one basket, she meant it."

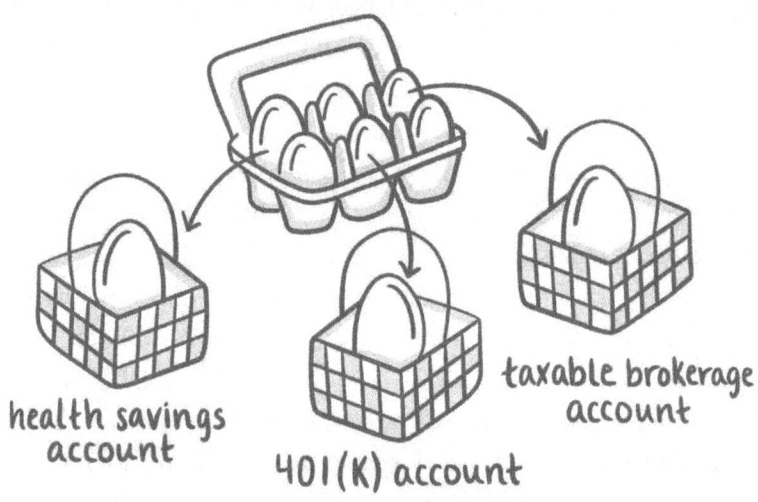

INVEST ACROSS DIFFERENT TAX TREATMENT CATEGORIES to minimize tax, maximize retirement income

- health savings account
- 401(K) account
- taxable brokerage account

OPTIMIZE YOUR ROTH CONTRIBUTIONS during financial ups and downs

- 2025: contribute to your Roth
- 2026: contribute more this year
- 2027: no contributions

Tax diversification is the idea that you should invest across different tax treatment categories to help minimize taxes and maximize your income in retirement. For example, in an earlier chapter, we discussed the idea of Roth versus Traditional contributions and splitting those contributions when contributing to your workplace retirement plan each paycheck.

This is a component that illustrates the principle of tax diversification. The average American will pay $524,625 in taxes throughout their lifetime—that's one-third (34.7%) of all estimated lifetime earnings ($1,494,986) spent on taxes.

In addition to the concept of splitting Roth and Traditional contributions, there is also the idea of optimizing your Roth contributions when your lifestyle allows it. Many of us don't always know what our tax situation and lifestyle are going to look like from one year to the next.

During those financial ups and downs which cannot be planned for, you may be able to make Roth contributions when, in other years, that is not something that works for your particular circumstances.

Tax diversification can apply beyond the bounds of Roth versus Traditional, although that's where the concept comes up the most. Other ways you may be thinking about tax diversification may be in the way of other accounts and how to diversify overall account types such as your health savings account, taxable brokerage account, and overall account set-up.

Consider your overall account structure and how you are optimizing your tax-efficient account strategy, but consider that this strategy is likely always in flux. While you can plan for your circumstances, there are things that are out of your control. One of the greatest things out of your control is that the government works in 10-year budget cycles and you cannot change updates in the Internal Revenue Code which may impact your tax strategy, but you can be nimble and update your plan over time.

 How diversified is your portfolio from a tax perspective? What changes might you need to consider, particularly when there are updates in the tax code?

63. Roth Conversions

"Our circumstances are always changing, which includes our tax situations."

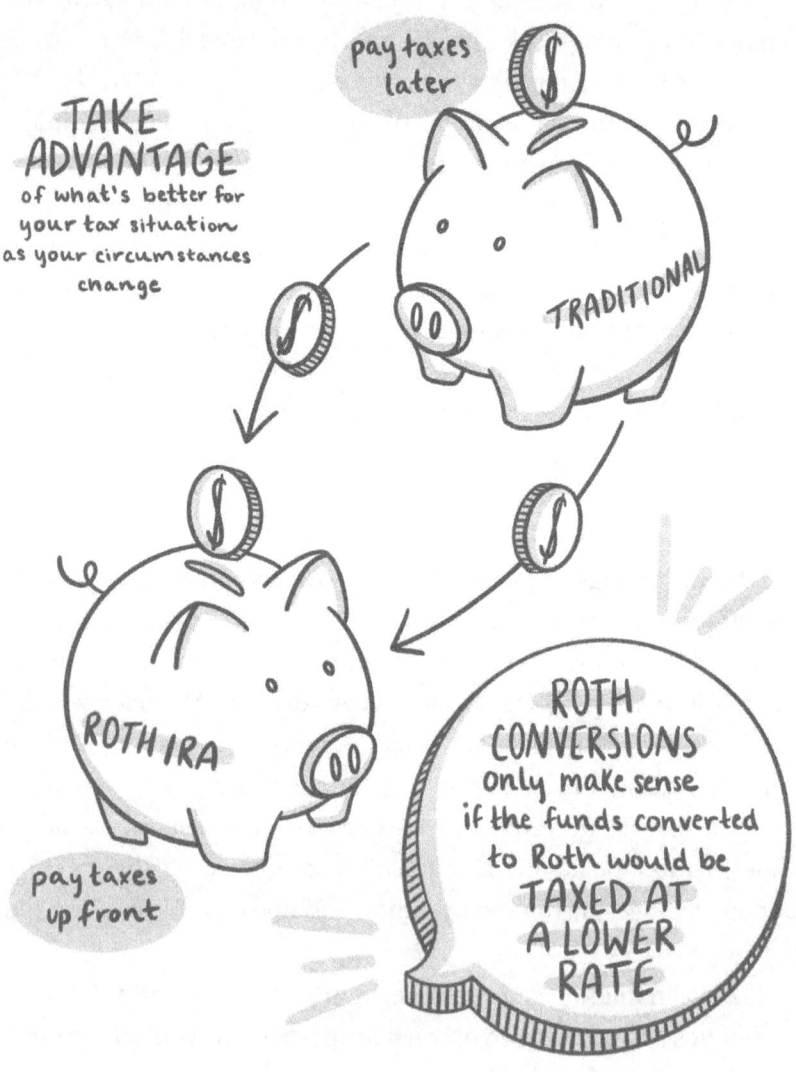

We have talked about making elections of Roth and Traditional, but what about changing once you already made the election?

The process of moving from a Traditional contribution to a Roth contribution is called a Roth conversion. This is available in both tradtional IRAs and your workplace retirement account (so long as the plan allows it).

The reason to go through the process of a Roth conversion is that unless you anticipate that your tax bracket will be the same on the day you contributed the funds and the day you withdraw your funds, then you may want to consider an analysis of whether a Roth conversion might be beneficial. Roth conversions essentially allow you to take advantage of what's better for your tax situation as your circumstances change.

Another benefit of Roth conversions is that Roth IRAs do not have Required Minimum Distributions (RMD) requirements; otherwise, RMDs commence at age 73 (unless otherwise changed by the rules).

You can optimize your tax strategy with a little planning. The challenge, however, can be determining when to do a conversion and how much. The trade-off between paying taxes today for those funds being converted to a Roth versus paying later (for those traditional funds that remain in the account) means that Roth conversions only make sense financially if the funds converted to Roth would be taxed at a lower rate today than they would be by leaving them alone until a later date.

> Have you considered the benefits of a Roth IRA in your savings? If so, have you considered the impact of a Roth conversion in your retirement planning and how that might impact your future?

64. Retirement Planning for Small Business Owners

"There is a structure for businesses of all sizes to be able to save for themselves as business owners and to be able to help their employees save."

TRADITIONAL RETIREMENT VEHICLES
- IRAs
- 401(K)s
- defined benefit plans

irregular pay streams
offering plans to employees
day-to-day challenges

EXPLORE OPPORTUNITIES THAT:
> help you with long-term saving
> provide tax breaks to your company
> help make your company more attractive to existing & potential employees

Although we typically associate IRAs as our own individual accounts (as discussed elsewhere in this book), there are technically three types of vehicles that can be offered to employees:

1. IRAs
2. Defined contribution plans
3. Defined benefit plans.

Don't most of us associate owning a small business with the American dream? Well, this stat might not feel that way. When it comes to their own retirement savings, 85% of self-employed/microbusiness owners know they should be saving more for retirement, 75% aren't sure if they are saving enough, and 42% worry they will never be able to retire.

For business owners of a small business, planning for retirement through a traditional vehicle can be very difficult. They are balancing offering a plan for their employees so that they can remain competitive with larger organizations (and also save themselves), while at the same time dealing with small business challenges such as irregular payment streams and the day-to-day challenges of being a small business owner wearing many hats.

For many small business owners, the notion of saving and retirement is even further removed than it is for the average saver because the focus is on meeting the next challenge or fire of each day. If you are a small business owner, particularly given recent legislation from SECURE 2.0, consider if there are opportunities to explore saving in a retirement plan that could help with your long-term saving, while providing a tax break to the company and also making the company much more attractive to potential and existing employees.

Also, keep in mind that legislative changes are beginning to require that employers of all sizes have an employer-sponsored plan of some kind, so you might as well optimize it to meet your savings needs and gain a tax credit at the same time.

※ If you are a small business owner, do you have a retirement plan today? If so, are you getting the most bang for your buck to take advantage of potential tax benefits?

Your Retirement Notes

Your Retirement Sketches

CHAPTER VI

MANAGING RETIREMENT INCOME

- Public Policy Risk
- Taxes in Retirement
- Knowledge in Retirement
- When to Retire
- Power of Delaying Retirement
- Guardrails
- Adaptive Spending
- Smart Income
- When to Claim Social Security
- Taxation of Social Security
- Power of Delaying Social Security
- Rule 72(t) Penalty Taxes
- Permission to Spend

- Traveling in Retirement
- IRMAA
- RMDs
- Reverse Mortgages
- Tapping Home Equity in Retirement
- Lines of Credit
- Navigating Sequence Risk
- Time Segmentation
- Retirement Planning Checkups

CHAPTER VI.
Introduction

A good savings plan gets you to retirement. A retirement income plan gets you through it.

You've done the work—you've saved, you've envisioned, you've prepared. Now it's time to put your retirement income plan into action. This is the point where the question shifts from: Do I have enough? to: How do I make it last? Managing a retirement income plan is all about making sure your goals are met and that you do not outlive your money.

Managing retirement income is where strategy meets real life. It's not about chasing returns or micromanaging every dollar—it's about creating a sustainable, adaptable income strategy that allows you to live the life you want without running out of money or living in fear of doing so.

This phase is dynamic. You'll need to juggle multiple moving pieces: your withdrawal strategy, taxes, benefits, spending needs, healthcare, and even debt. Retirement income management isn't just math—it's decision-making with consequence. It's about balancing what's coming in with what's going out, while being thoughtful about how and when you pull money from each account.

From accumulation to distribution

In your working years, the goal was simple: grow your money. But now, you're in the distribution phase—and the rules change. You need to figure out how to convert your assets into reliable income, ideally in a way that minimizes taxes, maintains flexibility, and protects against longevity and market risk.

That's where withdrawal strategies come in. Whether it's the 4% rule, a guardrails approach, a bucketing strategy, or time segmentation, the goal is the same: Withdraw enough to support your lifestyle—but not so much that you deplete your assets prematurely.

This is where the "sequence of returns risk" becomes real. If the market drops early in retirement and you're withdrawing heavily, you risk locking in losses that can permanently damage your portfolio. Managing your withdrawal rate and having access to lower-volatility or guaranteed income sources (like annuities, bond ladders, or cash) can help buffer this risk.

Taxes: the hidden expense

Let's not overlook one of the biggest (and most controllable) retirement expenses: taxes. You might be done working, but Uncle Sam isn't done with you. Every dollar you withdraw from a Traditional IRA or 401(k) is taxed as ordinary income. Add in Social Security taxes, Medicare premiums tied to income, and RMDs, and your tax bill can eat up more of your retirement income than you expected.

That's why managing withdrawals strategically across multiple account types—Roth, Traditional, taxable—is so important. It allows you to smooth out your tax liability, reduce RMD pressure, and avoid pushing yourself into a higher bracket unintentionally. A well-timed Roth conversion, qualified charitable distribution (QCD), or capital gains strategy can help keep more of your money working for you.

Maximize what you can control

What is one of the most overlooked ways to stretch your retirement income? Reducing unnecessary costs. Managing investment fees, minimizing lifestyle inflation, shopping around for Medicare plans, and eliminating unused subscriptions can make a surprising difference.

This isn't about cutting back joy—it's about being intentional with your money so you can direct it where it matters most.

The same goes for benefits. Maximizing Social Security—whether that means delaying benefits, coordinating spousal strategies, or understanding survivor options—can add tens of thousands of dollars over the course of retirement. It's not just a paycheck—it's one of the most valuable guaranteed income sources you have.

Rethinking debt in retirement

Debt in retirement often carries a negative connotation—but when used wisely, debt can actually enhance your flexibility. Whether it's tapping a home equity line, refinancing a mortgage to preserve liquidity, or using strategic borrowing during down markets, debt can be a tool, not just a burden. The key is managing it within your broader plan—not letting it manage you.

Income is a system, not a single source

Remember: Managing retirement income is about more than just drawing from a single account. It's a system—Social Security, pensions, retirement savings, brokerage accounts, health savings, part-time work, rental income, annuities, benefits, and more—all working together to support your life.

That system needs periodic tuning. Life will change. Markets will move. Policies will shift. And as they do, your income strategy must remain fluid but grounded—adaptable, but always tethered to your goals and needs.

So in this chapter, don't just think about dollars and percentages. Think about sketching out your income strategies and systems. Think about actions that can impact your plan and income.

65. Public Policy Risk

"Retirement is personal, but public policy is universal. Your retirement plan needs to account for both."

When it comes to retirement planning, you can budget carefully, diversify wisely, and save like a champ. However, there's one wild card you can't fully control: public policy.

According to a recent survey, 86% of Americans believe Washington doesn't understand how hard it is to save for retirement. And let's face it, they might be right. The rules around taxes, Social Security, Medicare, and retirement accounts form the very foundation of our retirement system, but they're written by people in suits who may never have balanced a middle-class budget.

The US retirement system is deeply tied to federal policies. The tax code influences how we save. Social Security, Medicare, and Medicaid shape how we retire. Employee Retirement Income Security Act (ERISA) helps govern our workplace retirement plans. All these policies are supposed to offer structure and security, but they can also shift very quickly.

What if tax rates rise? What if Social Security benefits are reduced? What if changes to Medicare increase out-of-pocket costs? These possibilities are what we call public policy risks, and they're not just theoretical.

The tricky part is that these risks are nearly impossible to eliminate. The government can, and often does, change the rules mid-game. That's why staying flexible is so important.

So what can you do?

Start by staying informed. Changes don't usually come overnight. Be proactive. Read, listen, and learn. And yes, *vote*. If you want your voice heard, the ballot box is the place to use it.

Next, diversify. Don't place all your retirement hopes on one system or one type of account. Spread your savings across different asset classes, different tax treatments (like Roth, Traditional, taxable accounts), and different income sources. The more flexible your plan, the better you can weather whatever comes.

Also, try not to rely too heavily on just one government benefit. Social Security is an important pillar, but it shouldn't be the whole house. A strong retirement strategy includes multiple income streams.

 How are you preparing for possible changes in public policy that could impact your financial future?

66. Taxes in Retirement

"Death and taxes are inevitable… but with smart planning, at least taxes can be less painful."

CHAPTER VI

They say two things in life are certain: death and taxes. Retirement might free you from early alarms, office politics, and endless Zoom calls—but the IRS? It's still very much on the clock.

Here's the jaw-dropper: The average American pays over $524,000 in taxes over their lifetime, roughly one-third of everything they'll ever earn. And depending on your state, that number could be even higher.

You've spent decades saving, investing, and planning. You're finally ready to enjoy your golden years. And then there's the big surprise. Your pension, 401(k), and Traditional IRA all come with tax strings attached. Those pre-tax contributions you faithfully made? Now it's payback time, and Uncle Sam wants his share.

It gets more complicated when you factor in the variety of income sources you might draw from in retirement: Social Security, annuities, brokerage accounts, even part-time work or a monetized hobby. Each is taxed differently. Social Security benefits are partially taxable based on your total income. Long-term capital gains from investments have their own tiered tax rates. And withdrawals from traditional retirement accounts? They're taxed as ordinary income.

The first year of retirement can be especially chaotic from a tax perspective. Many retirees are surprised by how much they owe. Setting up proper withholdings early can help you avoid headaches.

A big tax trap to plan for? RMDs. Starting in your early 70s, you're required to withdraw a minimum amount from certain accounts. Even if you don't need the money, the IRS does. These withdrawals can bump you into a higher tax bracket, increasing your overall liability.

Learn how each income stream is taxed. Know your tax brackets. Explore options like Roth conversions before RMDs begin, or space out withdrawals to keep your taxable income level.

You may not be able to dodge taxes, but with smart planning, you can minimize their bite and keep more of your hard-earned retirement for the things (and people) you love.

 Do you have your withholdings properly set-up to avoid penalties? Do you know what adjustments you will make to withholdings in retirement?

67. Knowledge in Retirement

"Start learning the ropes of retirement now. The more you know now, the happier you will be later."

Planning for retirement is like planning a trip to a country you've never been to… and don't speak the language. You wouldn't land in Tokyo with no map, no translator, and no clue what the yen is, right? Same goes for retirement. It's an entirely new phase of life, and the only way to win at it is to learn about it.

Here's the hard truth: On average, Americans score a dismal 31% on retirement income literacy. That's not even a passing grade at Hogwarts.

Sure, most of us pick up basic financial skills over the years. We learn about compound interest, saving for the future, and avoiding credit card doom. But retirement income planning? That's a whole different beast. This is where you need to think differently: You're not earning money anymore. You're spending it. Wisely. Strategically. Like a boss.

So what can you do? Get educated. Read a book. Take a quiz. Watch a webinar. Consult a pro. This stuff isn't just for Wall Street whizzes. It's created for you, the future retiree. And no, your cousin Larry who "likes stocks" doesn't count.

And here's the kicker: Some retirement decisions are one-way doors. You can't "undo" claiming Social Security too early or rolling into the wrong tax strategy. So if you're not confident in your knowledge (or just don't want to nerd out on IRS rules), bring in the big guns and hire a professional to guide you.

Retirement isn't the time to cross your fingers and hope for the best. It's the time to make smart, confident choices based on knowledge, not guesswork.

Think of it this way: Retirement isn't the end of the financial journey, it's the beginning of a brand-new adventure. One where you're in control, but only if you know how to steer. Whether it's creating a withdrawal strategy, figuring out how to make your savings last 20+ years, or understanding how taxes and healthcare can eat into your income, every decision matters.

✴ What areas of your retirement planning do you feel least confident about, and how can you improve your knowledge in these areas?

68. When to Retire?

"There is no perfect age for retirement. But choosing the right time can lead to a perfect retirement."

The average retirement age in the US today is about 62. Back in 1991, it was 57. As people live longer, retirement is slowly shifting later. However, that doesn't mean later is always better.

Deciding when to retire may be the most personal (and powerful) decision of your retirement journey. It affects everything: your income, your lifestyle, your freedom, and your future.

So how do you know when it's time? There is no perfect age. What matters is that the timing makes sense for you, financially, emotionally, and practically.

Here are a few questions to help guide your decision: Can you afford it? Have you saved enough to support the lifestyle you want? Are you eligible? Social Security kicks in as early as 62, and Medicare starts at 65. Are you ready mentally and emotionally? Retirement means a new routine, new identity, and a lot of free time to fill.

Do your life goals align with retiring now? Do you want to travel? Start a new hobby? Care for family? Pursue passion projects? Do you still enjoy working? If your job brings you purpose and community, why rush? Is your health helping make the decision for you? Sometimes the choice isn't fully ours.

Working just a few more months or years can make a huge difference. It means more income, fewer years of drawing from savings, and potentially higher Social Security benefits. But if working longer starts to chip away at your health or happiness, that matters too.

One great rule of thumb? Retire to something, not from something. Have a plan for what's next. Whether it's adventure, rest, volunteering, or creative projects, make sure you're stepping into a life you're excited to live.

 What matters most to you in deciding when to retire? And how will you know when it's your time?

69. Power of Delaying Retirement

"Delaying retirement can pay off. But remember: Your bucket list has an expiration date."

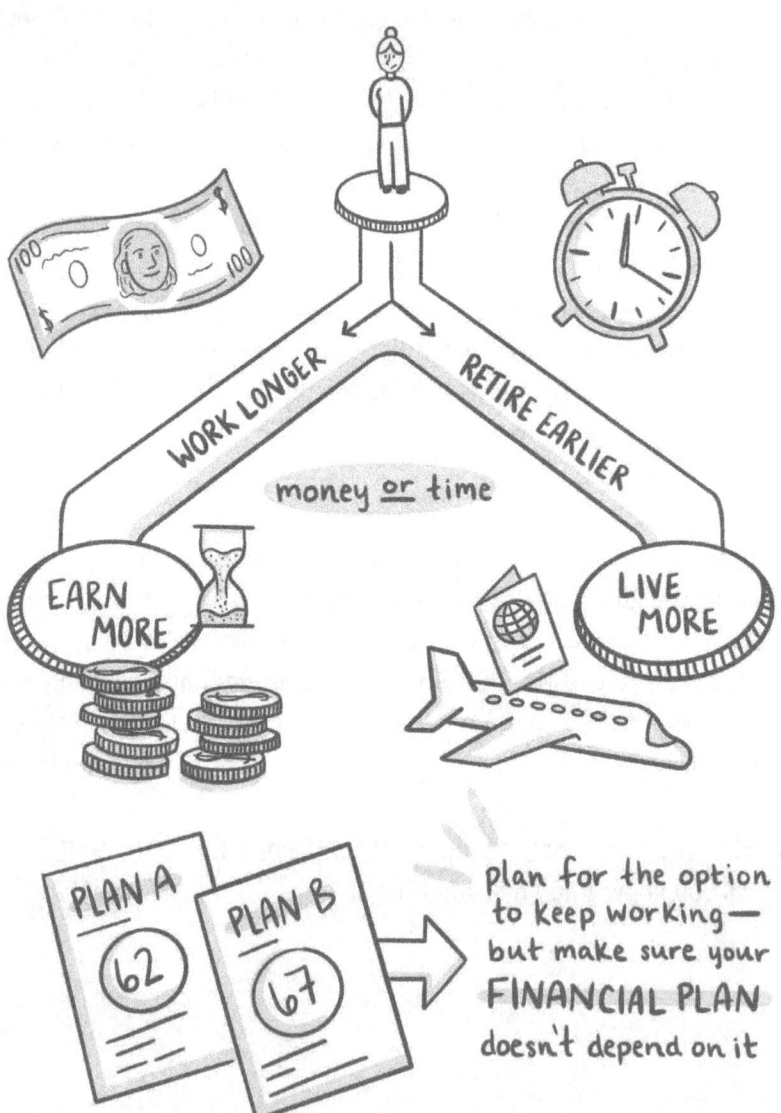

Retirement doesn't always go according to plan. You might think you'll hang up your hat at 67, but life might have other ideas (like 62… or next Tuesday). According to the 2024 EBRI Retirement Confidence Survey, while 22% of workers say they plan to retire between 60 and 64, 38% of retirees say that's when they actually did. Translation? There's a pretty big gap between what people expect and what actually happens.

Many workers picture themselves happily punching the clock into their 70s, but reality often throws a curveball—like health issues, caregiving responsibilities, or just plain burnout. In fact, while three out of four workers plan to work for pay in retirement, only 30% of retirees actually do. Turns out, it's harder than expected to find a flexible gig once you've started collecting AARP magazines.

Now, let's not knock delayed retirement completely. If you can work longer, it can pay off big time. You'll build up more savings, earn higher Social Security benefits, and potentially hang on to employer perks like health insurance.

Plus, staying mentally and socially active at work can be a win for your overall well-being (especially if you love what you do—or really hate daytime TV).

But let's talk trade-offs. Delaying retirement might mean fewer years spent traveling, spending time with grandkids, or just doing nothing in a hammock with iced tea in hand. And if you're working longer because you have to, not because you want to, that's a red flag your plan may need a second look.

So what's the takeaway? Delaying retirement can be a smart move, but it's not a guarantee. Plan for the option to keep working—but make sure your financial plan doesn't depend on it.

✸ What are the factors that you need to take into account to determine your retirement date? How will personal factors such as health, retirement income needs, family, and other factors impact your decision and planning?

70. Guardrails

"Don't dismiss the value of a good guardrail."

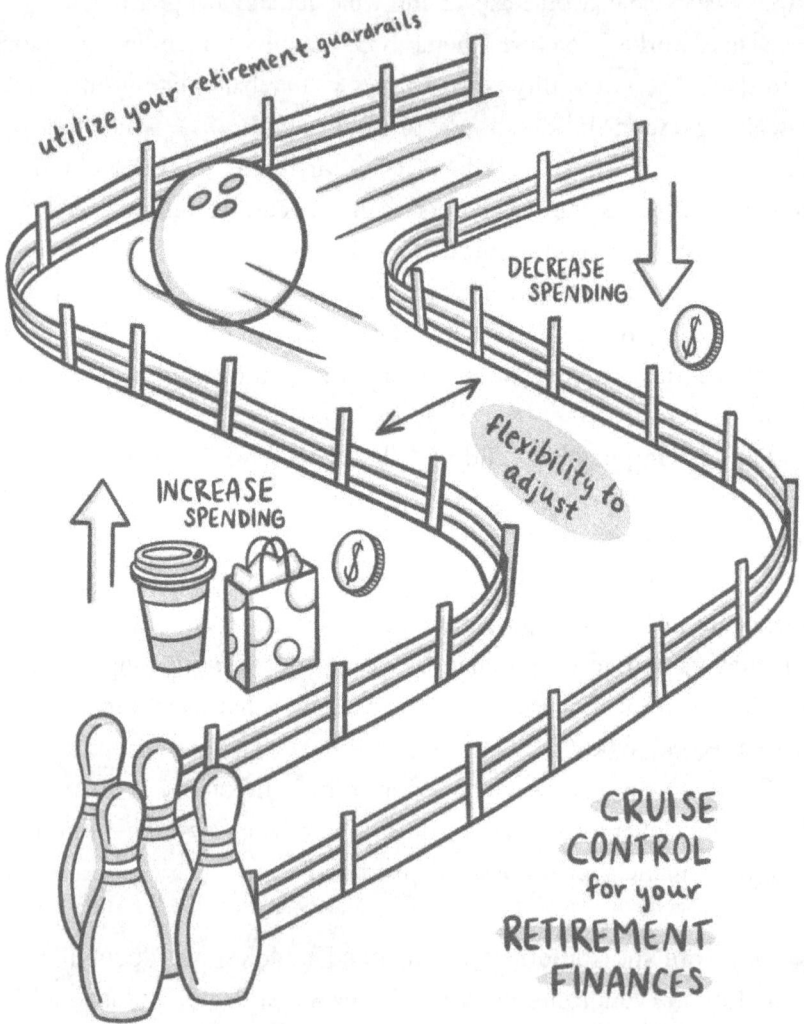

You've had guardrails your whole life. Guardrails on highways keep you alive. And guardrails in bowling alleys keep your ego intact.

Well, guess what? Retirement has guardrails too, and they're just as important (and way more fun than avoiding a gutter ball).

Here's how it works: If your investments take a hit and your portfolio drops by 20%, your lower guardrail kicks in and says, "Hey buddy, let's ease up a bit," and you dial your spending back by 10%.

But if your portfolio's been crushing it and goes up by 20%, your upper guardrail throws you the keys to the fun bus and says, "Go ahead, treat yourself!" and you get to increase your spending.

It's a flexible system that protects your nest egg from going splat, while also giving you permission to enjoy the good times guilt-free.

Think of it as cruise control for your retirement finances—with just enough flexibility to adjust for potholes and straightaways.

You're not locking yourself into a rigid budget or living in fear of buying an extra latte. You're giving yourself wiggle room with wisdom.

Guardrails don't just protect your money. They protect your peace of mind. When you've got a system in place that automatically tells you when to slow down or speed up, you're not stuck constantly second-guessing every spending decision. You're free to enjoy your retirement without the looming fear of running out of money. It's about creating a sustainable rhythm. With guardrails in place, your retirement plan doesn't just survive market ups and downs. You will be able to thrive in spite of them.

Retirement is usually a winding road. And with the right guardrails, you'll cruise through it with confidence, comfort, and maybe even a convertible.

 How can implementing guardrails enhance your confidence that your savings will last?

71. Adaptive Spending

"Being successful in retirement is not about IQ, it is about AQ—Adaptability Quotient. It's all about how willing you are to change your expenses and spending when things get tough."

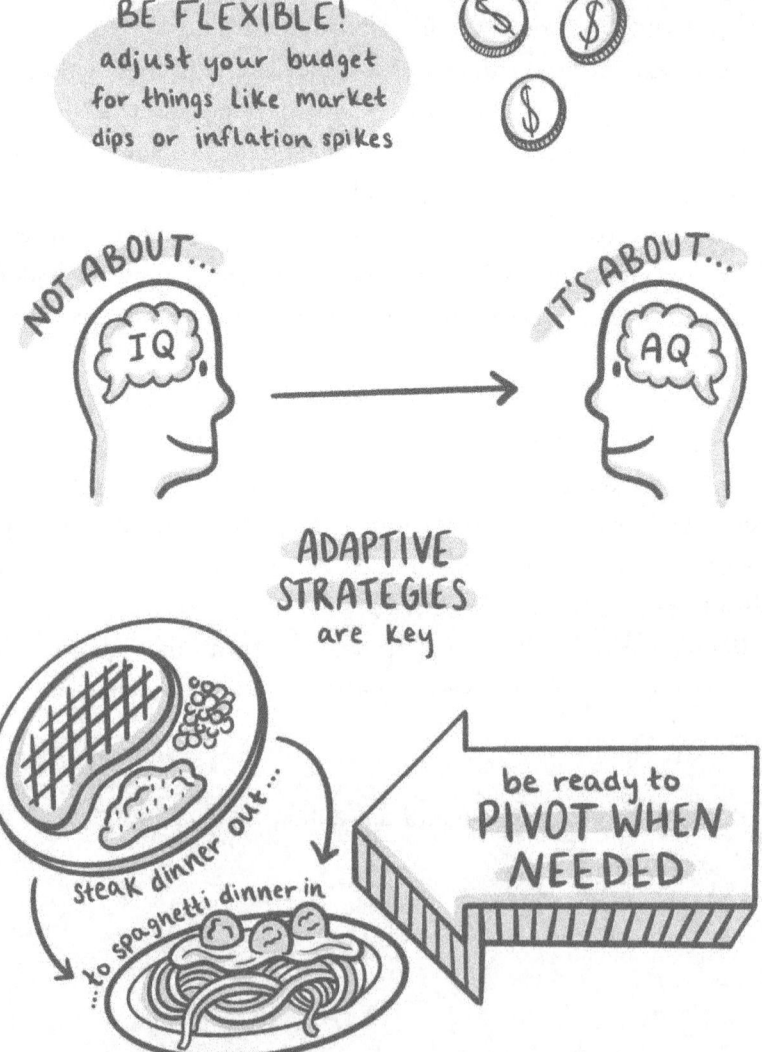

If you aim to spend 5% of your investment nest egg each year but are open to adjusting your spending based on how your portfolio is doing (even trimming it down to just 3% when times get tough), you're five times less likely to run out of money over 30 years. That's some serious staying power!

Think of it like this: In everyday life, when the budget's tight, we cut back—fewer lattes, more leftovers. Retirement's no different. The trick is to stay nimble. If the market dips, inflation spikes, or you realize you're going to live to 107, it's time to tweak that budget.

According to the very brainy folks David M. Blanchett and Larry R. Frank, Sr., adaptive strategies are the best way to make sure your money will last through your retirement.

Think about it this way: Life throws curveballs. Markets dip. In response, you do what any responsible adult does: You adjust. You cut back. You swap steak nights for spaghetti nights. It's not about suffering; it's about surviving fabulously.

Be flexible. Be fierce. And most of all, be ready to pivot when needed.

When you build adaptability into your retirement strategy, you're taking control instead of crossing your fingers and hoping for the best. It's about making small, thoughtful changes that can have a massive impact over time. Cutting back temporarily doesn't mean giving up on fun—it means making sure the fun lasts. Think of it as playing the long game: preserving your lifestyle, reducing financial stress, and giving yourself the confidence to weather whatever the market (or life) throws your way.

✷ Is your retirement plan ready to zig when life zags? Are you emotionally prepared to be flexible when it comes to budgeting in retirement?

72. Smart Income

"In retirement, your money should be working smarter, not harder."

SUSTAINABLE — long-lasting money e.g.: delay Social Security

MAXIMIZING — don't leave free money or perks

AUTOMATE — set up bill pay, auto retirement withdrawals

REINVEST income you aren't spending

TAX-EFFICIENT — strategize with Roth IRAs, HSAs, & smart deductions

Retirement is not the time to freestyle your finances. There are no do-overs once you retire!

That's why you need SMART income: Sustainable, Maximize, Automate, Reinvest, and Tax-efficient.

Sustainable means your money needs to last longer than your favorite TV series. We are talking about annuities or possibly delaying Social Security to increase your returns.

Maximizing involves getting the most out of your benefits. Don't leave free money or government perks on the table.

Automate everything you can. Set up bill payments, automate retirement withdrawals, and manage your financial assets. No one retires to spend their time doing paperwork.

Reinvest any income you're not spending—idle cash is just money taking an unearned vacation.

Tax-efficiency is key. Keep more of your money by using strategies like Roth IRAs, HSAs, and smart deductions.

Remember: 94% of people save more when it's automated, so set it up and forget about it (but with a good check-in now and then).

Having a SMART income plan isn't just about managing money. It's about creating freedom. When your finances are structured to support your lifestyle, you're not worrying about every market dip or unexpected expense. You're living. Traveling. Volunteering. Spoiling the grandkids. SMART planning gives you the clarity to make confident decisions and the flexibility to adapt as life evolves. It's the difference between hoping your money lasts and knowing it will—because you built a system designed for success.

In retirement, let your money hustle so you don't have to.

> How can you adopt the core elements of SMART income today? What could you automate to review your finances and look for duplicate subscriptions? Could you automate your investments or bill payments?

73. When to Claim Social Security

"Claiming Social Security too early is like starting every race in a full sprint without knowing the distance. Sometimes it will work out, but if you have to run a marathon you are going to wish you had saved that energy for later."

Deciding when to claim Social Security might not sound thrilling, but it can make a huge difference in your retirement game plan. For most Americans, Social Security isn't just a side dish—it's the main course of retirement income. And since it's a lifetime, inflation-adjusted paycheck, getting the timing right really matters.

Social Security provides benefits to those who've paid into the system—or who qualify through a spouse. And when one spouse passes away, the surviving spouse keeps receiving the higher of the two benefits, not both. So it's important to plan strategically—because this decision doesn't just affect you, it can affect your partner too.

Around 34% of eligible retirees claim Social Security benefits at the earliest possible age of 62, often resulting in significantly reduced lifetime benefits. However, by delaying Social Security benefits to age 70, instead of claiming at age 62, increases monthly benefits by 77%.

The decision of when to claim Social Security benefits can significantly impact your financial security in retirement.

Consider delaying Social Security benefits if possible, as this can increase your monthly benefits by about 8% each year you delay past your full retirement age up to age 70. The Social Security claiming decision is a mostly permanent decision once made. If you plan to live past average life expectancy or have no other sources of lifetime inflation-adjusted income, you might want to consider deferring benefits out as far as possible.

Consider your health, longevity, other resources, and goals when making your decision.

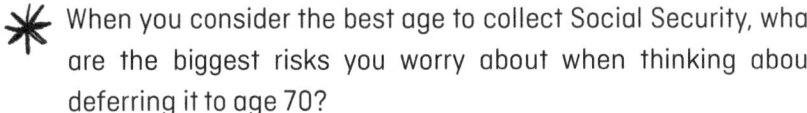

When you consider the best age to collect Social Security, what are the biggest risks you worry about when thinking about deferring it to age 70?

74. Taxation of Social Security

"Yes, you still have to pay taxes in retirement, even on Social Security. But hey, at least it's not the full amount."

UP TO 50% OF YOUR BENEFITS ARE TAXABLE IF YOUR INCOME IS:

$25,000 –to– $34,000 individual

$32,000 –to– $44,000 married couple

UP TO 85% OF YOUR BENEFITS ARE TAXABLE IF YOUR INCOME IS:

more than $34,000 individual

more than $44,000 married couple

BE STRATEGIC ABOUT HOW MUCH YOU WITHDRAW FROM DIFFERENT ACCOUNTS

SOCIAL SECURITY · 401(K) · ROTH IRA

Here's the truth no one loves to hear: Social Security benefits can be taxed. Retirement doesn't give you a free pass from the IRS.

In fact, depending on your income and filing status, up to 85% of your benefits could be taxable. If your total income is more than $25,000 as a single filer, or $32,000 as a married couple filing jointly, you may have to pay federal income taxes on your Social Security benefits. The percentage that gets taxed depends on how high your combined income goes.

Here's how the IRS breaks it down: Up to 50% of your benefits are taxable if your income is:

- $25,000–$34,000 (individual)
- $32,000–$44,000 (married couple).

Up to 85% of your benefits are taxable if your income exceeds $34,000 for individuals and $44,000 for married couples. What exactly is "combined income?" It's a mix of your adjusted gross income (line 11 on your tax return), plus any non-taxable interest, plus half of your Social Security benefits.

Example: Let's say you're single and taking $40,000 from your 401(k) and receiving $1,500 a month in Social Security. That's $18,000 per year in benefits. The IRS counts half of that ($9,000), adds it to your $40,000 in retirement income, and calculates a combined income of $49,000. That puts you in the range where 85% of your Social Security benefits—or $15,300—would be taxable.

Important reminder: No one pays taxes on more than 85% of their benefits, no matter how high their income is. Manage your income sources wisely. You may be able to reduce taxes by adjusting how much you withdraw from different types of accounts. Know your state laws. Most states don't tax Social Security benefits.

Plan ahead for payment. You may owe taxes quarterly or choose to have them withheld from your monthly Social Security check.

> How does Social Security taxation fit into your overall tax planning strategy? Are you doing what you can now to manage your retirement income in a tax-efficient way?

75. Power of Delaying Social Security

"When it comes to your Social Security checks, timing is everything."

IF YOU WAIT UNTIL AGE 70 vs 62, YOUR MONTHLY CHECK COULD BE UP TO 77% HIGHER

you earn delayed retirement credits for every year you delay past your full retirement age

boosts monthly payments

Here's the deal: When it comes to Social Security, patience really can pay off. If you wait until age 70 to claim your benefits instead of starting at 62, your monthly check could be up to 77% higher. That's not a rounding error—that's real money.

Your Social Security benefit is based on three key things: the number of years you've worked, your lifetime earnings, and the age you start taking your benefit.

The Social Security Administration rewards those who wait. For every year you delay past your full retirement age (up to age 70), you earn delayed retirement credits which boost your monthly payout.

Despite this, most people don't wait until 70. Why? Sometimes life doesn't give you the luxury of choice. Health issues, job loss, or lack of other income may push people to claim earlier. And in some cases, that's the right move.

But if you're healthy, have income from other sources, and can afford to wait, delaying Social Security can be one of the smartest financial decisions you make.

No one can see the future, but if you expect a long retirement, delaying benefits can really pay off over time.

Additionally, spousal benefits can be impacted by the age and timing of your claim. In some cases, your decision affects both your benefit and your spouse's. If your Social Security check is higher than your spouse's, delaying could increase the survivor benefit they receive after you pass.

Timing isn't just about your age. It's about your health, your household, your goals, and your income needs. Think of it like a puzzle, where every piece affects the big picture.

✳ What's influencing your decision on when to claim Social Security? Could waiting give you a financial edge and more peace of mind in retirement?

76. Rule 72(t) Penalty Taxes

"Rule 72(t) can be a lifeline for early retirees. With the right strategy and discipline, it turns locked-up retirement savings into a reliable income stream, without the penalty price tag."

Some financial experts estimate that fewer than 5% of eligible individuals use this unique tax strategy. Yet it can be so powerful for those who need early access to retirement savings and do not want to pay the typical early withdrawal penalty.

Rule 72(t) applies only to certain retirement accounts, including Traditional IRAs, the earnings portion of Roth IRAs, and qualified employer-sponsored plans like 401(k), 403(b), and 457(b) accounts—as long as you're no longer employed by the sponsoring employer. If you're planning to retire early or need a bridge to cover expenses before age 59½, this little-known rule could be your financial lifeline.

Typically, tapping into your retirement funds before 59½ means facing a double hit: regular income tax plus a 10% early withdrawal penalty. But under Rule 72(t), there's a key exception. If you take a series of substantially equal periodic payments (SEPPs), you can avoid the penalty. You'll still owe income tax, but the extra 10% fee is waived, as long as you follow the rules.

There are three approved calculation methods for SEPPs: the RMD method, the fixed amortization method, and the fixed annuitization method. Each yields a different annual withdrawal. Once you choose one, you're required to stick with it.

So, if you start at age 50, you must take payments for 9½ years until age 59½. Start at 57, and the commitment is just five years. But be warned: If you stop payments too early or alter the plan outside of limited exceptions, the IRS can retroactively impose the 10% penalty plus interest on every withdrawal made.

For early retirees, Rule 72(t) offers a structured, penalty-free way to access funds when you need them most. It's not for everyone—but if planned carefully, it can provide flexibility, cash flow, and peace of mind during the early years of retirement.

 If you're considering retiring before age 59½, how could using Rule 72(t) help you manage your income needs while avoiding early withdrawal penalties?

77. Permission to Spend

"Give yourself permission to spend with joy, not guilt. You've earned it."

For decades, we're told to save, save, save. We chase that "magic number" for retirement like it's a high score on a video game. But here's the twist: When the game changes from saving to spending, many retirees freeze up. Nearly half of retirees struggle with actually spending the money they've worked so hard to save—a phenomenon known as the "saver's dilemma." And it's not just those with modest means—even wealthy retirees tend to underspend.

Why? Because we've been conditioned to believe that spending equals failure, or worse, loss. We build our lives around accumulating wealth, and suddenly we're expected to reverse that behavior overnight? No wonder it feels uncomfortable.

But retirement isn't about hoarding your wealth like a dragon guarding gold. It's about using what you've saved to live fully, joyfully, and on your own terms. Spending in retirement should feel good—not like a trip to the principal's office.

Here's the key: Build a spending plan that helps you enjoy life while keeping your savings sustainable. If you're holding back because you're afraid of running out, consider transferring some of those big "what-ifs." Life insurance can protect your legacy. Long-term care insurance can handle health costs. An annuity can provide reliable income for life. These tools aren't just about safety—they're about freedom. Freedom to spend without guilt. Freedom to say yes to travel, grandkid spoiling, or even just better coffee.

If spending doesn't feel joyful, it's time to reassess. After all, what's the point of a well-funded retirement if you're too nervous to enjoy it?

 What mental or emotional barriers might be preventing you from comfortably spending your retirement savings, and how can you address them?

78. Traveling in Retirement

"Plan for a retirement like you would for the ultimate vacation. Set your plan in advance, budget for adventure, and don't wait to chase the bucket list."

People often spend more time planning a two-week vacation than their entire retirement. But here's the twist: Retirement might just be the longest vacation you'll ever take. So imagine all the time you'll finally have to plan trips, explore new places, and chase your bucket list dreams!

According to AARP, over 65% of retirement-aged individuals plan to take a leisure trip this year, often spending 5–10% of their annual budget on travel. That may sound like a lot—but ask any retiree, and they'll tell you: Money spent on memories is money well spent.

But here's the key: Traveling in retirement doesn't just happen—it takes smart planning. You'll want to budget for travel like you would for groceries or healthcare. In fact, you might consider front-loading your travel budget. Take those big, physically demanding trips early in retirement—your "go-go years"—before the "slow-go" and "no-go" phases sneak in.

Also, don't forget the practical stuff. Where you live matters—are you close to a major airport? Near family and friends? As time goes on, travel may shift from far-flung adventures to heartwarming reunions. That's still travel—just a different kind.

Pro tips to stretch your travel dollars: Travel during off-seasons, consider longer stays (hello, Airbnb discounts!), and plan ahead for travel inflation. You might even want to budget more than you think, because let's be honest—retirees love to travel more than they admit!

Oh, and don't forget healthcare. Make sure your Medicare or supplemental coverage works where you're headed, especially if you're going international.

Finally, make your bucket list—and rank it by adventure level. Knock out the big ones early. You don't want to be climbing Machu Picchu in your 80s... unless you're into that sort of thing.

 How important is travel to you in retirement, and how are you planning to financially accommodate this priority?

79. IRMAA

"If you've ever heard someone say Medicare isn't free, they're right."

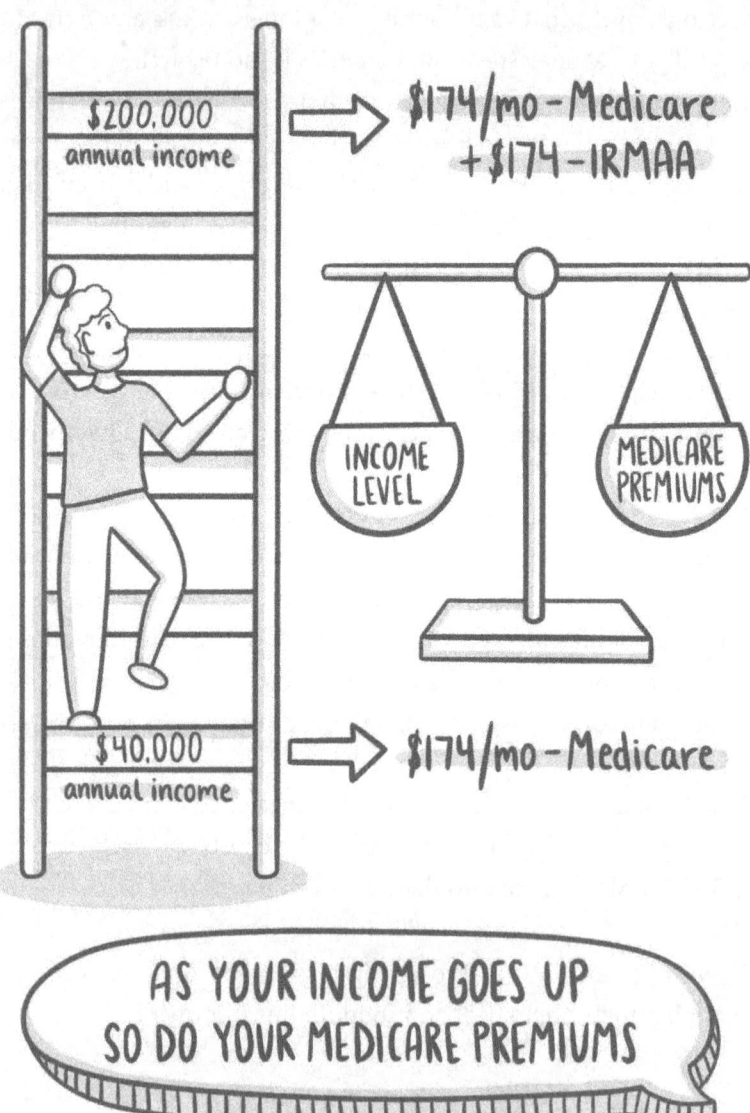

AS YOUR INCOME GOES UP SO DO YOUR MEDICARE PREMIUMS

If you're a high earner in retirement, you might get hit with a little something extra called IRMAA—the Income-Related Monthly Adjustment Amount.

So what is IRMAA? Think of it like a surcharge. The government looks at how much money you made two years ago and says, "You've got extra income, so you can afford to pay a bit more for Medicare." This applies to both Part B (doctor visits) and Part D (prescription coverage).

The Social Security Administration (SSA) decides if you owe this fee by reviewing your modified adjusted gross income (MAGI). That's your regular adjusted gross income plus some non-taxable items—like tax-free interest from municipal bonds. Each year, the SSA sets income brackets, and if you land in one of the higher ones, you'll get a notice in the mail telling you how much more you owe.

As of 2024, about 7% of people on Medicare Part B and 8% on Part D pay IRMAA charges.

Here's how it might look: Person A earns $40,000 a year. They pay the standard $174.70/month for Medicare Part B. Person B earns $200,000 a year. They pay $174.70 + an IRMAA charge, which could bump their monthly cost up to $349.40 or more.

But IRMAA can change every year. That makes it a variable expense in retirement and something you'll want to plan around.

So, keep an eye on your income. Higher MAGI means higher IRMAA, and large IRA withdrawals or capital gains can trigger higher charges.

If you experience a life-changing event like retirement, divorce, or death of a spouse, you can request a lower IRMAA using Form SSA-44. You can also ask a financial advisor or tax professional to help you make tax-smart decisions that may reduce or avoid IRMAA altogether.

So yes, Medicare is a great program, but it is not free. Be prepared for variable costs, and know that higher-income retirees may get a higher price tag.

 Have you thought about how IRMAA could affect your retirement budget? What strategies can you use now to help manage or avoid this extra expense?

80. RMDs

"The government wants its tax money, so you can't just let your retirement savings sit and grow forever."

Once you turn 73, the IRS says it's time to start withdrawing from your tax-deferred retirement accounts—like IRAs, 401(k)s, SIMPLE IRAs, and SEP IRAs. These withdrawals are called Required Minimum Distributions, or RMDs. And yes, they are required.

During the years when you contributed money into these accounts, you got a tax break. Now, Uncle Sam is ready for his cut.

Interestingly, nearly 30% of retirees only take the minimum required RMD and no more. That might mean they have plenty of other income and don't need additional funds. But it could also mean they're unsure about their plan and are hesitant to withdraw more than necessary.

RMDs begin at age 73 (or 75 if you were born in 1960 or later). Roth IRAs do not have RMDs during your lifetime, since taxes were already paid. But beneficiaries of Roth IRAs do have to take RMDs.

If you're still working at 73 and participating in your employer's plan, you may be able to delay RMDs from that account.

Qualified charitable distributions (QCDs) allow you to give up to $115,000 (indexed for inflation each year) per year directly to a qualified charity from your IRA, counting toward your RMD and excluding the amount from taxable income. You can always take more than the minimum if needed to fund your retirement lifestyle or rebalance your tax situation.

Work with a financial advisor to calculate your RMD correctly. It is based on your account balance from the end of the previous year divided by a life expectancy factor from the IRS's Uniform Lifetime Table.

Missing an RMD results in a 25% penalty on the amount not withdrawn. If you correct it quickly, the penalty drops to 10%, but that's still money you probably don't want to lose.

To simplify things, consider consolidating retirement accounts so you don't accidentally miss an RMD from a forgotten or old account. You can also set up automatic withdrawals to ensure you never miss your annual deadline.

> Are you preparing ahead to simplify your RMDs, reduce your tax burden, and avoid penalties? How can you make this a smoother part of your retirement income plan?

81. Reverse Mortgages

"A reverse mortgage isn't just a last-ditch lifeline. It can be a smart retirement power move."

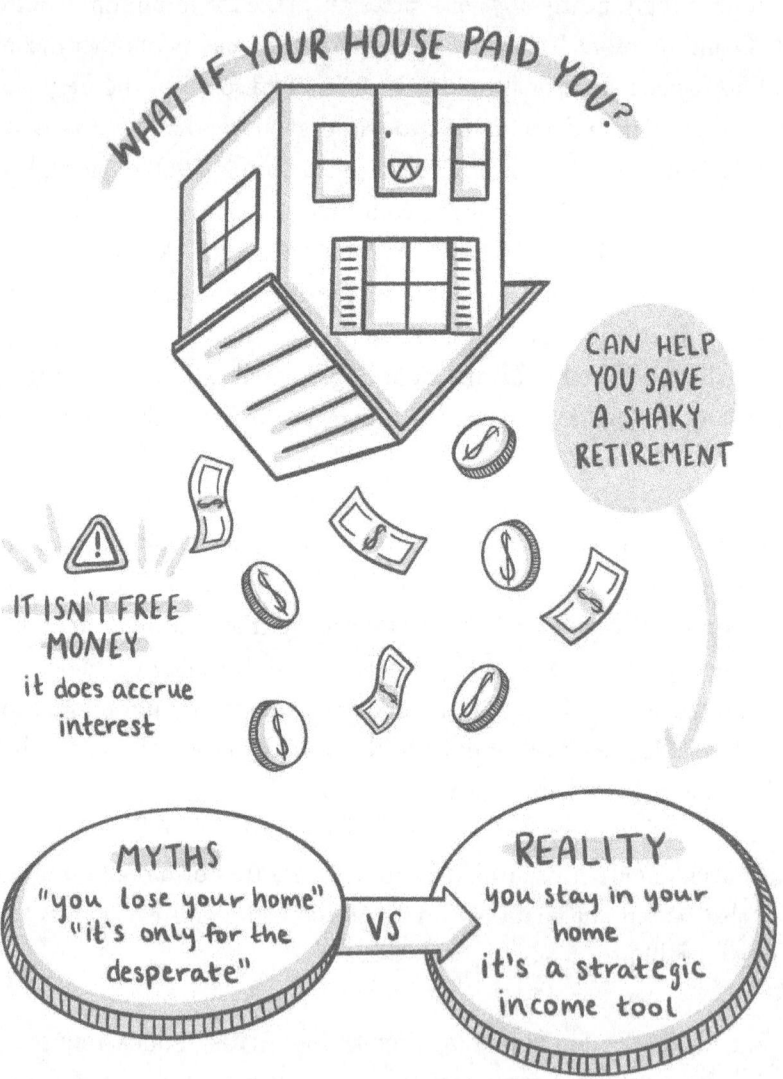

Let's bust a myth: Reverse mortgages aren't just a last resort for when your couch cushions are empty and your bank balance hits rock bottom. In fact, when used strategically, a reverse mortgage can help reverse the course of a shaky retirement plan.

Despite being a potentially powerful tool, only about 2% of eligible homeowners actually use one to fund retirement. That's like having a golden ticket to Willy Wonka's Chocolate Factory… and using it to get a parking discount.

So, what's a reverse mortgage anyway? It's kind of like a mortgage flipped upside down. Instead of you paying the bank every month, the bank pays you—either monthly, in a lump sum, or as a line of credit. You get access to the equity you've built in your home, and the best part? No monthly payments required while you're still living there.

Now, this isn't free money—it does accrue interest—but it's designed so you'll never owe more than your home is worth. It's a non-recourse loan, meaning your heirs won't be stuck with a scary bill when you're gone. Nice, right?

Here's the catch: Many people wait until the very end to use it, treating it like financial duct tape. But that's actually the worst time. Instead, think of it as a financial sidekick that can smooth out rocky market years, help fund big expenses like a new roof, or just give your investment accounts a break.

Used early and wisely, a reverse mortgage can be a savvy way to stretch your retirement income—and maybe even boost your lifestyle a bit (hello, upgraded recliner). Be willing and open to the idea that you can let your home pitch in for your retirement.

✷ Are you comfortable tapping home equity for retirement income in retirement and would you be open to borrowing in the form of a reverse mortgage if it meant you would have more income in retirement?

82. Tapping Home Equity in Retirement

"When used wisely, home equity is more than just square footage. It's financial fuel that can turn a struggling retirement into a thriving one."

Here's a fun fact: For over 80% of retirees, their biggest asset isn't in a bank or a portfolio. Instead, it's sitting right under their feet. Yep, it's the house! But here's the kicker: While it's your biggest asset, it can also be your biggest money drain. The good news? It doesn't have to be.

Too many retirees treat their home like an untouchable heirloom—saving it for the kids or waiting until they absolutely have to tap into it. But what if your home could actually boost your lifestyle instead of just collecting dust and property taxes?

Your home doesn't just have to be where you live—it can be your financial secret weapon. Whether it's downsizing to free up equity, refinancing smartly, using a line of credit, or even considering a reverse mortgage, your house can start working for you in retirement, not the other way around.

Think about it: You've spent decades paying into your home—why not let it return the favor? If you've got a low mortgage rate, maybe keep it and let your investments grow. If cash flow's tight, a reverse mortgage could take those payments off your plate.

Or maybe it's time to cash out some equity for a kitchen upgrade, travel adventures, or that dream deck with the hot tub. (We won't judge.)

Housing costs are usually your biggest retirement expense. But they can also be your biggest opportunity. With the right strategy, you can turn a so-so retirement plan into one that actually feels like retirement—flexible, sustainable, and maybe even a little luxurious.

 How could you use your home equity more strategically in retirement than you might have previously been thinking?

83. Lines of Credit

"A line of credit in retirement is like an umbrella. You hope you never need it, but when the roof starts leaking, you'll be glad it's there."

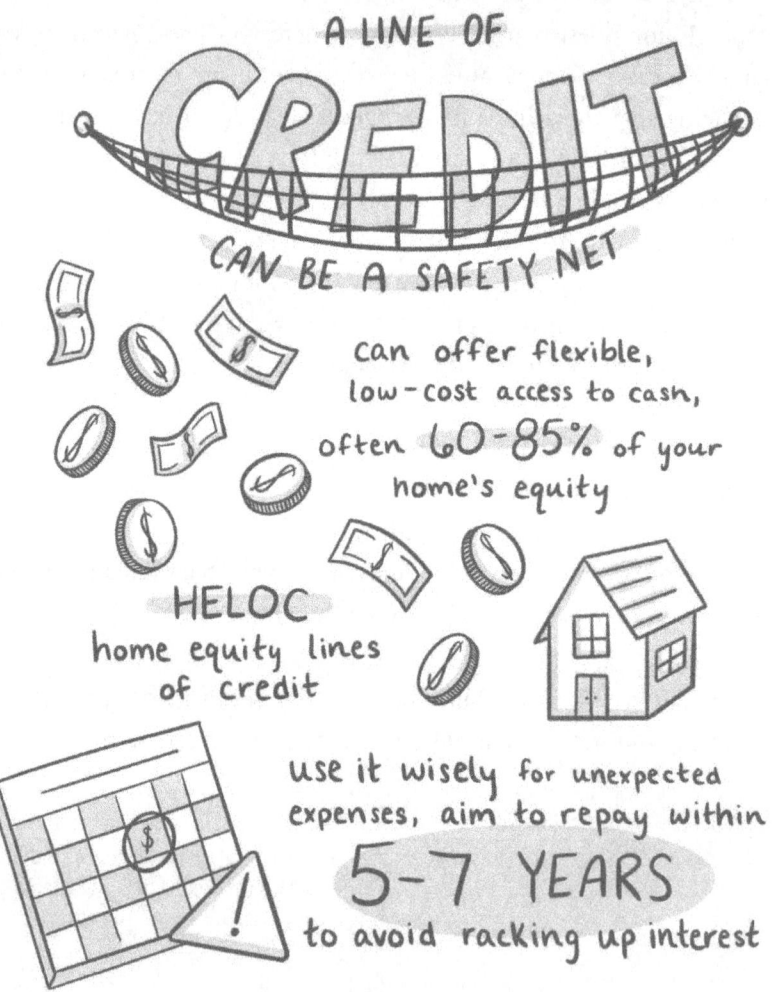

A line of credit can be a financial lifeline in retirement, especially when unexpected expenses pop up. Retirement can be filled with major expenses. Remember, not only are you aging, but your home is aging with you. This means you may have to replace your roof, or perform home renovations to make your living space more senior-friendly. Having a line of credit available can help you handle these costs.

In fact, nearly 40% of Americans carry some form of home equity debt in retirement, with cash-out refinances and home equity lines of credit (HELOCs) leading the way in borrowing after age 62.

When managed wisely, a line of credit offers flexible, low-cost access to cash—often up to 60–85% of your home's equity. Many HELOCs come with little to no setup cost and can serve as a reliable financial cushion without putting your nest egg or your home at major risk.

Think of it as a safety net: It's there when you need it, but it's important to use it responsibly. Aim to repay any borrowed amount within five to seven years to avoid racking up interest, and always keep an eye on current interest rates versus your investment returns. If rates are high, tapping into savings or other assets may be the better move.

Setting up a line of credit—whether a traditional HELOC or a reverse mortgage line of credit—early in retirement can offer peace of mind. It's a smart strategy to ensure financial flexibility without having to liquidate investments in a downturn.

A line of credit can enhance any retirement plan.

> Have you considered setting up a line of credit today to better understand how they work and how it could be useful to supplement your income when big expenses arise?

84. Navigating Sequence Risk

"We can't control the market's mood swings, but we can control how prepared we are when they happen."

Retirement is about enjoying life, not stressing about every headline. Yet, retirees face a variety of risks: inflation, interest rates, longevity. One of the sneakiest of these challenges is called sequence of returns risk.

So what is it?

It's about when you get returns from your investments. The sequence, or order of returns, especially in the early years of retirement, can dramatically affect how long your money lasts.

Imagine retiring in 2007. Just a year later, the market fell by nearly 50%, and US households lost more than $16 trillion in net worth. If your retirement income was based on those assets, the damage would have been painful—and possibly permanent.

Sequence risk is especially dangerous for:

- People who retire just before a market downturn
- People who enter retirement during a long stretch of flat or low returns.

Bad timing can trigger a downward spiral when you're withdrawing from a shrinking portfolio. That makes recovery harder and faster depletion more likely.

You can't prevent sequence risk, so as retirement approaches, consider reducing equity exposure and increasing bonds or income-producing investments to help buffer volatility.

Consider adjusting your spending when markets dip. Spending a little less in a downturn can preserve your portfolio for the long haul.

Create a retirement budget that accounts for potential shocks, including inflation, healthcare costs, and market dips, so you can ride out the market's ups and downs while keeping your retirement on track.

※ How regularly do you review your retirement plan in depth? Do you have access to anyone who could help you with this review, particularly if the market has been volatile?

85. Time Segmentation

"With time segmentation, you're not just investing for retirement. You're investing for each chapter of retirement."

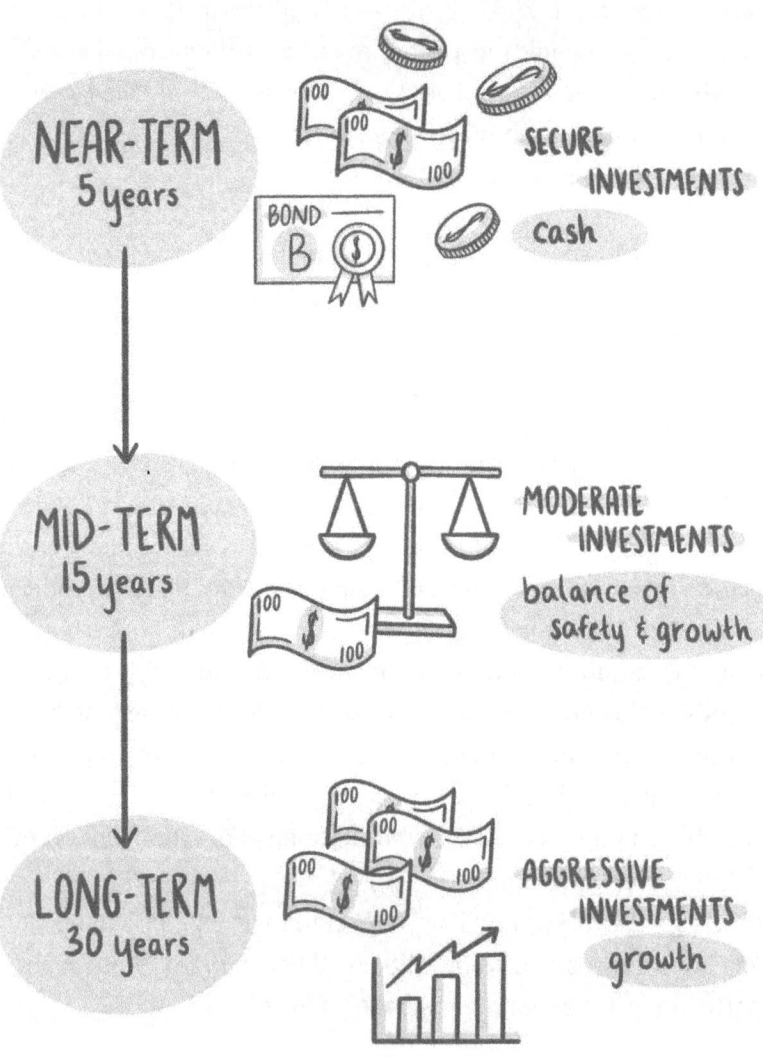

Many people find it difficult to picture how their retirement savings will turn into a steady income they can count on. That's where time segmentation comes in. It's a strategy that makes retirement planning more tangible and structured by aligning your investments with when you'll actually need the money.

Think of retirement as a series of life chapters. Time segmentation helps you prepare for each one, from your early years of travel and adventure to your later years of rest and reflection. You divide your savings into segments based on timing: near term, mid term, long term.

The money you'll need soon is kept safe and stable in things like cash or short-term bonds. These funds are there to cover your everyday living costs without depending on the ups and downs of the stock market. As you move into the middle stretch of retirement, you might shift into a mix of investments that balance safety and growth—assets that continue to support your lifestyle while also preparing for the future. For the distant years ahead, when you'll need to stay ahead of inflation, growth-oriented investments like stocks help build the wealth that supports your later-life needs.

This method isn't just about investments. It's also about peace of mind. Matching your future expenses with specific investments—often called liability matching—makes retirement feel less like a guessing game and more like a well-prepared journey. It can help reduce the fear of outliving your money and give you a sense of control over your financial future.

As your life changes or the markets shift, you can revisit your plan and make adjustments. That flexibility helps you stay on track without being thrown off course by unexpected bumps along the way.

※ Would it help to break down your retirement into time-based segments and match your investments to those phases? Could this approach make your financial future feel more stable and easier to manage?

86. Retirement Planning Checkups

"The biggest mistake in retirement planning? Thinking you can set it and forget it."

According to the Employee Benefit Research Institute (EBRI), only 33% of US workers feel very confident in their ability to retire comfortably, and 60% of workers plan to retire after age 65—or not at all. Yet, most people aren't checking in on their progress. Only 13% of people check their retirement account balance daily, and only about half of workers have ever tried to estimate how much they actually need to save.

Yet, confidence in retirement planning starts with clarity, and clarity comes from routine checkups.

Your retirement plan deserves a regular review, say annually, and you don't have to make sweeping changes each time. The goal is to make sure you're still on track and aligned with your goals.

Use this checklist as your personal retirement plan "report card":

- Savings rate—Are you saving enough based on your income, goals, and timeline? Could you bump it up a little?
- Investment allocation—Are your investments aligned with your age, risk tolerance, and retirement horizon? Has your allocation drifted?
- Other savings opportunities—Beyond your 401(k) or 403(b), are you making use of HSAs, IRAs, or other tax-advantaged accounts?
- Account fees—Do you know what fees you're paying? Are there lower-cost options that fit your needs?
- Beneficiaries—Are the beneficiaries on your retirement accounts still accurate and up to date?

You can do this review on your own or, better yet, with help. If you have access to a workplace retirement plan, you may already have resources—like financial advisors or planning tools—available at no cost. Take advantage of them.

Your retirement won't run on autopilot. A little intentional maintenance each year can go a long way toward helping you retire on your own terms.

 How often do you check in on your retirement plan? And do you have someone who can help guide the review?

Your Retirement Notes

Your Retirement Sketches

CHAPTER VII

LIVING IN RETIREMENT

- Retirement is Not Binary
- Stop Saving Right Before Retirement
- Retirement Housing
- Downsizing in Retirement
- Managing Debt in Retirement
- Continuing Care Retirement Communities
- Inflation
- The Four Percent Finding
- Learn Everything You Can
- Changing Your Identity
- Silver Divorce
- Social Network in Retirement
- Changing Interest Rates
- Refilling Buckets
- Medicare
- Aging in Place

- Aging and Frailty
- Health is Wealth
- Long-Term Caregivers
- Cognitive Decline and Financial Decision-Making
- Pet Care and Planning in Retirement
- Second Careers
- Finding Meaning in Retirement

CHAPTER VII.
Introduction

Once the retirement party ends, the real work—and the real joy—begins. You're now living in retirement. No more countdowns, no more projections—you've arrived. But unlike the world of work, retirement doesn't hand you a schedule or a rulebook. That's the beauty, and the challenge.

This chapter of life is about much more than managing money—it's about designing a lifestyle. One that brings meaning, connection, autonomy, and well-being. Time is now your most valuable currency. How you spend it—and with whom—is entirely up to you.

Retirement is a chance to reclaim your time and recenter your life around what matters most. And that starts with asking some big questions:

- What do I want my days to look like?
- Who is in my circle—my community, my tribe?
- Where do I want to live, and what does "home" mean now?
- How will I take care of my body, my mind, and my future self?

Building your retirement community

Loneliness in retirement is real—and often underestimated. As we leave the workforce, we also leave behind structured relationships, shared goals, and a sense of place. That's why community matters more than ever in retirement. Whether it's friends, family, neighbors, faith groups, volunteer circles, or pickleball partners—your people are your lifeline.

Be intentional about community. Make the calls. Invite others in. Reinvest in old relationships and cultivate new ones. Connection doesn't happen by accident—it's built with effort. And studies show that strong social bonds are one of the best predictors of health and happiness in later life.

Housing: aging with intention

Next comes one of the biggest lifestyle decisions: where you live. That's not just a financial choice—it's an emotional and physical one, too. Will you age in place or move closer to family? Downsize or renovate? Stay in your community or explore something new?

Aging in place can provide continuity and comfort—but it may require home modifications, support systems, and access to care. Retirement communities offer built-in social networks and amenities, but come with rules and costs. Multi-generational living, co-housing, or snowbirding might suit others. The point is: There's no one-size-fits-all solution—only what's right for you.

Ask yourself:

- Will this home serve me well if my mobility changes?
- What services or help might I need to stay independent?
- Who's nearby that I can count on?

Housing isn't just about real estate—it's about future-proofing your lifestyle.

Planning for care before you need it

Let's talk about the topic nobody likes to think about: care. Eventually, most of us will need help—whether for a short recovery or long-term support. The best time to plan for it is when you're still healthy and independent. That way, you stay in control.

Ask yourself:

- Where do I want to receive care—at home, with family, in a facility?
- Who do I trust to help—and have I talked to them about it?
- Have I built a plan—financially and logistically—for when care is needed?

These aren't easy conversations, but they're loving ones. You plan so you can live the best life possible, even in challenging seasons.

Your time, your purpose

One of the biggest gifts in retirement is time. But without direction, time can slip away unnoticed. So, how will you fill your days? What will give you purpose, joy, and challenge?

Maybe it's volunteering, mentoring, part-time work, caregiving, writing, painting, traveling, or just being present. Retirement can be full or spacious, fast or slow—it's yours to design. The only mistake is assuming you'll figure it out later. Be proactive. Purpose doesn't find you—you create it.

Your greatest asset: your health

Finally, let's talk about health. No retirement plan is complete without a wellness plan. You can't fully enjoy freedom if your body or mind doesn't support it. This isn't about perfection—it's about commitment to self-care. Health is wealth in retirement.

Move your body regularly. Stay sharp mentally. Sleep well. Nourish your spirit. Get your checkups. Retirement isn't about slowing down—it's about investing in the energy you want to bring to this chapter of your life.

Retirement is not the end of your story—it's a chance to rewrite the next chapters with clarity, care, and creativity.

Use this sketchbook not just to imagine retirement, but to live it with intention—from your home to your health, from your people to your purpose.

87. Retirement is Not Binary

"A successful retirement is about living life on your terms."

Let's flip the script on retirement. It's not a simple pass/fail scenario or some final exam where you either ace it or flunk out. Retirement is about designing a life that works for you—on your terms, at your pace, and with what matters most to you.

Here's something interesting: 77% of retirees say that social support is one of the biggest contributors to a successful retirement. Not hitting a certain dollar amount. Not following a rigid financial formula. Real people. Real connection. Real purpose.

Despite that, many still believe in the "magic number" theory. You know the one—hit that specific retirement savings target and you're good to go. Miss it, and you're not "ready." Add to that, most retirement tools and calculators boil things down to a probability of success or failure. Will your money last or won't it?

That kind of black-and-white thinking misses the point. Life doesn't work that way. And neither should retirement planning.

Here's a better way to look at it: Retirement is dynamic. It shifts. It evolves. And your ability to adapt is more powerful than any spreadsheet. Being flexible—whether that means spending less in down years, picking up part-time work, or shifting your lifestyle—can make your savings go further and your retirement more fulfilling.

There's no universal income number that guarantees happiness. What truly matters is aligning your plan with your lifestyle, goals, and values. The more adaptable you are, the less you need to stress over hitting some idealized financial target.

Retirement is not just about whether your assets last forever. It's about your life satisfaction, your freedom to pivot, and your ability to shape your next chapter.

 What does a successful retirement really look like? How will you define a truly successful retirement beyond that of mere numbers?

88. Stop Saving Right Before Retirement

"The last few years before retirement are your chance to live well enough to keep going, and by doing so, retire even better."

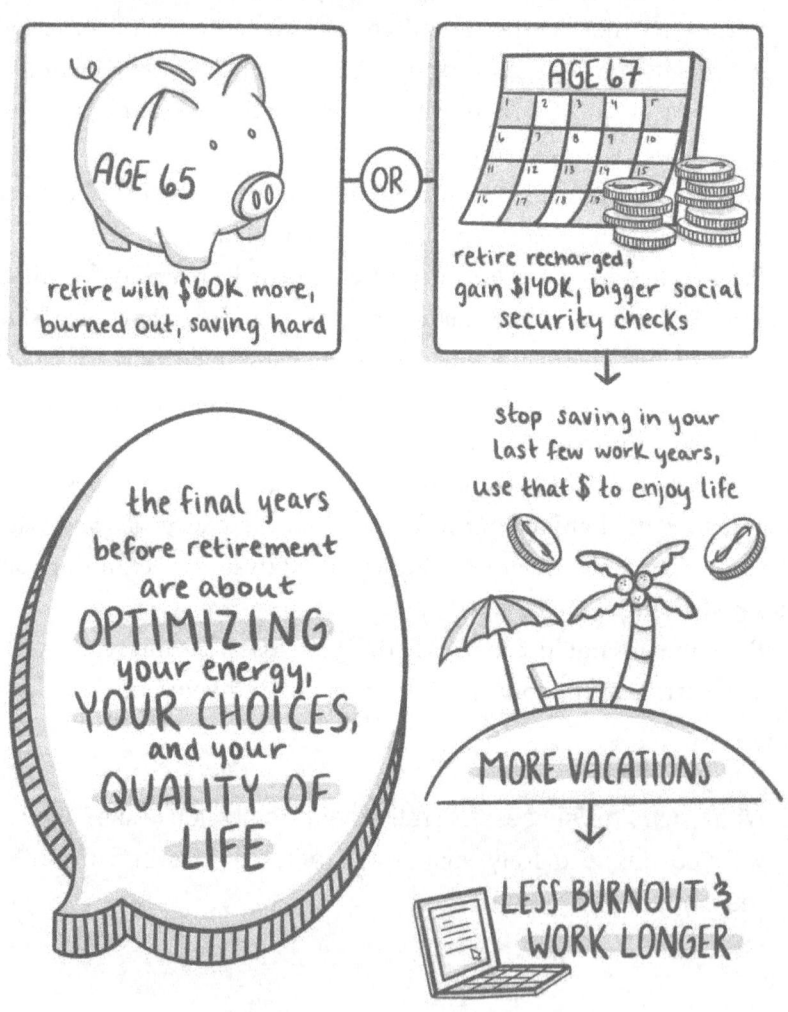

Let's rethink a long-standing retirement myth: the idea that you should keep saving aggressively right up to your retirement date. Sounds smart on the surface, but there's a twist: What if not saving at the very end actually puts you in a better financial position?

Here's the surprising part: Working just a little bit longer can have a greater impact on your retirement security than socking away more money in your final working years. According to the National Bureau of Economic Research (NBER), in some cases, working just three to six months longer gives your retirement income a bigger boost than saving an extra 1% of your salary for the past 30 years. That's a big deal.

Most people focus so much on saving that they overlook a critical part of the equation—how long they work. If you stop saving in the last few years of your career and instead use that money to enjoy life or reduce stress, it could give you the energy and motivation to stay in the workforce a little longer. And those extra working years? They make a huge difference.

Imagine you're earning $100,000 annually and saving 20% of it. Over your last three working years, that's $60,000 in savings. Now, picture spending that $60,000 instead. Maybe you travel, or invest in hobbies, or just improve your day-to-day life. You feel recharged and push retirement out by two years. That means two more years of income, two fewer years relying on your savings, and two additional years of delaying your Social Security benefits, which increases your monthly check. Compared to retiring at 65 and saving that $60,000, retiring at 67 could leave you more than $140,000 better off financially.

This approach doesn't mean retirement savings aren't important. Of course they are. But it shows that the final years before retirement aren't always about saving more. These years are about optimizing your energy, your choices, and your quality of life.

 Have you considered the long-term impact of stopping your retirement contributions early? What might allow you to stay in the workplace longer?

89. Retirement Housing

"In retirement, your home isn't just about where you live. It's how you live. The right choice balances comfort, community, and cash flow."

We've all heard it before: location, location, location. But when it comes to retirement, there's a new mantra in town: cash flow, cash flow, cash flow.

Sure, where you live matters. But how your home supports your lifestyle matters even more. In fact, about 83% of retirees say they want to stay in their homes for as long as possible. The dream? Comfortable surroundings, familiar neighbors, and a fridge that's always stocked just how you like it.

But here's the twist: Housing in retirement isn't a one-and-done decision. It's a journey. What makes sense at 65 might not at 85. And with housing being one of the biggest retirement expenses, your choice has major financial ripple effects.

There are tons of options beyond the classic "stay put" strategy. You could age in place, share your home with a friend (think modern-day Golden Girls), relocate somewhere new, downsize, rent, move into a continuing care community, join a 55+ neighborhood, or even live with family. Each option has its perks—and its quirks.

Want to boost your cash flow? Renting out a room or moving in with a friend can free up income while adding a little social spice to your day. But hey, we get it. That's not for everyone. Some people thrive in shared spaces, others just want their own peaceful corner of the world. The key is finding your sweet spot.

And don't forget to look beyond just the price tag. Think about accessibility, community vibe, walkability, proximity to healthcare, and whether you'll actually enjoy spending time there. Moving might mean leaving behind familiar grocery stores and beloved coffee shops, perhaps even changing friends and local routines. On the flip side, it could mean a fresh start in a sunnier, easier-to-manage home.

Here's the bottom line: Where you live in retirement isn't just about real estate. It's about lifestyle, longevity, and financial freedom. So take your time. Weigh your options.

✳ What kind of home will support the kind of retirement you really want?

90. Downsizing in Retirement

"Downsizing in retirement isn't about having less— it's about making room for more of what matters."

NOT DOWNSIZING. RIGHTSIZING!

lower costs, less maintenance, more travel, closer to family, peace of mind

DOWNSIZING ISN'T ABOUT HAVING LESS. IT'S ABOUT MAKING ROOM FOR MORE OF WHAT MATTERS!

Downsizing can help you create a lifestyle that fits who you are now, not who you were 20 years ago.

More than half of adults over 50 say they want to downsize, and it's easy to see why. Less house often means lower costs, fewer chores, and more time and money for the things you actually want to do—like traveling, picking up new hobbies, or just enjoying a slower pace.

But let's shift the thinking from "downsizing" to "rightsizing." This isn't just about shrinking your living space. It's about aligning your home with your life. Maybe it means moving to a smaller place with no stairs, less lawn to mow, and easier access to the things you care about. Or maybe it means swapping your old house for a newer, more efficient one that costs more, but fits your needs better.

Downsizing can absolutely lighten your financial load, but it's not just a numbers game. The emotional side is real. That old house might hold decades of memories, family milestones, and stories in every corner. And once you sell it, it's tough to go back. So any decision to move should be made with both head and heart.

Ask yourself: Will this move reduce stress? Will it free up money or time? Does it put me closer to family, friends, or medical care? Does it support the kind of life I want in retirement?

Before you make a move, run the numbers and visualize the lifestyle shift. Talk to a financial advisor to understand how a sale or purchase might impact your taxes, retirement income, and long-term plans. Consider renting first in a new area to test the waters before committing. And don't overlook the emotional benefits of letting go: less clutter, less upkeep, and more freedom to focus on what truly matters.

Remember, housing will likely be your biggest expense in retirement. So the goal isn't just to go smaller. It's to go smarter.

 What would rightsizing in retirement mean for your quality of life, your peace of mind, and your financial health in retirement?

91. Managing Debt in Retirement

"In retirement, debt can be a lever or a liability. The difference is whether you're using it with intention or letting it use you."

WELL-MANAGED DEBT CAN FUNCTION AS A TOOL

64% of Americans say paying down debt is their top financial priority

POORLY USED DEBT CAN NEGATIVELY AFFECT YOUR RETIREMENT PLAN

DEBT SHOULD NEVER BE IGNORED, BUT IT DOESN'T HAVE TO BE FEARED

Not all debt is bad. Used wisely, it can preserve liquidity, provide flexibility, and even enhance your lifestyle in retirement. Used poorly, however, debt becomes dead weight—more like cinderblock shoes in the ocean than a financial strategy, slowly dragging down even the best-laid plans.

According to the 2024 Northwestern Mutual Planning and Progress Study, 64% of Americans say paying down debt is their top financial priority—before even saving for retirement. That's a staggering number, and it reveals just how central debt is to the American financial experience. Most people don't enter retirement with a blank slate. Whether it's a mortgage, personal loans, or credit card balances, debt management is a reality—and often a necessity—in retirement.

That said, not all debt should be feared. For retirees, debt can serve a variety of strategic purposes. You might take out a mortgage on a downsized home to preserve capital. You may open a home equity line of credit to fund aging-in-place renovations. In some cases, using a reverse mortgage can improve cash flow without having to sell off investments in a down market. Borrowing isn't always bad—it just has to be intentional.

On the other hand, unmanaged debt can quietly eat away at a retirement plan. Carrying high-interest balances or letting loans grow unchecked can add stress and financial strain. That's why managing debt in retirement means more than just making payments—it means creating a plan. Whether you focus on eliminating high-interest debt to reduce long-term costs, or you strategically borrow to reduce taxes or avoid selling off assets, the key is balance. Debt should never be ignored, but it doesn't have to be feared.

Instead of asking, "Should I carry debt into retirement?" ask, "How can I use debt to support my goals without compromising my peace of mind?" The goal isn't to eliminate all debt at all costs—it's to use it wisely, with clarity, control, and purpose.

> What types of debt do you currently have, and which—if any—do you truly need to carry into retirement? Are you using debt as a tool to enhance flexibility, or is it limiting your financial freedom?

92. Continuing Care Retirement Communities

"The best time to consider a continuing care retirement community is before you think you need one. Planning early gives you more choice, more freedom, and more peace of mind."

Here's the paradox with Continuing Care Retirement Communities (CCRCs): Most people think they're not old enough to consider one. And when they do feel ready, they may no longer qualify. It's the classic retirement Catch-22.

In fact, 63% of people are drawn to CCRCs because of the security they offer: the ability to age in place with a continuum of care. But nearly half of those same people say they hold off on moving in because they just don't feel "old enough" yet. So when is the right time?

CCRCs are designed to evolve with you. They offer a full range of care options, starting with independent living, then transitioning to assisted living or skilled nursing care as needs arise. You might start in a standalone home, apartment, or condo and stay within the same community as your lifestyle and health change. This kind of setup can be especially valuable for couples who may have very different care needs over time.

Of course, making the move is a big decision. Most CCRCs require a significant upfront payment (think of it like buying into a retirement plan), along with monthly fees that vary based on the level of care and services. Some contracts allow you to prepay certain long-term care costs, which may even be partially tax deductible. Others operate more like pay-as-you-go models.

It's essential to do your homework. Look into the financial health of the organization. Ask about the quality of their medical care, community life, food, services, and living spaces. Talk to current residents and their families. Understand the terms of the contract. And yes, dig into their financial history. While some CCRCs have struggled, state governments have occasionally stepped in to protect residents and ensure continued care.

Despite the complexities, surveys show that most residents are highly satisfied with their decision to move to a CCRC. Many wish they had done it sooner. The blend of independence, built-in support, and peace of mind can be a powerful recipe for a secure and fulfilling retirement.

> How does a CCRC fit into your retirement picture? Have you ever visited a CCRC? Should you consider a trip to look at a local facility to understand it better?

93. Inflation

"Inflation doesn't retire when you do. Make sure your plan keeps up with the rising cost of living."

When everyday essentials like groceries, rent, gas, and utilities cost more, it's a lot harder to stash away money for the future. Especially when that "future" feels far off, like retirement.

According to a recent Nationwide study, 42% of people said inflation has made it tougher to manage their daily expenses. And honestly, it's easy to see why. Inflation doesn't just stretch your current budget—it reshapes how you plan for the years ahead.

Where you are on the retirement timeline really affects how inflation hits you. If you're already retired, rising costs can be more than inconvenient—they can force some hard decisions. Maybe you planned to spend a certain amount on food, utilities, or healthcare, only to find those costs have blown past your original budget.

If you're still saving for retirement, inflation is just as critical—but a little trickier to see. Your retirement savings don't automatically adjust with rising prices. A million dollars today won't buy you what it will 10 or 20 years from now. That's why it's essential to build inflation protection into your long-term plan.

Some financial advisors proactively plan for this with inflation-adjusted investment strategies. Others don't. That's why it's important to ask: Is my retirement plan built to keep up with rising costs? What assumptions are we making about inflation over the next 10, 20, or 30 years?

The good news? You're not powerless against inflation. There are strategies to help cushion the impact, like investing in assets that historically outpace inflation (such as stocks or Treasury Inflation-Protected Securities), delaying Social Security to increase your benefit, or allocating part of your portfolio to income sources that grow over time. Even small adjustments, like trimming non-essential expenses or reevaluating your withdrawal rate, can help stretch your retirement dollars further. Inflation may be inevitable, but with the right plan, it doesn't have to derail your retirement goals.

Whether you're already living in retirement or still planning for it, inflation isn't just a passing headline. It's a long-term factor that can reshape your financial future.

 Is your retirement plan ready for the rising costs of life?

94. The Four Percent Finding

"In retirement, it's not the average return that matters. It's all about sustainability. The 4% rule isn't a license to spend, but a guide to help your savings last as long as you do."

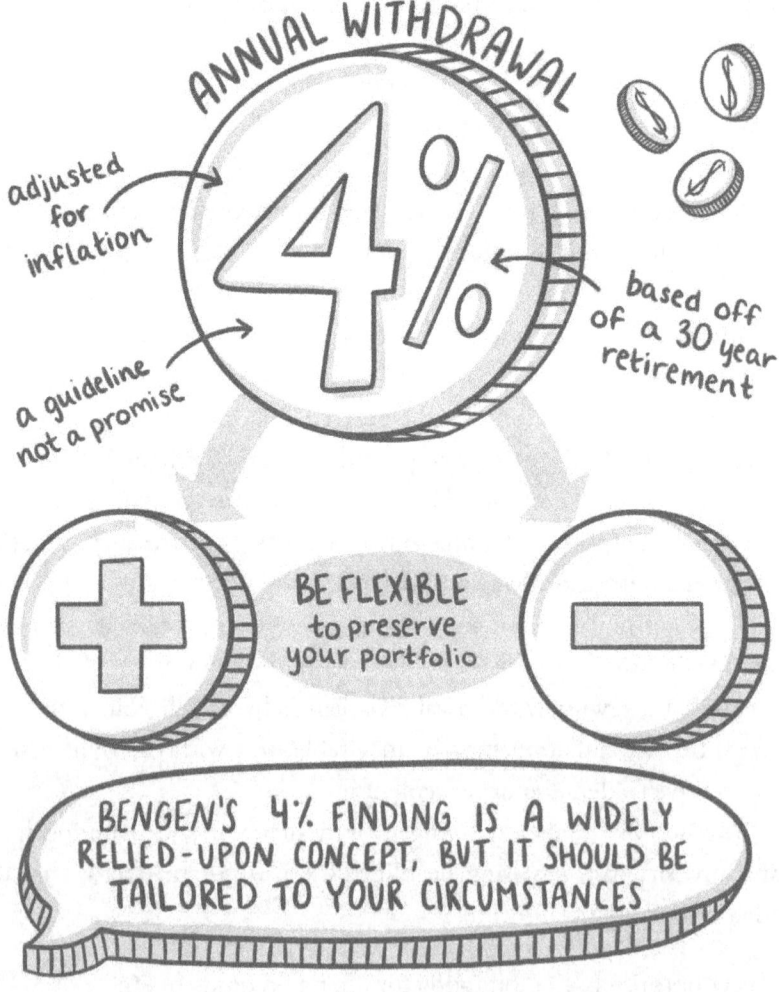

Just because your investments might average an 8% return during retirement doesn't mean you can safely spend 8% a year. This is one of the most common misunderstandings about managing retirement income. The key here is sustainability. Historically, a well-balanced portfolio (roughly 50% US large-cap stocks and 50% bonds) has been able to support a 4% annual withdrawal rate, adjusted for inflation, without running out of money over a 30-year retirement period in the United States.

This idea, known widely as the "4% rule," came from research originally conducted by financial planner Bill Bengen. *Morningstar* has since revisited and expanded on this research, reinforcing the value of this rule as a starting point, but not a guarantee.

The 4% rule is based on historical market data, but while markets might average higher returns over long periods, the sequence of those returns really matters. If you experience poor investment performance in the early years of retirement—a phenomenon known as sequence-of-returns risk—your portfolio could take a serious hit, which can reduce your sustainability.

Since the 4% figure is based on a 30-year retirement, you should review your withdrawal strategy regularly and make adjustments based on market conditions, your own risk tolerance, and how long you expect your remaining retirement to last.

Flexibility is also important. If you're willing to scale back spending in tough years, especially when markets are down, your overall average spending rate could exceed 4% while still preserving your portfolio for the long haul. The 4% rule also helps set a good savings target: Generally, you should aim to save about 25 times the annual income you want in retirement. For instance, if you want to spend $40,000 a year, you'd need to save $1 million.

Bill Bengen's original work laid the foundation for a critical principle in retirement planning. But like all financial strategies, it should be tailored to your personal circumstances.

 Is a 4% return a good fit for your retirement plan? Or do today's market conditions, your lifestyle, and your goals point toward a different approach?

95. Learn Everything You Can

"Education is often the most valuable asset in your portfolio. Your ability to learn as much as possible before making important decisions will drive your success in retirement."

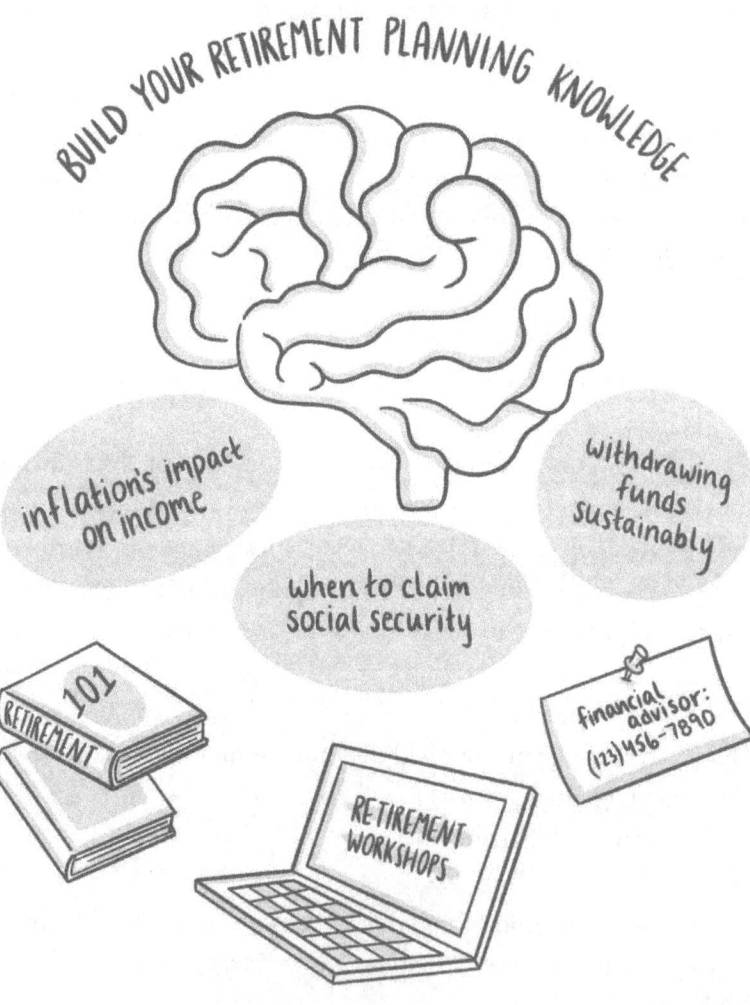

We can only make decisions based on the experience and knowledge we currently have. And when it comes to retirement, that presents a challenge. Most of us haven't lived through retirement yet, so we're making plans for something we haven't personally experienced. That's why it's so important to focus on building retirement planning knowledge before stepping into that phase of life. The more informed you are, the more confident and prepared you'll be to make good decisions.

Despite this need, many Americans are not as ready as they should be. The majority of people approaching retirement struggle with basic concepts like how inflation impacts income, how to withdraw funds sustainably, and when to start claiming Social Security.

While general financial understanding tends to improve with age, retirement-specific knowledge often remains weak. Many people over 50 have a decent grasp of topics like savings, budgeting, and compound interest. But when it comes to managing retirement income, taxes, and investment risk over a long retirement, there's a significant knowledge gap.

That's why ongoing education matters. Reading books, attending workshops, and talking with a financial advisor can all help. You might also try a retirement literacy quiz to see where you stand. If learning the finer points of retirement planning doesn't appeal to you, it might be worth hiring a professional who can help you make informed choices.

Some of the biggest decisions in retirement, like when to claim Social Security, when to convert to a Roth IRA, or when to actually retire, can't be reversed later. These choices often come with lasting consequences.

That's why it's so important to make these decisions based on accurate, up-to-date information, not guesswork or assumptions.

 What areas of retirement are you least confident in? What steps can you take to improve your understanding?

96. Changing Your Identity

"Retirement is not just a significant change in lifestyle. In many ways, it can mean changing your identity."

Retirement can seem like one giant change in lifestyle: One day you're working, the next day you're not. But in reality, it's more like a three-part journey—and how you move through each phase can have a big impact on your mental and emotional well-being.

Retirement isn't just a change in schedule. It's a full-blown identity shift. For most, this experience can be incredibly unsettling. To deal with this, there are three unique phases to help with the transition.

Phase One: Preparing to retire

Start planning about what life will look like without the job title, the paycheck, and the daily grind. You dream about what comes next. You talk to your partner, your friends, your coworkers. You try to map out a version of life that's both exciting and sustainable.

Phase Two: The act of retiring

This is the moment of truth. Do you pop champagne or quietly slip out the door? For some, it's a long-awaited celebration. For others, it comes faster than expected. Whatever it looks like, it marks the end of one identity and the beginning of something new.

Phase Three: Living in retirement

Now you're not planning retirement—you're living it. And that requires figuring out who you are without the 9-to-5. Some people thrive. Others struggle to find their rhythm. The challenge? Replacing structure with purpose, and busyness with fulfillment.

Think of it this way: Some retirements erupt like a volcano—fast, dramatic, life-altering. Others unfold like a stream carving its way through stone—slowly, quietly, but with lasting impact. Either way, the landscape shifts. And how it shapes you depends on how prepared you are to walk that path with intention.

❋ What steps can you take to smooth the transition from your current state to a fully retired state?

97. Silver Divorce

"No one plans for a divorce in retirement, but failing to plan can turn a difficult transition into a devastating one."

NO ONE PLANS FOR A DIVORCE IN RETIREMENT, BUT PLANNING AHEAD CAN SOFTEN THE BLOW

CHAPTER VII

Divorce touches nearly every part of life—finances, family, community, emotions, and everything in between. But when it happens later in life, during or near retirement, its impact can feel even more profound. This is what's often called a grey divorce—named for the silver strands of hair that usually accompany this stage of life.

According to AARP, divorce among people over the age of 65 has tripled since 1990. There are many reasons why people divorce later in life. Some experience "empty nest syndrome," when the kids move out and realize they've grown apart. Others face retirement and suddenly find themselves spending far more time at home with someone they may not feel connected to anymore. Health challenges, lifestyle differences, or simply wanting something different from the years ahead can all play a role.

While divorce is hard at any age, the financial consequences of a grey divorce can be especially steep.

It might sound unromantic, but thinking ahead can protect both your heart and your financial well-being. The old saying "good fences make good neighbors" applies here too. For those entering marriage later in life, a prenuptial agreement might make sense. And if you're already married or facing a divorce, working with professionals—attorneys, tax advisors, financial planners—may come at a cost, but the cost of not doing so can be even greater.

Key things to consider include changes to health insurance coverage (especially for dependents), new tax filing status, and day-to-day budgeting. Even little things—like who pays for that sudden home repair or emergency expense—can become much bigger when you're on your own.

No one gets married planning for divorce, but smart planning means being prepared for every possibility—even the ones we hope never happen.

✳ Are you financially and emotionally prepared to navigate the unexpected, whatever your relationship status may be?

98. Social Network in Retirement

"Retirement done right means finally spending time with the people you love most."

RETIREES WITH DEEP SOCIAL TIES ARE HEALTHIER, HAPPIER, & LIVE MORE FULFILLING LIVES

Retirement is more than just a pleasant social shift. Taking the plunge into a new phase of life is vital to your health. According to recent research, older adults with strong, supportive relationships actually age one to two years more slowly than those without those connections.

In retirement, your social circle becomes more than just your friend group. It becomes your lifeline. A strong, active network can keep you mentally sharp, emotionally grounded, and even physically healthier. And countless studies back this up—retirees with deep social ties are healthier, happier, and live more fulfilling lives.

So how do you build that circle? You invest in it—just like you did your 401(k). Join a club. Volunteer. Take a class. Say yes to coffee invites and community events. Find people who share your passions or challenge your thinking. And don't forget to budget for it. Yes, really.

Think beyond just rent or healthcare—think about what it costs to stay connected. Can you afford to live near your closest friends or family? What about joining a gym, a gardening club, or a travel group? These aren't luxuries—they're strategic investments in your well-being.

Whether you're exploring a 55+ community, a co-housing setup, or simply making more room for social experiences in your daily life, prioritize connection as part of your retirement planning. Financial security is important, but a life filled with purpose and people? That's the real retirement dream.

 What are you doing today to build the kind of social network you'll want to have in retirement? And looking back, what community has brought you the most joy in life so far?

99. Changing Interest Rates

"To maximize your retirement plans, make sure that interest rates are working for you and not against you."

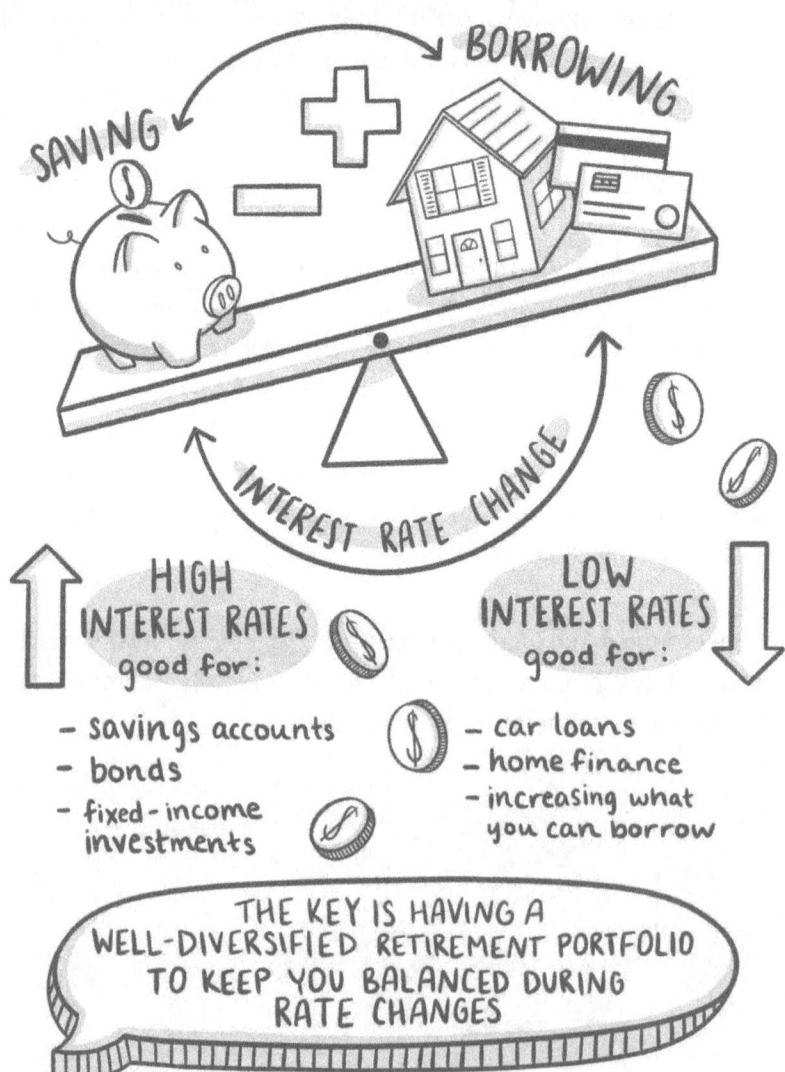

CHAPTER VII

Imagine you borrow $10 from a friend to buy cupcakes. Your friend agrees, but says that when you pay the money back next week, they want $1 extra as a thank-you. That extra dollar is the cost of borrowing money, or from the other perspective, the reward for lending it.

An interest rate is simply the percentage added to the amount you borrow or earn on top of what you invest. This rate shows up all throughout life—in car loans, credit cards, mortgages, and investment portfolios.

From an investing point of view, interest rates can work in your favor. When rates rise, savings accounts, bonds, and other fixed-income investments often start yielding more. That's good news if you hold those types of assets. But interest rates don't stay still. They change over time, often influenced by the Federal Reserve, which adjusts rates based on economic conditions. Market trends, bond yields, and decisions by financial institutions also play a role in setting interest rates.

A recent study by Charles Schwab looked at 14 instances of federal interest rate cuts and found that the S&P 500 posted positive returns in the following 12 months 86% of the time. This shows that rate changes don't just affect loans and savings—they can have a significant impact on investment performance too.

In retirement, changing interest rates can influence both your income and your overall financial plan. For example, lower interest rates can help when financing a big purchase like a car. But if you rely on high-yield savings accounts, CDs, or money market funds, rate cuts can shrink your income from those sources. So you should think carefully about how much of your portfolio is exposed to interest-sensitive assets.

Spreading your investments across a mix of asset types allows you to benefit when rates rise, while also protecting you when they fall. Understanding your exposure to interest rate changes is an important part of planning for long-term financial security in retirement.

> ✳ Will falling interest rates hurt your income stream? Would rising interest rates give you an opportunity to adjust your investments?

100. Refilling Buckets

"The art of refilling buckets in retirement is a bit like watering plants. Wait too long, and everything starts to wilt. Do it too often, and you risk drowning the roots."

The basic idea behind a bucket strategy is simple: Divide your retirement savings into separate "buckets" based on when you expect to need the money. Typically, the first bucket holds one to two years' worth of cash or cash-like assets for immediate expenses. The next might hold more conservative investments for medium-term needs, and a third would be invested in long-term growth assets. The problem isn't in the setup. Instead, it's in the refill.

Most retirees find the first bucket depletes faster than expected, especially compared to a systematic withdrawal strategy. That's when the real challenge begins: How and when do you refill it? Pulling too soon from growth assets may hurt long-term returns. Waiting too long might leave you short during a market downturn. This is where a static, set-it-and-forget-it approach tends to fall short. A bucket strategy only works well if the refill process is dynamic and flexible enough to respond to market conditions and portfolio performance.

Morningstar's 2023 research on retirement income strategies confirms this. Bucket strategies don't consistently outperform simple withdrawal strategies unless they're carefully managed and customized. A rigid approach can leave you exposed, but a thoughtful, opportunistic refill strategy can improve outcomes significantly.

There are a few ways to manage this more effectively. One is to watch for times when your long-term investments, like stocks or bonds, are doing particularly well. Those moments can be ideal for taking profits and using them to refill the cash bucket. Another option is to reduce the size of your cash bucket to lessen the performance drag that too much cash can cause.

Ultimately, refilling your income bucket isn't just a logistical task. It's an emotional one. Having cash on hand during turbulent market periods helps reduce the urge to panic. It gives you room to breathe, space to think, and the ability to ride out market storms without locking in losses. Being able to draw from more stable sources during tough times, and then replenish when the markets rebound, can make a huge difference in your long-term retirement success.

 How can a bucket strategy help you manage both your income and your emotions throughout retirement?

101. Medicare

"Medicare isn't just a card. It's a critical part of your retirement health plan. The more you understand it, the better protected you'll be."

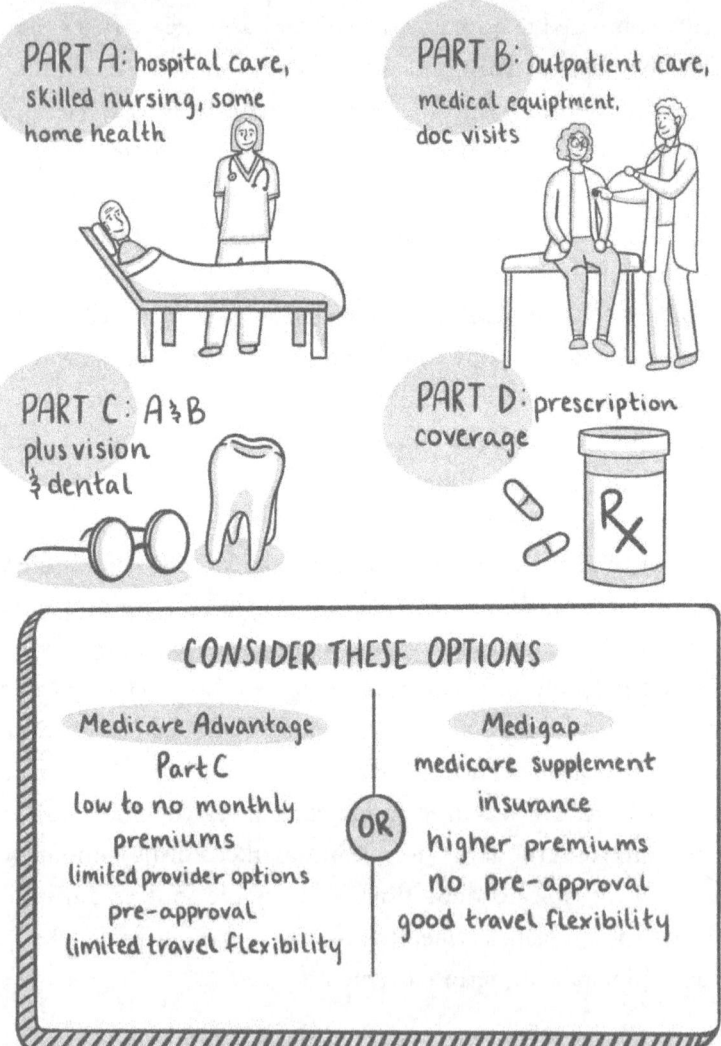

PART A: hospital care, skilled nursing, some home health

PART B: outpatient care, medical equipment, doc visits

PART C: A & B plus vision & dental

PART D: prescription coverage

CONSIDER THESE OPTIONS

Medicare Advantage
Part C
low to no monthly premiums
limited provider options
pre-approval
limited travel flexibility

OR

Medigap
medicare supplement insurance
higher premiums
no pre-approval
good travel flexibility

Medicare is a federal health insurance program in the United States, mainly for people over age 65 and younger people with disabilities. While Medicare provides coverage to many Americans, most Americans don't understand the program.

According to NerdWallet, only 26% of Americans under 65 were aware that Original Medicare does not cover services like vision, dental, or hearing. Further, among Americans 65 and older, 58% know that Medicare is run by a federal agency, and only 32% know how coverage works when traveling abroad.

Understanding Medicare is important for your retirement planning, as it is your health insurance in retirement.

Medicare is divided into four primary parts:

1. Part A: Covers hospital care, skilled nursing facility care, hospice, and some home health services.
2. Part B: Covers doctor visits, outpatient care, preventive services, and medical equipment.
3. Part C: Private insurance plans that include Parts A and B and often extend to additional services not covered in Parts A and B such as vision/dental.
4. Part D: Prescription drug coverage.

Once enrolled in Medicare, you will pay monthly and can pay online or through the mail. As you approach 65, it is critical to understand your options beyond Parts A and B. There are two options you should consider: (1) a Medicare Advantage (MA) plan, which is Part C, or (2) the Medicare Supplement (Medigap) insurance to cover extra costs.

When choosing between the two options, there are trade-offs to consider. Medicare Advantage has low or no monthly premiums, but they restrict your choice of providers and require preauthorization for high-cost treatments. Medigap coverage doesn't have those same obstacles to treatment but it comes at a cost of paying higher monthly premiums.

 How well do you understand what Medicare covers, and what plans do you have in place for the expenses it does not?

102. Aging in Place

"Aging in place is not just a financial choice. It's about staying where the walls know your story."

CHAPTER VII

For many retirees, the idea of aging in place means more than simply avoiding a move. It's about holding onto independence, routine, and the comfort of a home filled with memories. Nearly 90% of those over age 65 and 75% of adults over age 50, want to stay in their homes as long as possible.

Aging in place means continuing to live in your own home as you grow older, rather than relocating to a retirement community or assisted living facility. Home is where your favorite chair sits by the window, where your neighbors greet you by name, and where life just feels like yours.

But staying home successfully takes more than sentiment. It takes planning: Does your home need adjustments to remain safe and accessible, like installing grab bars in bathrooms, wider doorways for mobility devices, walk-in showers, or ramps instead of stairs.

Next, look at your financial picture. Will your income sources—Social Security, pensions, retirement savings, or long-term care insurance—support your desire to age in place? Will you be able to afford in-home care or other support services if your health needs change? Consider setting aside a reserve fund for unexpected home repairs, health-related costs, or caregiving expenses.

It's also important to plan beyond the house itself. How will you stay socially connected? Will you have access to transportation, healthcare, and community services? A strong network of support makes all the difference.

And while aging in place is the ideal for many, it's still wise to explore other options—downsizing to a more manageable home, moving closer to family, or joining a community that offers graduated care. Being prepared doesn't limit your independence—it strengthens it.

 What modifications or support systems would you need to stay in your home long term? How emotionally attached are you to your current home? Do you see yourself staying where you are, or do you imagine moving as your needs evolve?

103. Aging and Frailty

"You don't stop living because you age—you adjust how you live to keep doing what matters most."

Retirement isn't about slowing down because you're older. It's about moving more deliberately—because you have purpose.

As we live longer, we don't just plan for more birthdays—we plan for more changes. Physical frailty becomes more common with age, even among otherwise healthy adults. According to clinical guidelines, frailty affects about 4% of people aged 65–69, rising steadily to 26% of those over 85. It doesn't happen all at once. It sneaks up in the form of sore knees, stiffer mornings, slower recoveries, and a few more "I'll do that tomorrow" days.

We tend to focus on the big-ticket issues like medical bills and long-term care, but some of the most impactful expenses of aging are the slow, creeping kind. Mowing the lawn. Putting up holiday lights. Changing a lightbulb in a ceiling fixture. Shoveling snow. These once-routine chores often become outsourced necessities—and those little costs can quietly stack up over time.

Planning for frailty isn't just about anticipating major health events. It's about recognizing that someday, you might not want to—or be able to—climb ladders, bend down to pull weeds, or carry groceries upstairs. Outsourcing these tasks may not just be convenient, it might be essential.

That means preparing not only your body but your budget. You might want to explore financial products like LTCI policies to help cover care needs, or set aside a portion of your retirement income for these creeping costs of independence. Equally important is your support system—family, friends, neighbors, or professionals—who can help when you no longer want to do it all yourself.

Think of these household tasks as unpaid jobs you've been doing for years. One day, someone else will need to do them. The question is: Have you planned for that?

✷ What steps are you taking to prepare—physically, emotionally, and financially—for the realities of aging and potential frailty?

104. Health is Wealth

"You can't buy good health, but you can invest in it every single day."

You can't enjoy your wealth if you don't have your health.

As retirement approaches, most people double down on savings—but far fewer focus on what really fuels a fulfilling retirement: their physical and mental well-being. According to a 2024 MassMutual study, while 64% of near-retirees increased their focus on saving, only about half reported prioritizing their health. Even fewer gave attention to maintaining strong social connections, despite their direct link to happiness and longevity.

Here's the reality: Good health is a form of wealth. It gives you the energy, ability, and freedom to actually enjoy the life—and the financial security—you've worked so hard to build.

The financial side of health can't be ignored either. Fidelity estimates that a 65-year-old individual may need $165,000 in after-tax savings just to cover healthcare expenses in retirement. That number has been steadily rising and is expected to continue growing. If you want to protect your finances later, the time to invest in your health is now.

Living a long and active life starts with daily habits. Simple, consistent actions can protect your body, mind, and retirement dollars. That includes preventive care, regular exercise, smart nutrition, good sleep, and maintaining a strong social circle. Keeping your brain sharp also matters—whether through learning, games, or conversations, staying mentally active helps support both your independence and your identity.

At the same time, plan for healthcare costs like any other major expense. Build those costs into your retirement budget. Understand what Medicare does and doesn't cover. Explore supplemental insurance, long-term care coverage, or health savings accounts while you're still working.

The goal is to stay well so you can live well—and ensure that the years ahead are not just long, but rich in experience and energy.

✴ How are you and your loved ones prioritizing your health today to help secure a more vibrant and financially stable retirement tomorrow?

105. Long-Term Caregivers

"Caregiving isn't just about giving care. It's about sharing love, support, and respect in a way that honors everyone involved."

PLAN FOR YOUR CAREGIVING NEEDS TO EASE STRESS ON LOVED ONES & ENSURE YOUR EXPECTATIONS ARE MET

Most retirees will need some form of long-term care, and women tend to need care for longer periods. They also make up the majority of unpaid caregivers in the US—providing care to spouses, aging parents, and other loved ones, often without formal support.

In fact, more than 65% of older adults rely solely on family and friends for their long-term care needs. These informal caregiving networks are vital—but they can also create real emotional, physical, and financial strain on caregivers.

When planning for long-term care, it's essential to consider not only where care will be delivered, but who will provide it. Each option has trade-offs: familiarity versus professionalism, emotional comfort versus logistical limits, affordability versus availability.

Will you be comfortable receiving help with personal tasks like bathing or dressing? Would you prefer that help comes from a family member or a trained professional? What happens if your children live far away or work full time? These are sensitive questions, but they're necessary ones.

Talk openly with your loved ones. Let them know what kind of care you want—and what kind of care you don't. Give them permission to use your resources to pay for your care, so honoring your life with the dignity you've planned for.

You can also explore LTCI, Medicaid planning, or building funds for professional assistance. It could also mean planning for respite care, hiring part-time help, or even creating caregiver contracts that formalize expectations if a family member is providing regular care.

Caregiving should be discussed, planned for, and supported. When you plan ahead, those difficult "what if" questions become clear "when needed" decisions—guided by your voice, your values, and your preparation.

 How are you planning to support your caregivers? Have you thought about what would make it easier for a loved one to help care for you?

106. Cognitive Decline and Financial Decision-Making

"Cognitive decline doesn't announce its arrival. The best time to prepare for cognitive decline is before it begins, when your judgment is sharp and your voice is clear."

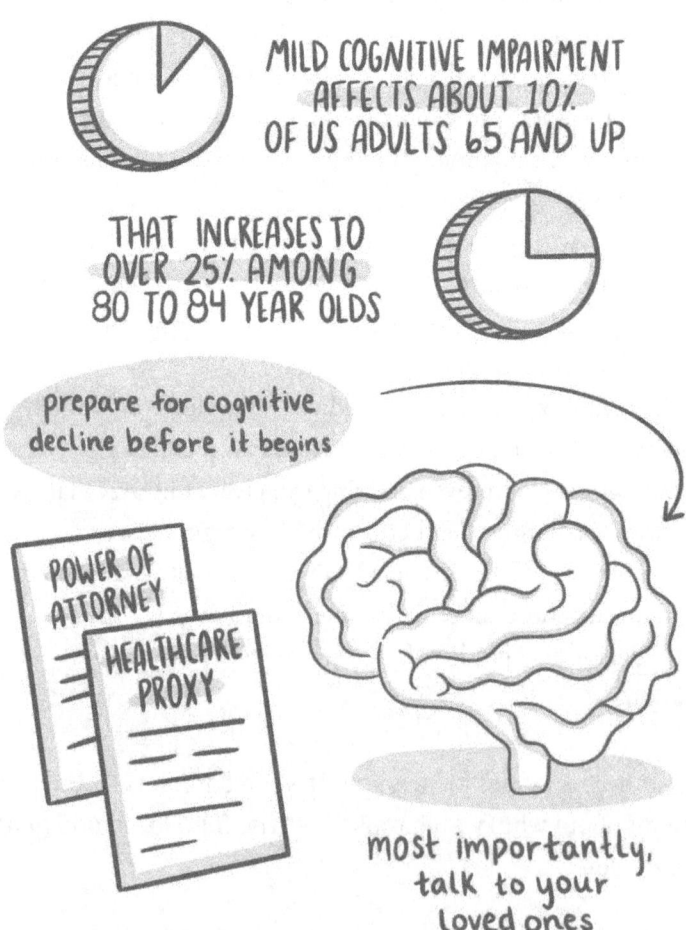

MILD COGNITIVE IMPAIRMENT AFFECTS ABOUT 10% OF US ADULTS 65 AND UP

THAT INCREASES TO OVER 25% AMONG 80 TO 84 YEAR OLDS

prepare for cognitive decline before it begins

POWER OF ATTORNEY

HEALTHCARE PROXY

most importantly, talk to your loved ones

Mild Cognitive Impairment (MCI) affects about 10% of US adults aged 65 and older. Among those aged 80 to 84, that number climbs to more than 25%.

Cognitive decline is one of retirement's most overlooked risks. It doesn't arrive all at once—and that's part of the challenge. Over time, memory fades, reasoning slows, and tasks that once felt second nature become confusing. What's more, many people continue to feel confident in their decision-making even as their abilities gradually diminish. This disconnect can lead to delayed bill payments, poor investment decisions, and increased susceptibility to scams. And when there's no plan in place, the consequences can be deeply damaging.

The time to plan isn't when the decline starts. Preparing for cognitive changes means putting up protective guardrails while you're still in control.

Start with legal documents. A durable power of attorney and healthcare proxy ensure someone you trust can step in if needed. Next, look at your financial life and ask: Can this be simplified? Consider consolidating accounts, setting up automatic bill payments, and scheduling withdrawals. The more you can automate and streamline now, the less stress there will be later.

Most importantly, talk to your loved ones. Share your intentions. Give them permission to speak up if something seems off. These conversations can be emotional, but avoiding them doesn't make the risk disappear. It just leaves everyone more vulnerable.

Protecting your future isn't just about safeguarding your finances. It's about honoring your autonomy, even in moments when your voice might not be as strong as it once was.

Is your financial life simple and automated enough that it could function smoothly if your cognitive abilities started to decline? What steps can you take today to prepare your loved ones—and yourself—for the possibility of needing help in the future?

107. Pet Care and Planning in Retirement

"In retirement, a pet can be more than a companion. Pets can be a source of purpose, joy, and better health. Plan for them like family, because to them, you are."

Owning a pet can reduce your risk of mortality by 24%.

IF A PET IS A PART OF YOUR RETIREMENT VISION, FACTOR THEM IN BOTH YOUR FINANCIAL & LIFESTYLE PLANS

According to the American Heart Association, owning a pet can reduce your risk of mortality by 24%. Whether furry, scaly, or feathered, pets offer companionship, purpose, and surprising health benefits that can be especially meaningful during retirement.

But as much joy as pets bring, they also come with responsibilities: financial, physical, and logistical. It's important to consider how a pet fits into your lifestyle. Would a bouncy puppy make sense, or would a calm senior cat better match your pace? Your retirement phase may even help determine your pet's age, type, and care needs.

Here are four key considerations for pet ownership in retirement:

1. Budgeting for pet care: Plan for food, grooming, vet visits (both routine and emergency), boarding, toys, and other supplies. Unexpected medical expenses can add up quickly.
2. Travel and backup care: Whether it's a weekend getaway or an unexpected trip, have a plan (and a person) in place to care for your pet. Factor in costs for boarding or pet sitters.
3. Mobility and physical limitations: Consider your own physical capabilities. Walking a strong dog or cleaning a litter box can be challenging as you age.
4. Long-term and estate planning: Who will care for your pet if you're no longer able to? Incorporate pet care instructions into your estate plan or designate a guardian in case of long-term illness or death.

If a pet is part of your retirement vision, factor them into both your financial and lifestyle plans. They can provide unmatched emotional support—but only when you're fully prepared for the commitment. A well-planned pet partnership can bring joy, routine, and even better health to your retirement years.

✻ Have you considered how your pet, or future pets, might enrich your life in retirement? Are they included in your long-term financial and care planning?

108. Second Careers

"Retirement isn't the end of your story. It's your chance to write the chapter you've always dreamed of."

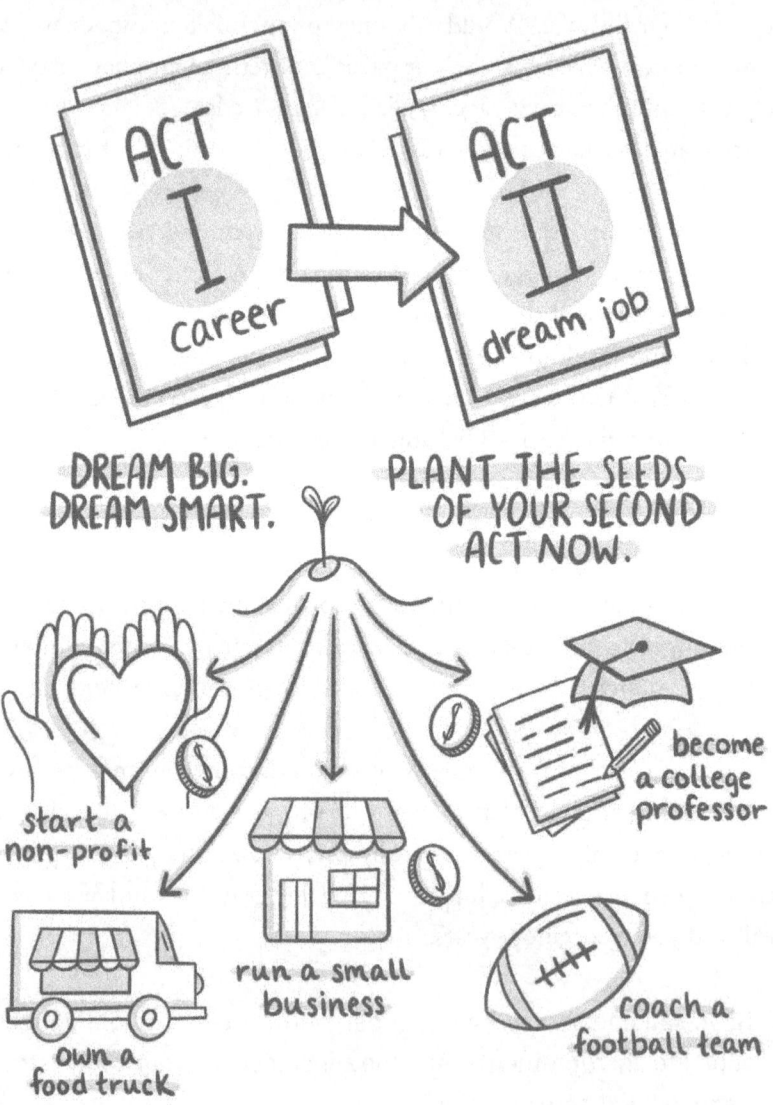

Think of a second career in retirement as the mid-story plot twist. This is going to be the part of the book that surprises you, redefines the narrative, and, hopefully, makes the story even better.

Retirement used to mean hanging up your hat for good. Now? Not so much. Around 20% of retirees are still working in some capacity after age 65, and about 11% are still active after age 75. But this time, it's different. They're often chasing passion, purpose, and fulfillment, not just a paycheck.

Second careers are becoming more common, not only because some retirees need the extra income but also because people are realizing retirement doesn't mean "stop working"—it means "stop working just for the money." That shift opens up all kinds of exciting possibilities.

Most people who successfully launch second careers in retirement have two things in common: They still benefit financially from working, and they genuinely enjoy what they're doing. If you can check both of those boxes, you've found your sweet spot.

But here's the key: Dream big, yes, but also dream smart. This is where a little realism goes a long way. Maybe you'd love to be a college professor, a travel photographer, or coach an NFL team. Great! Now take the first step today to build toward that goal. Start volunteering, take a class, join a group, or build your network. Plant the seeds now, and let them grow into something meaningful down the road.

Sometimes, your second act might require saving a little more now so you can afford to pursue that dream job later. Maybe you want to open a bookstore, start a nonprofit, or run a food truck just for the joy of feeding people. Whatever it is, give yourself the runway to make it happen.

Because at the end of the day, retirement isn't the end of your career story. It's just the start of a new chapter.

> What will your second act look like? And if you could do any job in retirement, what's stopping you from starting that journey right now?

109. Finding Meaning in Retirement

"Retirement isn't the end of the road. It's the beginning of the path you finally choose for yourself."

Retirement isn't just about leaving work behind. It's about moving toward something that matters.

After decades of making a living, this is your time to make a difference. Yet for many, the transition isn't as easy as it sounds. About 27% of retirees report feeling unmotivated or overwhelmed, and nearly 20% say they feel depressed or alone. At the same time, 85% agree that finding meaning is essential to their happiness in retirement.

So what does meaning look like? It's different for everyone. It might be spending more time with grandchildren, mentoring others, volunteering for a cause, traveling with purpose, learning something new, or simply having a strong social circle. The key is that it's not about being busy—it's about being fulfilled.

Before you retire, take time to reflect on where and how you'll find that meaning. Where will you live? Who will be around you? How strong is your social network outside of work? Many people find value in living in communities where others share their pace and passions, whether that's a retirement community or simply being near close friends or family.

The happiest retirees tend to be those who remain connected—to people, to hobbies, to purpose. They stop working for income and start working for joy.

But purpose doesn't stand alone. Your finances must support the life you want to live. If meaning for you involves travel, charitable giving, or helping family with expenses, those goals should be woven into your financial plan. It's not about having the most money. It's about having enough to live a life that feels full and aligned with your values.

A meaningful retirement isn't measured in spreadsheets. It's measured in impact, joy, and connection. It's about waking up excited for the day ahead. It's about knowing that your legacy—big or small—will outlive your working years.

 What brings you joy? What activities make you lose track of time? What could you do today to start building more of that into your retirement?

Your Retirement Notes

Your Retirement Sketches

CHAPTER VIII
WHEN FINALITY BECOMES REALITY

- Estate Planning Basics
- The Digital Afterlife
- Digital Estate Planning Process
- Inherited Accounts
- Trusts: Revocable versus Irrevocable
- Prepare for a Good End of Life
- Medicaid Spend Down
- Long-Term Care Delivery
- Longevity
- Elder Abuse
- Medicaid
- Leaving a Legacy
- Giving Back: Charitable Giving

- Qualified Charitable Distributions
- Giving to Grandchildren
- The G3 Summit

CHAPTER VIII.
Introduction

We are a death-denying society. We avoid the topic, change the subject, and push off hard conversations until it's too late. But here's the truth: Denying death doesn't delay it. What it does delay is the chance to prepare with purpose, protect those we love, and bring peace to what is often the most emotionally and financially complex moment in our lives—the end.

This chapter of your retirement sketchbook is about stepping into that truth—not with fear, but with intention. It's about recognizing that when finality becomes reality, it's not just about loss—it's about legacy. It's about the impact you leave behind: the stories, the support, the values, and the stability you offer your family, your community, and the causes you care about.

Death is inevitable— disorganization is optional

Too often, families are left to sort through grief and paperwork at the same time. But by engaging in end-of-life planning, you give your loved ones something far more valuable than money: clarity, compassion, and direction.

This planning includes:

- A well-crafted estate plan—wills, trusts, powers of attorney, healthcare directives
- Beneficiary designations that reflect your current wishes
- Letters of instruction, ethical wills, or legacy statements
- Open conversations about your wishes, your values, and even your beliefs about death and the afterlife.

These aren't cold legal documents—they are acts of love. They say, "I've thought of you. I've protected you. I've planned so you won't have to worry."

Legacy is more than wealth

When people think of legacy, they often think of money—and yes, part of this process includes leaving behind financial support for spouses, children, grandchildren, and chosen family. But your legacy is more than that. It's the lessons you teach, the stories you share, the causes you champion, and the example you set by living a life of intention.

What do you want to be remembered for? What do you want to pass on that can't be deposited in a bank account?

Take time to reflect:

- What values do I want to live by in my final years?
- How can I pass those on?
- What kind of example am I setting through my retirement choices?

Planning for a charitable impact

Many people also find great meaning in giving back. Retirement is a powerful time to explore charitable giving—whether through donations, donor-advised funds, charitable trusts, or naming nonprofits in your estate plan. Giving can be structured for tax-efficiency and aligned with your long-term goals—but at its core, it's a deeply human act. It's one more way to ensure your life's work extends far beyond your own timeline.

Charitable planning isn't reserved for the ultra-wealthy. Anyone can leave a mark. Anyone can plant seeds that grow long after they're gone.

Integrating end-of-life planning into your retirement

Your retirement plan should include more than income and investment strategies. It should also reflect your exit strategy—a roadmap for how your affairs will be handled when you're no longer here to direct them. This includes:

- Assigning key roles (executor, trustee, power of attorney)
- Reviewing and updating documents regularly
- Discussing your wishes openly with those involved
- Aligning your healthcare preferences with your legal documentation
- Planning for your digital assets and online legacy.

The reality is that death often brings logistical chaos. But it doesn't have to. A clear, organized, and communicated plan brings comfort to everyone involved.

These conversations are good and healthy

Talking about death doesn't hasten it. It frees us. It allows us to live more fully in the now—knowing that the people we care about are taken care of, our affairs are in order, and our life meant something. Conversations about death, religion, the afterlife, and legacy are good and healthy. They connect generations, clarify values, and ground us in the truth that life is precious because it's finite.

You don't have to have all the answers. But you can start the conversation.

So in this chapter, you're not just sketching your retirement—you're sketching your legacy. You're giving your future self, and your future family, the gift of peace, purpose, and preparation.

Because when finality becomes reality, your plan becomes your voice—and your love, your wisdom, and your care carry on.

110. Estate Planning Basics

"Estate planning is not just about managing money or wealth. It's also about taking care of your loved ones and leaving them with a plan instead of just heartbreak and headaches."

CHAPTER VIII

An estate plan is a comprehensive set of legal documents and strategies that outline how your assets, responsibilities, and healthcare decisions should be handled in the event of your death or incapacity. While there can be some shortcuts using online resources, typically a specialized attorney in this field assists in setting up an estate plan which is not a one-and-done. As your life circumstances change, the estate plan may need to be revisited from time to time.

An estate plan can accomplish a few different goals, including but not limited to, helping to execute on your wishes after your death, minimizing the cost of probate and legal fees, minimizing taxes for others when planned accordingly, and planning for your own mental incapacity and inability to make decisions as you reach your endpoint.

The primary documents in your estate plan may include the following, but it is important to note that this may be governed by state laws, not federal laws.

1. Will: Defines who will inherit your property and identifies who will take care of your children, if applicable.
2. Trust (e.g., revocable living trust): Holds assets to avoid probate and manage distribution efficiently. This may incorporate by reference your will depending on the set-up in your state.
3. Power of attorney (POA): Appoints someone to handle finances if you become incapacitated.
4. Healthcare directive/living will: Specifies your medical preferences and appoints a decision-maker.

Nobody wants to think about these decisions, but it is important not to leave your family and friends with a mess after you are gone. Work with an estate planning attorney to draft or update your will, establish trusts if necessary, and ensure all beneficiary designations are current.

✸ When was the last time your estate plan was updated? Do the appropriate parties know who to contact for questions?

111. The Digital Afterlife

"In a digital world, our online presence and story won't end upon our death but instead live on as a digital afterlife."

The average American has hundreds of accounts and values their digital assets at $191,516. While over 90% of American adults use digital services, fewer than 10% have a plan for their digital assets after death.

Digital assets comprise all electronically stored pieces of information used and owned, including emails, text messages, photos, social media posts, NFTs, biometric data, financial and medical records, and all of the accounts that hold this information.

The planning and management of digital assets is vastly different from managing more traditional assets like our house and money. Digital assets require specific language in wills, trusts, and powers of attorney to allow your executor or fiduciary to be able to manage and transfer these assets.

The terms of service agreement with service providers typically state that you cannot transfer your username, account, or anything related to the account to anyone else.

So your estate and other instructions should say what accounts you want to delete, passed if possible to someone else or memorialized. If you don't take care of this planning it can lead to online accounts being around for decades, opening up your heirs to potential online fraud or theft.

Managing digital assets is an often overlooked aspect of estate planning. Digital assets require specific language in wills, trusts, and powers of attorney to allow your executor or fiduciary to be able to manage and transfer these assets.

✳ Have you considered how to manage your digital legacy? What steps have you taken to secure your digital assets? How much value do you believe you have in your online accounts? What would you pay to get them back if you lost access to every email and online account you own?

112. Digital Estate Planning Process

"A well-lived life deserves a well-planned legacy. Your digital footprint doesn't vanish when you do."

Your digital life shouldn't become a digital mess. Fewer than 10% of American adults have a plan in place for their digital assets after death.

Nearly every state now recognizes a legal framework called RUFADAA (Revised Uniform Fiduciary Access to Digital Assets Act), which offers guidance on managing digital assets after death. Here's a 10-step process to get your digital estate in order:

1. Identify your digital assets: Email accounts, cloud storage, social media, bank logins, crypto, loyalty programs, digital subscriptions.
2. Know where everything is stored: Note where each asset exists.
3. Document access information: Use a password manager or encrypted document to securely record usernames, passwords, security questions, two-factor details.
4. Evaluate the value: Some digital assets are priceless emotionally (like family photos), while others carry financial value.
5. Focus on high-risk assets first: Which accounts would cause the most chaos if no one could access them?
6. Understand ownership rules: Some companies restrict account transfers after death. Review the terms of service around access to key platforms.
7. Create a digital disposition plan: Outline what should happen to each digital asset and who is in charge. Do you want your Facebook account deleted or turned into a memorial?
8. Update your legal documents: Appoint a digital executor in your will or trust—someone who can manage your online world.
9. Inform the right people: Make sure your digital executor or family knows where to find this plan—don't keep it a secret.
10. Revisit and refresh: Your digital life evolves quickly. Update your plan every year or when you go through major life changes.

If something happened tomorrow, could your spouse access your email, bill payments, or investment accounts? Do your loved ones know how to unlock your digital life?

113. Inherited Accounts

"Your heirs may or may not be happy with the money you left them if it comes with a heavy and unexpected tax burden."

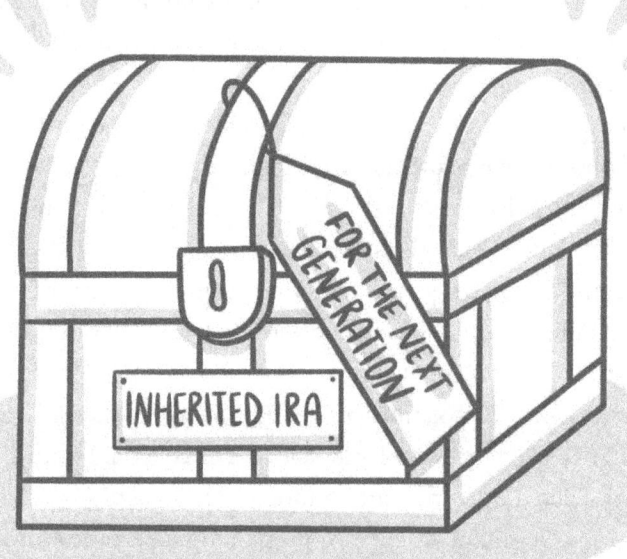

THERE ARE OVER $12 TRILLION IN IRAs

Here're the good and bad news: As of 2023, there was approximately $12 trillion in IRAs. That means there was a generation that saved well and will likely leave some money to their heirs—it also means that there is potentially a lot to be collected in taxes.

When a retirement account passes to an heir, such as (1) a spouse, (2) non-spouse (including a child or sibling), or (3) an eligible designated beneficiary, which could include a minor child or disabled individual, that is an inherited account they are receiving.

It's not so simple as to just pass, as depending on what type of account and who it passes to, there are special rules which involve taxation. As we learned about with RMDs, beneficiaries are still subject to RMD rules (which must begin by the end of the year after death).

Spouses may keep the inherited account or rollover that account into their own IRA.

For those that aren't an eligible designated beneficiary, then the inherited account needs to be emptied/withdrawn within a 10-year period (or else take a lump sum with a hefty immediate tax bill). If it is an eligible designated beneficiary, however, there is more time to spend the money because there is an exception, such as with a child who wouldn't even be of an appropriate age to access the money yet.

You should seek advice regarding inherited accounts. First, if you may be in a position to inherit an account, consider how that will impact your financial plan and how you will be able to withdraw those funds from the associated account within the associated timeframe.

Alternatively, if you are planning your estate plan, consider how you may be impacting those to whom you will leave your estate. Consider counseling them in conjunction with a financial professional regarding the impact of potential inherited accounts. Finally, inherited accounts are the target of tax law changes from time to time.

 Are you aware of how inherited retirement accounts are treated under current law, and how might this affect your estate planning for yourself and your heirs?

114. Trusts: Revocable Versus Irrevocable

"Have trust in your trust. And if you're not sure, make it revocable."

Trusts are like the Batman's Utility Belt of estate planning: flexible, powerful, and sometimes a little intimidating until you understand how they work. About 20% of estate plans include a trust, and whether you go revocable or irrevocable depends on your personal goals, how much control you want to keep, and how much you're willing to give up.

So what's the difference?

Think of a revocable trust like a tote bag. You can open it, add things, take things out, or even toss the whole thing if you change your mind. These trusts are often set up to make things easier after you're gone—avoiding probate, streamlining asset distribution, and keeping things private—but you remain in charge while you're alive. You're the boss of the bag.

Now, an irrevocable trust? That's a vault. Once you drop something in, it's locked in. You can't casually open it up and take things back out. This type of trust is often used when you're ready to make a permanent move—whether it's gifting assets, reducing your estate for tax purposes, or shielding assets from future liabilities. Once set up, control usually shifts to a trustee, and you step back.

All trusts eventually become irrevocable upon your death. The question is whether you want to hand over the keys to the vault now or keep them in your pocket for a while longer.

Both types of trusts can help you avoid probate, reduce estate costs, provide for loved ones, support charitable causes, and create a lasting legacy.

Revocable and irrevocable trusts do it in different ways. That's why it's important to sit down with an estate planning attorney to assess your situation and choose the right structure for your financial and legacy goals.

✳ Are you ready to permanently transfer or separate assets now in an irrevocable trust? Or do you want to maintain flexibility with a revocable trust and make changes as life evolves?

115. Prepare for a Good End of Life

"A good end-of-life plan isn't just a legal checklist. It's a final gift to those you care about most and a way to bring them clarity, comfort, and peace."

It's one of the most important conversations you'll ever have—and one of the most avoided. According to research, over 90% of people say that talking about end-of-life care is important. Yet only about 30% have actually had that talk with their families.

Why the disconnect? Because it's hard. It's emotional. And honestly, it's easy to put off. But preparing for the end of life isn't just about having a will tucked away in a file cabinet. It's about making sure your loved ones know what matters most to you—your healthcare preferences, your financial wishes, your values, your voice.

These conversations can help prevent confusion, reduce conflict, and provide peace of mind. They help your family understand how to care for you, not just what decisions need to be made. They let you say, "It's okay to talk about this," and "Here's what I want," and "I trust you."

So how do you begin?

Start by gathering your thoughts and writing down what matters most to you. Then set up a time to talk with your family. It doesn't have to be dramatic or formal. It just needs to be honest.

You might also want to include your financial advisor, attorney, or healthcare providers in the conversation. Legal documents like a healthcare proxy, power of attorney, and living will are essential, but they don't replace real communication. Keep these documents updated and stored in an easy-to-find location, and make sure someone knows where to find them.

And remember, this isn't just about forms and signatures. It's about giving your loved ones permission—permission to make decisions, to care for you the way you want, and to carry out your wishes with confidence and love.

 Have you clearly communicated your end-of-life wishes? Have you created space for your family to ask questions and understand your values?

116. Medicaid Spend Down

"Medicaid is the safety net, but getting there often means walking a narrow financial tightrope."

only about **20%** of Americans are currently eligible for Medicaid

SPEND DOWN REFERS TO THE PROCESS OF REDUCING YOUR ASSETS & INCOME TO BECOME ELIGIBLE FOR MEDICAID

Medicaid is a vital program that helps cover long-term care costs for those who meet certain income and asset limits. But what happens if your resources are just above those limits? That's where the concept of "Medicaid spend down" comes in.

Spend down refers to the process of reducing your assets and income to become eligible for Medicaid. For most individuals, this means reducing countable assets to under $2,000. While that number might sound shockingly low, Medicaid does allow some key exceptions. In most states, you can keep your primary residence, one vehicle, a small life insurance policy, and personal items.

Medicaid spend down is essentially a strategy of using your own funds for care until you've reached the eligibility threshold—and only then turning to Medicaid for help. It's a last-resort option, but for many, it becomes a necessary part of the long-term care journey.

To put this into context, only about 20% of Americans are currently eligible for Medicaid. The wealthiest 5% can likely afford to self-fund their care. That leaves about 75% of the population in the middle, facing the uncomfortable question: How will I afford long-term care?

For many in this group, self-funding may work for a time, but costs can add up quickly. This is where spend-down becomes relevant. It offers a way to qualify for public assistance once other resources have been exhausted.

Planning ahead can make a world of difference. If you expect Medicaid may one day be part of your care strategy, it's wise to speak with a Medicaid planning professional. They can help you navigate the rules, avoid costly missteps, and make the most of your remaining assets.

Long-term care is expensive. And while no one hopes to rely on Medicaid, understanding how it works can provide a sense of control during uncertain times.

 What are your thoughts on using Medicaid spend down as a strategy for long-term care, and what are your other options?

117. Long-Term Care Delivery

"You can't control if you'll need care, but you can control how prepared you are when that day comes."

Here's the reality: About 70% of people over the age of 65 will need some form of long-term care in their lifetime. Around 20% will need that care for more than five years. Long-term care isn't a rare event—it's a high-probability chapter in retirement, and it deserves attention in your planning.

Many people assume long-term care just means a nursing home, but the truth is it can take many forms. You might receive care in an assisted living facility, a continuing care retirement community, a skilled nursing facility, or even at home. While care in hospitals is possible, it's relatively uncommon in this context.

Despite all these formal care settings, most long-term care in the United States actually happens at home. Often, it's delivered by spouses or adult children, unpaid and untrained, juggling their own lives while trying to meet the growing needs of a loved one. This can be physically, emotionally, and financially draining—for both the caregiver and the person receiving care.

That's why planning ahead is so important. It's not just about deciding how to pay for care, though that matters. LTCI or hybrid financial products may help, but you also need to think about where you want to receive care and who you hope will provide it.

Many people say they want to age in place, surrounded by familiar walls and familiar faces. But in reality, most people in the United States still pass away in institutional settings. That gap between what we want and what happens is often due to a lack of planning.

If you want care at home, start planning for it now. Think about how it will be funded, who might be involved, and what kind of support those caregivers might need. Make your wishes known and documented—don't assume your loved ones know what you want or are prepared to handle it when the time comes.

✳ Where do you want to receive care as you age? Have you communicated those wishes, and are you doing what you can now to make them possible?

118. Longevity

"Longevity isn't just about adding years to your life. It's about adding life to your years."

Today, the average person retiring at age 65 can expect to live about 20 more years. On average, a 65-year-old man will live to around 84, and a 65-year-old woman to about 87. But here's the catch: Averages are just that. Half of people will live longer than the average. If you only plan for the average, you're rolling the dice with your future.

That's why longevity is often called the biggest risk in retirement. But calling it a "risk" can be misleading. Living longer is a gift. It's what humans have aspired to for generations. The real challenge is that longevity multiplies every other risk: More years mean more chances to experience market downturns, health problems, inflation, cognitive decline, or the loss of a partner or social connections.

So instead of fearing longevity, embrace it—and plan for it wisely.

Here are a few smart steps:

- Consider delaying Social Security benefits. You get a bigger monthly check the longer you wait, up to age 70.
- Look into longevity insurance or annuities designed to provide income later in life.
- Keep some of your portfolio growth-focused, especially if you retire in your early 60s. A 30- or even 40-year retirement is not uncommon.
- Think beyond averages. If you plan to live only to the average life expectancy, your odds of outliving your money are—statistically speaking—about 50/50.

Also, remember that longevity is about more than finances. It's about living with purpose, staying connected to your community, maintaining your health, and finding joy in the years ahead. A longer life should be a richer one too—filled with love, fulfillment, and vitality.

How long do you think you'll live in retirement? What are you doing today to support a long and meaningful life?

119. Elder Abuse

"You don't plan for elder abuse because you expect it. You plan for it because you deserve to be protected, no matter what the future holds."

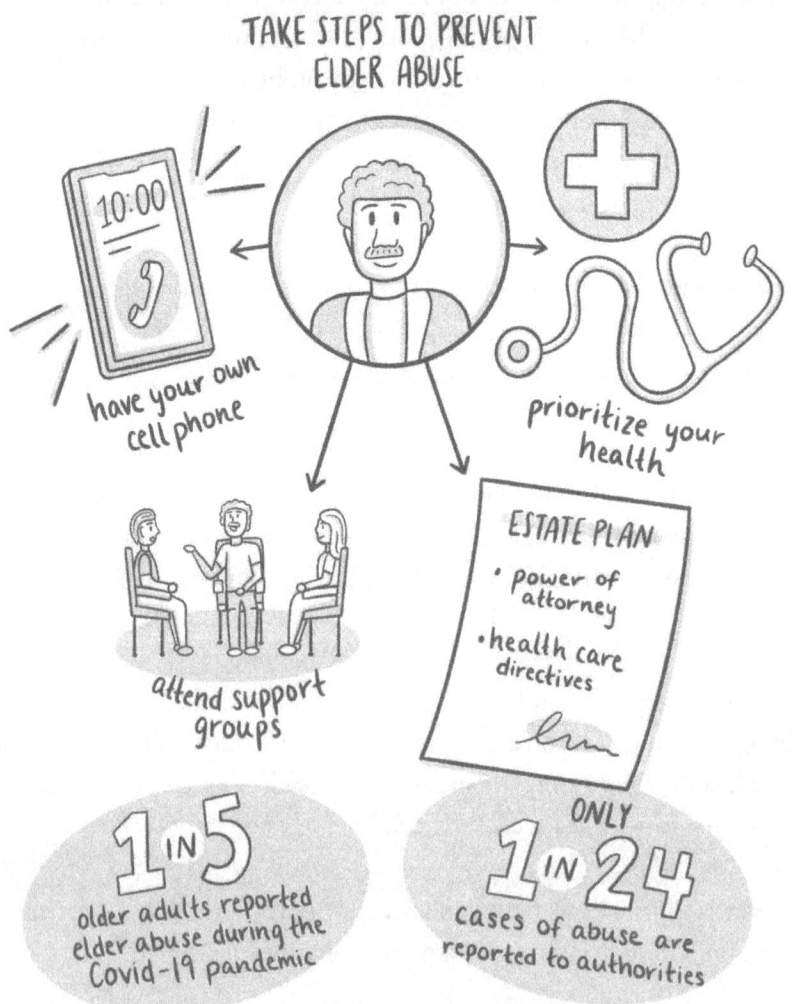

When you go from being the protector to being protected, it can be uncomfortable, but essential. But, how are you proactively protecting yourself in these positions?

The statistics regarding elder abuse are frightening. Pre-pandemic sources estimated approximately one in 10 Americans age 60+ have experienced some form of elder abuse. A newer study found that roughly one in five older adults reported elder abuse during the Covid-19 pandemic. Yet only one in 24 cases of abuse are reported to authorities.

Elder abuse comes from family members, financial professionals, caretakers, and many others. It can be difficult to spot if children live far away, or if the other spouse is also suffering from mental impairment, or if there is a general feeling of not wanting to "rock the boat" among family members when one family member may be the cause of the problem.

There are both civil and criminal penalties for elder abuse. But many cases go unreported.

There are tips for elders to work toward to prevent elder abuse, including the following:

- Make health a priority.
- Attend support groups if you believe you may be a victim of any form of abuse.
- Plan for your future in advance by considering estate planning basics including the appropriate healthcare directives and powers of attorney, which may be a cause of some elder abuse.
- Stay connected to your community and maintain your own lines of communication such as having your own phone.

While this is not an exhaustive list, consider planning ahead and learning more as we never think these things will happen to us, but we should be prepared in the event they do.

What steps have you taken to protect yourself or your loved ones from the risk of elder abuse in the event you are no longer able to support one another?

120. Medicaid

"Understanding Medicaid today can help protect your future, your health, and your dignity in retirement."

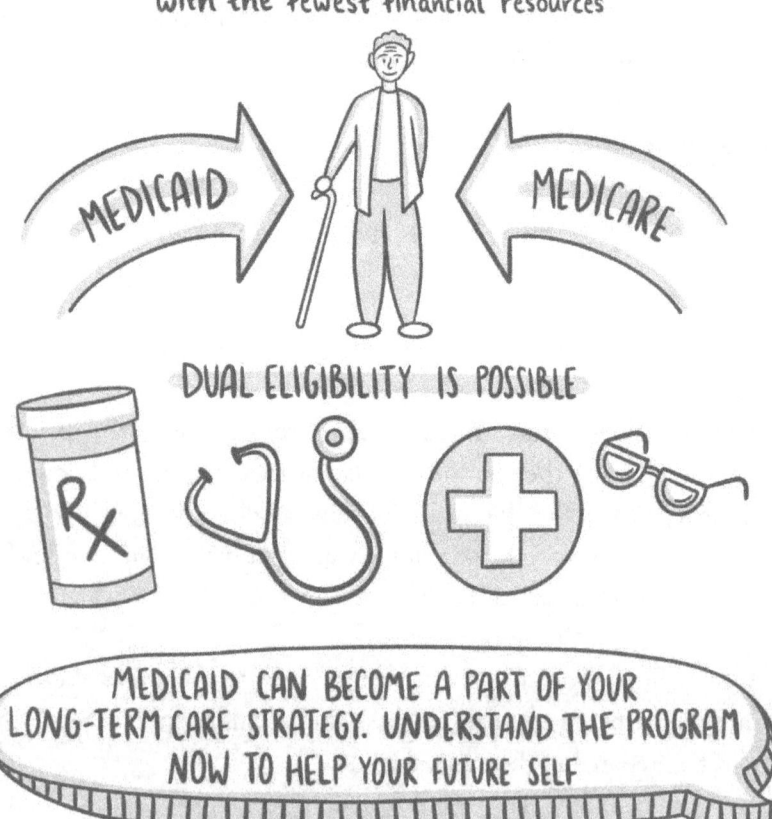

Sometimes, Medicare and Medicaid are used interchangeably, but they're not the same thing.

Medicare is a federal program, primarily for people age 65 and older or younger individuals with specific disabilities or conditions. Medicaid, on the other hand, is a joint federal and state program that provides health coverage for individuals and families with limited income and assets. It's designed to help those with the fewest financial resources get the care they need.

It's possible to have both programs. If someone is 65 or older and meets the financial requirements, they may qualify for both Medicare and Medicaid. This is called being dually eligible, and it can provide broader healthcare coverage with reduced out-of-pocket costs.

As of 2022, over 90 million Americans were enrolled in Medicaid. That's nearly double the number from a decade earlier. Today, Medicaid is responsible for about one-fifth of the nation's healthcare spending—a major player in the healthcare landscape.

Medicaid is administered at the state level, so your eligibility, benefits, and application process will depend on where you live. While all states follow federal guidelines, each state sets its own rules. Generally, Medicaid covers a wide range of services including preventive care, hospital stays, prescription drugs, and long-term care.

Medicare only covers short-term stays in a nursing facility or rehab center. If you need long-term support, Medicaid is often the only public program that will step in to cover the costs.

For many people, planning for Medicaid eligibility becomes a part of their long-term care strategy. That might include spending down assets, setting up irrevocable trusts, or purchasing Medicaid-compliant annuities to meet the financial criteria. In many states, that means having income below 138% of the Federal Poverty Level and assets under $2,000 for an individual.

Medicaid is not a one-size-fits-all solution, but it can be a critical piece of your end-of-life planning. Understanding the program now, before the need arises, can make a big difference later.

 Have you considered how Medicaid might fit into your long-term care strategy? Do you know the eligibility rules in your state?

121. Leaving a Legacy

"The legacy you leave tomorrow begins with how you live today."

Living your legacy doesn't require a dramatic gesture or a public platform. It could be something as heartfelt and lasting as a handwritten note to your children. Or it might take the form of planned giving, using tools like QCDs to support a cause that matters to you.

There's no single roadmap to leaving a legacy. It's not about grandeur or scale. It's about authenticity. About shining your light in a way that helps others find their own.

Alice Tang, who grew up in a modest home in Hong Kong and later immigrated to the United States, provided an interesting question: "Will you send the elevator back down for someone else?"

Tang became a successful financial advisor. She founded the Women's Million Dollar Conversations Club, encouraging women not only to build wealth, but to lift others along the way. That's her legacy: helping more people, especially women, reach the milestone of a $1 million net worth.

Currently, fewer than 10% of Americans have a net worth above $1 million. Alice is working to change that, not through charity alone but also through mentorship, empowerment, and creating pathways for others to follow.

But a legacy doesn't have to be about money. It can be about family, health, values, wisdom, or simply the way you made people feel. A legacy is the imprint your life leaves on others. It's made up of your actions, your beliefs, and the values you share with the world—whether with loved ones, colleagues, or people you may never meet.

The idea is simple. The execution? That's where it gets personal.

Here are a few things to reflect on:

- What are the core values or lessons you want to pass on?
- What are you already known for? What's your personal "secret sauce?"
- Who do you want to influence or inspire with your message?
- How far do you want that message to reach?
- Is there a way you're already living your legacy—and could you do more?

※ If you were gone tomorrow, how would you want to be remembered? Are you living today in a way that reflects that vision?

122. Giving Back: Charitable Giving

"It's not just about what you have. It's about what you do with it."

When we hear the phrase "charitable giving," we often picture writing a check to a favorite nonprofit. But it can also include your time, talents, possessions, investments, and energy. Whether you're volunteering at a food pantry, donating appreciated stock, or funding a new roof for the local animal shelter, it all counts.

Of course, when we're talking taxes, the term "charity" needs to be the real deal—a 501(c)(3). Otherwise, you're not making a charitable contribution. You're just giving a gift.

But charitable giving is a powerful way to find purpose, especially in retirement. Dr Joe Coughlin of the MIT AgeLab puts it this way:

> We have a longevity paradox. Now that we've achieved what humankind has long dreamed of—living longer—we don't have a great idea of what to do with all that extra time.

Giving back can be structured smartly. QCDs are a prime example. If you're age 70½ or older, you can donate directly from your IRA to a qualified charity. This donation can count toward your RMD and may reduce your taxable income at the same time. QCDs are subject to a yearly limit, which is indexed for inflation, but they pack a powerful one-two punch of philanthropy and tax-efficiency.

You could explore donor-advised funds. These allow you to make a charitable contribution, receive an immediate tax deduction, and then recommend grants to your favorite nonprofits over time. It's a bit like a charitable savings account, with you as the advisor.

Whatever your method, start with your motivation. Are you focused on tax strategy? Do you want to give your time? Are you hoping to involve your family in your legacy of giving? Maybe you're looking to take advantage of employer match programs while still working. Whatever your goals, there's likely a tool or tactic that aligns with your purpose.

 What causes are most important to you, and how do you plan to support them in retirement (or before)?

123. Qualified Charitable Distributions

"Giving money to charity doesn't have to wait until your will gets the final word."

If you are planning to leave a little something to charity, it's way more satisfying to see the impact while you're alive than to let your lawyer have all the fun later. Enter the QCD, the IRS-approved way to give generously and smartly.

Think of QCDs as the VIP lounge of charitable giving for folks 70½ and up with IRAs. Here's how it works: Instead of withdrawing money from your IRA and paying taxes on it, you can send it directly to a qualified charity—up to $100,000 a year, tax-free (yay!). And if you're married? Double that—talk about power couple goals.

Yes, there are other ways to donate: direct contributions, donor-advised funds, private foundations. However, they all come with strings like administrative fees, tax deduction limits, or piles of paperwork. QCDs are about as smooth and drama-free as charitable giving gets.

Here's the play-by-play:

- Tell your IRA custodian you want to make a QCD.
- Make sure the check goes straight to the charity (no pit stops in your checking account).
- You'll get a 1099-R for tax reporting—report it on Form 1040, line 4.

Note: You don't also get to deduct it on Schedule A. No double-dipping!

But wait, there's more! QCDs count toward your RMDs, which now kick in at age 73. That means you can shrink your taxable income and check off your RMDs, all while supporting a cause you care about. It's a win-win-win.

 Could using QCDs make your retirement plan a little more tax-savvy and a lot more heart-happy?

124. Giving to Grandchildren

"Love is powerful, but so is financial reality."

63% of grandparents said they would make financial sacrifices for their grandchildren's happiness

MAKE THOUGHTFUL, INFORMED DECISIONS THAT PROTECT YOUR FINANCES BUT STILL ALLOW FOR A MEANINGFUL GIFT

Let's be honest. Few things bring more joy than treating your grandchildren. Whether it's birthday gifts, helping with tuition, or slipping them a little cash just because, many grandparents find themselves happily opening their wallets. In fact, some are practically building junior-sized economic stimulus packages.

But here's something to think about. One of the authors of this guide happens to love Halloween. Yet even they'll admit that some of the real scares come from today's financial statistics. A 2024 study found that 63% of grandparents said their grandchildren's happiness is worth any financial sacrifice. Even more unsettling, more than one-third of those surveyed said they put their grandkids' needs ahead of their own financial stability.

There's no doubt that helping family can be emotionally rewarding. But it can also be financially risky if you're not careful. This isn't just about generosity—it's about the motivations behind it.

Emotions like guilt and shame often creep into our financial choices. Grandparents may overspend not only out of love, but because they feel they're making up for lost time or trying to compensate for something in the past.

Rather than letting guilt steer the ship, take a clear, honest look at your finances. Even if you wish you had done more in the past, remember that your future well-being matters too.

The most responsible thing you can do is make thoughtful, informed decisions that protect your financial security while still allowing for meaningful giving.

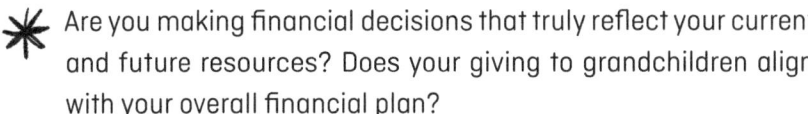 Are you making financial decisions that truly reflect your current and future resources? Does your giving to grandchildren align with your overall financial plan?

125. The G3 Summit

"Grace keeps you steady, gratitude keeps you grounded, and grit keeps you going. Together, they're the compass for a successful retirement and a life well lived."

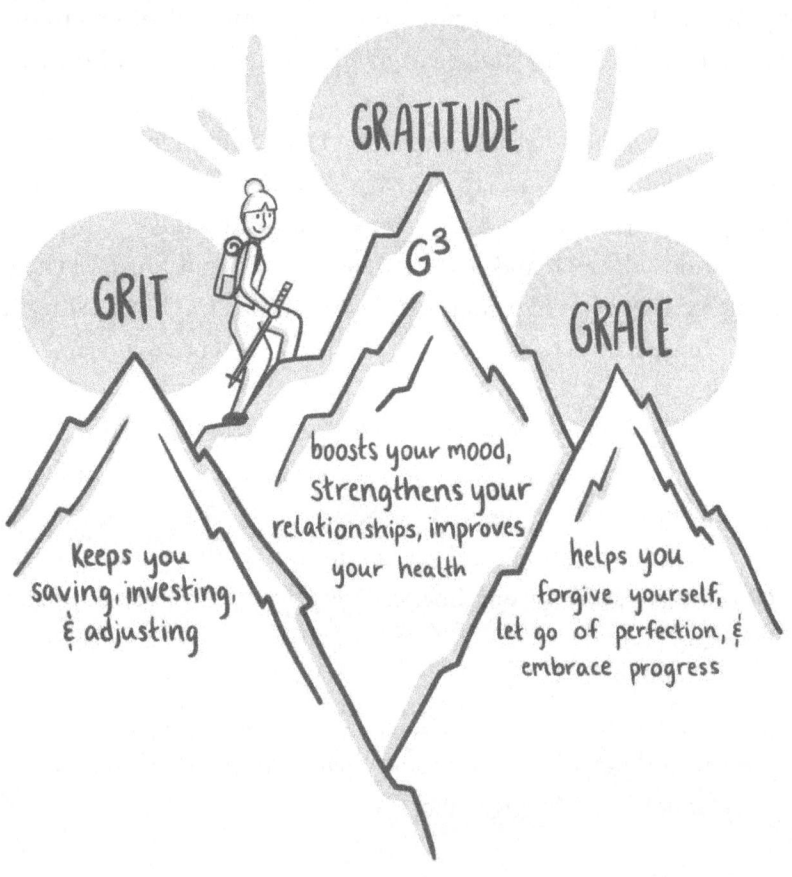

CHAPTER VIII

Retirement isn't just about having enough money. It's about having enough meaning. And that's where the G3 Summit comes in. No, it's not a global economic conference. It's an inner gathering of three powerful traits: grace, gratitude, and grit. Together, they create a mindset that transforms retirement into a time of strength, peace, and fulfillment.

Let's start with grit. Grit is what helps you keep saving, investing, and adjusting. Whether it's a market downturn, a job loss, or rising costs, grit gives you the perseverance to stay the course. At West Point, grit was the strongest predictor of success during the toughest training. In retirement, grit is what keeps you moving forward with purpose.

Now add grace. Retirement, like life, doesn't always go according to plan. Maybe you didn't save as much as you hoped. Maybe you had to retire earlier than expected. Grace is what helps you forgive yourself, reset, and adapt without shame or guilt. Grace gives you permission to revise your plan, let go of perfection, and embrace progress over pride.

And then there's gratitude, the quiet power that makes everything better. Gratitude boosts your mood, strengthens relationships, and even improves health. One study found that people with higher gratitude scores had a 9% lower risk of death over four years. In retirement, gratitude can help you celebrate what's going right, shift your focus from "more stuff" to "more freedom," and stay encouraged through every stage of the journey.

You don't have to master all three overnight. Just start where you are. Practice gratitude by noticing small wins. Offer yourself grace when you make a financial misstep. Lean into grit when things feel uncertain but you keep showing up anyway.

Retirement is more than a financial finish line. It's a new phase of life that deserves emotional strength and mental clarity.

> How might living with grace, gratitude, and grit shape your retirement experience? Is there one area where you could offer yourself more grace? And who is one person you could reach out to today to express your gratitude?

Your Retirement Notes

Your Retirement Sketches

CONCLUSION

Sketching forward—living the life you designed

Retirement isn't the final chapter of your story—it's the beginning of a new volume. You've spent your career preparing, saving, and imagining what this stage of life might look like. You've run the numbers, made hard decisions, reflected on your values, and started sketching out your ideal future. Now the pen is in your hand. The canvas is open. Retirement well lived is not just a math problem—it is a balance of art and science. The science is in the planning, but the art is in the living.

The art of retirement is why we wanted to incorporate sketches and artwork into this book. We wanted to draw that connection between a dynamic life and retirement planning. Retirement is also dynamic, it is about making changes through time.

What we covered

Retirement, like a great piece of art, doesn't begin fully formed. It starts with intention, evolves through stages, and comes to life with personal meaning. *Your Retirement Sketchbook* has walked you through the essential strokes, each chapter adding depth and clarity to the picture of your future.

In **Chapter I: Your Relationship with Money**, we explored the foundation—the blank canvas—shaped by your past, your mindset, and your financial beliefs. Before any real sketching begins, you must understand the medium you're working with.

Chapter II: Saving for Retirement was about laying the pencil lines—setting structure and direction. Saving is your framework, the outlines that guide the picture even when you don't see the final form yet.

With **Chapter III: Investing for Retirement**, you began shading—adding dimension and potential. Investing is where risk and return create contrast, turning a simple outline into something dynamic and full of life.

Chapter IV: Getting Ready to Retire marked the moment when the sketch becomes clearer. It's the decision point—the move from preparation to transition. You're no longer just drawing possibilities; you're deciding which lines to ink in permanently.

Chapter V: Preparing Your Retirement Income Plan is where the sketch becomes a blueprint. You start mapping how this art will sustain itself over time—how it will be displayed, supported, and preserved.

Then in **Chapter VI: Managing Retirement Income**, we stepped into the role of a steady hand. This phase is about balance and refinement—making real-time adjustments to preserve the integrity of your work against the erosion of time, inflation, and market uncertainty.

In **Chapter VII: Living in Retirement**, you added color and texture. This is where the drawing comes to life. The routines, passions, people, and places that fill your days—these are the vibrant hues that make the sketch not just complete, but deeply meaningful.

And finally, **Chapter VIII: When Finality Becomes Reality**, reminded us that even the most beautiful artwork has borders. End-of-life planning isn't the end of your legacy—it's the final brushstroke that frames your life's masterpiece and prepares it to be shared, remembered, and preserved.

Now, as you close this book, remember: Your sketchbook is still open. The tools are in your hands. And whether you're adjusting a line, adding new colors, or starting a fresh page, the art of retirement is in living it—authentically, intentionally, and fully.

CONCLUSION

From planning to living

There's a big difference between preparing for retirement and being retired. Most people don't make that transition overnight. You might still work part-time, consult, volunteer, or support your family. You'll adjust your routines, rethink your days, and ask yourself big questions like, "Is this what I want my life to look like?" And that's the beauty of it—retirement is iterative. Like a sketch, it gets refined, erased, and redrawn over time.

Don't wait for perfection before you start living. Perfection is a myth. Progress is real. Give yourself permission to enjoy today, not just protect tomorrow. Spend when it brings you joy. Gift when it reflects your values. Rest when your body calls for it. Work when your purpose demands it. You've earned the flexibility. Now embrace it.

Re-sketching along the way

Just like you revisit a budget or rebalance a portfolio, revisit your life sketch. Your values may evolve. Your family may change. Your health may shift. That's why flexibility is your greatest asset in retirement—not a stock, not a bond, not even a million dollar Roth IRA.

Set aside time each year to ask:

- What still fits in my life?
- What feels forced?
- Where do I need to re-sketch?
- What is going well?
- What is not going well?
- What brought me happiness?

And don't go through it alone. Retirement doesn't have to be a solo art project. Work with advisors, attorneys, medical professionals, and tax planners. Involve your loved ones. Share your vision, your fears, and your goals. The more you articulate your retirement dream, the more likely you are to live it.

Planning for the uncomfortable

Yes, we need to talk about aging. About loss. About frailty. About cognitive decline. These aren't topics we rush toward, but they are realities we can face head-on. And the truth is: When you prepare for decline, you create space for freedom. Structures like powers of attorney, living wills, and automated finances aren't just legal boxes to check—they're gifts to your future self and your family. They say, "I've thought this through. I've got this covered. You don't have to worry."

Preparation is a form of love.

Wealth that can't be measured

Some of the most meaningful parts of retirement won't show up on your net worth statement. Laughter around a dinner table. A grandchild's first recital. A sunrise walk with your spouse. Mentoring someone who reminds you of a younger you. These moments are the dividends of a life well lived.

You don't need to have the most money. You just need enough to live the life you want—and the courage to go live it.

Your retirement sketch starts today

So here we are, at the end of this book. But your sketchbook is far from finished. The rest is up to you.

Take a deep breath. Open your mind. Pick up the pen.

Your retirement isn't something that happens to you. It's something you create. Day by day. Choice by choice. Line by line.

This is your sketchbook. Make it beautiful. Make it yours.

ENDNOTES

Chapter I. Your Relationship with Money

Section 1: Rewirement—Talker Research, 2024, www.nypost.com/2024/08/27/lifestyle/how-americans-are-reinventing-retirement/.

Section 2: Success is Not a Straight Path—Nationwide Shifting Expectations Survey, InvestmentNews, www.investmentnews.com.

Section 4: Understand Your Why—Culture of Purpose Study by Deloitte, www.deloitte.com.

Section 5: Money Memories—Cambridge, www.telegraph.co.uk.

Section 6: Why Spending Feels Like Loss—Daniel Kahneman and Amos Tversky, "Prospect Theory: An Analysis of Decision Under Risk" (1979).

Section 7: Behavioral Biases in Retirement Decision-Making—Daniel Kahneman, "Thinking, Fast and Slow." (2012).

Section 8: Get Connected with Future You—H. Hershfield, D. Goldstein, W. Sharpe, et al., "Increasing saving behavior through age-progressed renderings of the future self," *Journal of Marketing Research*, (2011), pp. 23–37.

Section 9: Balancing Today and Tomorrow—Majority of Americans are More Concerned About Paying Bills Right Now Than Financial Future, www.allianzlife.com.

Chapter II. Saving for Retirement

Section 12: Matching Contributions—Vanguard: www.corporate.vanguard.com/content/dam/corp/research/pdf/are_employers_optimizing_their_401k_match.pdf.

Section 13: Retirement Plan Loans—How America Saves 2024, Vanguard Group, June 2024.

Section 14: Retirement Plan Hardships—Fidelity, Building Financial Futures 2024.

Section 15: Emergency Withdrawals from Retirement Plans—Empower study, "Over 1 in 5 Americans have no emergency savings," www.empower.com.

Section 22: Roth versus Traditional—Tax Policy Center, The Tax Policy Briefing Book, available at: www.taxpolicycenter.org/briefing-book.

Section 23: Social Security Funding—Status of the Social Security and Medicare Programs, A Summary of the 2025 Annual Reports, www.ssa.gov.

Chapter III. Investing for Retirement

Section 26: Bond Ladders—Morningstar.

Section 27: Target Date Funds—JP Morgan, 2024 Defined Contribution Plan Participant Survey Findings, available at: 2024 Defined Contribution Plan Participant Survey Findings.

Section 28: Digital Assets—Investopedia, www.investopedia.com/should-you-invest-in-crypto-for-your-retirement-11713843.

Section 29: Alternative Investments—Pew Research, Alts in Pension Funds, www.pew.org/en/research-and-analysis/issue-briefs/2025/04/increased-risk-complex-investment-landscape-require-prudent-pension-management-practices.

Section 30: Survivor Bias—ETF.com, Swedroe: How Survivorship Biases Happen www.etf.com/sections/index-investor-corner/swedroe-how-survivorship-biases-happen.

Section 31: Home Bias—Moritz Maier and Hendrik Scholz, authors of the January 2019 study "Determinants of Home Bias: Evidence from European Equity Funds."

Section 33: Annuities—Blanchett, David and Finke, Michael S., "Guaranteed Income: A License to Spend," June 28, 2021.

Section 34: Life Insurance in Retirement—Bankrate, "Life Insurance Facts and Statistics 2025," www.bankrate.com/insurance/life-insurance/life-insurance-statistics/#life-insurance-statistics-by-age.

Section 35: LTCI and Hybrid Policies—Urban Institute, What is the Lifetime Risk of Needing and Receiving Long-Term Services and Supports? www.aspe.hhs.gov.

ENDNOTES

Section 36: Cash Value Life Insurance as an Income Tool—Life Insurance as a Retirement Income Tool Russell DeLibero, Ph.D., CFPa, Wade D. Pfau, Ph.D., CFA Financial Services Review 26 (2017), pp. 221–240.

Section 37: Capital Gains Strategies in Retirement—2025 Tax Brackets, The Tax Foundation, www.taxfoundation.org/data/all/federal/2025-tax-brackets/.

Section 38: Working with an Advisor—American College Retirement Income Literacy Research, www.insights.theamericancollege.edu.

Chapter IV. Getting Ready to Retire

Section 39: Envision Your Future—Pengmin Qin, Georg Northoff, "How is our self related to midline regions and the default-mode network?," *NeuroImage* (2011).

Section 40: Retirement Preparedness—www.newsroom.fidelity.com/pressreleases/fidelity-research--america-s-retirement-preparedness-level-declines-amid-continued-volatility/s/c57ac0e9-9c5c-4f5c-938c-cdf82a3aa7b1.

Section 42: Going Beyond Goals to Aspirations—The Impact of Commitment, Accountability, and Written Goals on Goal Achievement Psychology, Dr Gail Matthews, 2007.

Section 43: Issue with Averages in Retirement—Empower Average Retirement Savings 2025 (August 29, 2025), www.empower.com.

Section 44: Pay Yourself First—TIAA 2024 Survey on Gen Z Savings, www.tiaa.org/public/about-tiaa/news-press/press-releases/2024/10-14.

Section 45: Planning Through the Decades—Voya, 2024, www.voya.com/news/2024/07/new-voya-financial-survey-finds-all-generations-wish-they-started-saving-earlier.

Section 46: Paycheck Replacement—Alternate Measures of Replacement Rates for Social Security Benefits and Retirement Income by Andrew G. Biggs and Glenn R. Springstead Social Security Bulletin, www.ssa.gov/policy/docs/ssb/v68n2/v68n2p1.html.

Section 47: The Retirement Change—Center for Ageing Better, Retirement Transitions in Later Life, www.ageing-better.org.uk/news/retirement-transitions-later-life.

Section 49: Part-Time Work in Retirement—Employee Benefit Research Institute. "2022 Retirement Confidence Survey—Expectations About Retirement," Pages 1-2.

Section 51: Forced Retirement—Economic Policy Research Center, "52% of Older Workers Forced into Involuntary Retirement" (October 5, 2018), www.economicpolicyresearch.org.

Section 52: Phased Retirement—Forbes, "Why More People Are Trying a Phased Retirement, 2024," www.forbes.com/sites/nextavenue/2024/08/26/why-more-people-are-trying-a-phased-retirement/.

Section 53: Retirement Planning for Couples versus Singles—Brad Breeding, "Single Seniors May Pay the Price When it Comes to Retirement Savings," My Life Site (October 12, 2021), www.mylifesite.net/blog/post/single-seniors-may-pay-the-price-when-it-comes-to-retirement-savings/.

Chapter V. Preparing Your Retirement Income Plan

Section 54: Retirement Income Planning—BiPartisan Policy Center, www.bipartisanpolicy.org/blog/new-survey-retirement-expectations-dont-match-reality/.

Section 55: Value of Lifetime Income—Jason Fichtner, Executive Director of the Alliance for Lifetime Income's Retirement Income Institute, "Welcome to the Peak 65° Zone: A New Chapter in America's Retirement Landscape."

Section 56: What is Retirement Income—Andrew G. Biggs and Glenn R. Springstead, "Alternate Measures of Replacement Rates for Social Security Benefits and Retirement Income," *Social Security Bulletin* (October, 2008), www.ssa.gov/policy/docs/ssb/v68n2/v68n2p1.html.

Section 59: Bucketing Approach—J. T. Cacioppo, and R. E. Petty, "Effects of message repetition and position on cognitive response, recall, and persuasion," *Journal of Personality and Social Psychology* (1979).

Section 60: Flooring Approach—Biennial Health and Retirement Study (HRS), a nationally representative survey of Americans over age 50 conducted by the University of Michigan.

Section 61: Retirement Risks—Ted Gobout, "Half of Households at Risk of Lower Living Standards in Retirement," ASPPA (May 22, 2023), www.asppa-net.org.

Section 62: Tax Diversification—A Life of Tax: How Much Tax Will Americans Pay Over Their Lifetime? www.self.inc/info/life-of-tax/.

Section 63: Roth Conversions—Peter Thiel Made $5 Billion in a Roth IRA, www.smartasset.com/retirement/peter-thiel-5-billion-no-taxes-roth-ira.

Section 64: Retirement Planning for Small Business Owners—Choosing a Retirement Solution for Your Small Business, www.dol.gov/sites/dolgov/files/EBSA/about-ebsa/our-activities/resource-center/publications/small-business-retirement-solutions-information-booklet-2023.pdf.

Chapter VI. Managing Retirement Income

Section 65: Public Policy Risk—2024 National Institute on Retirement Security, www.nirsonline.org/wp-content/uploads/2024/02/FINAL-2024-Public-Opinion-Research.pdf.

Section 66: Taxes in Retirement—Investment Accounts, Retirement Accounts, www.finra.org.

Section 67: Knowledge in Retirement—American College of Financial Services 2024 Retirement Literacy Survey, www.theamericancollege.edu/knowledge-hub/insights/unveiling-results-from-the-retirement-income-literacy-study.

Section 68: When to Retire—NerdWallet, MassMutual Survey 2024, www.nerdwallet.com/article/investing/social-security/average-retirement-age-us.

Section 69: Power of Delaying Retirement—John Manganaro, "Delayed Retirements Remain Elusive for Most Americans," Think Advisor (April 25, 2024), www.thinkadvisor.com/2024/04/25/delayed-retirements-remain-elusive-for-most-americans/.

Section 70: Guardrails—William J. Klinger, "Guardrails to Prevent Potential Retirement Portfolio Failure," *Journal of Financial Planning* (2016).

Section 71: Adaptive Spending—David M. Blanchett and Larry R. Frank, Sr., "A Dynamic and Adaptive Approach to Distribution Planning and Monitoring," *Journal of Financial Planning* (April 2009).

Section 72: Smart Income—Vanguard 2024, "How America Saves 2024," www.corporate.vanguard.com/content/dam/corp/research/pdf/how_america_saves_report_2024.pdf.

Section 73: When to Claim Social Security—Bob Carlson, "Here's More Evidence in Favor of Delaying Social Security Benefits," *Forbes* (February 24, 2023).

Section 74: Taxation of Social Security—Andy Markowitz, "How is Social Security Taxed?" AARP (October 10, 2018), www.aarp.org.

Section 75: Power of Delaying Social Security—Andy Markowitz, "3 Reasons to Claim Social Security Early," www.aarp.org/social-security/claim-benefits-early-or-late/.

Section 76: Rule 72(t) Penalty Taxes—Substantially Equal Periodic Payments, www.irs.gov.

Section 77: Permission to Spend—Spending Trajectories After Age 65, www.rand.org/pubs/research_reports/RRA2355-1.html.

Section 78: Traveling in Retirement—2024 Travel Trends, www.aarp.org/pri/topics/social-leisure/travel/2024-travel-trends.html.

Section 79: IRMAA—How to Request an Adjustment to Your IRMAA Medicare Premium, www.ncoa.org.

Section 80: RMDs—Retirement Topics, Required Minimum Distributions (RMDs), www.irs.gov.

Section 81: Reverse Mortgages—www.mercatus.org/research/working-papers/retire-house-possible-use-reverse-mortgages-enhance-retirement-security.

Section 82: Tapping Home Equity in Retirement—www.nrmlaonline.org/wp-content/uploads/2016/03/HECM-Survey-Report-10-31-15-Final-Draft.pdf.

Section 83: Lines of Credit—Karan Kaul and Linna Zhu, "More Older Americans Are Drawing Wealth from Their Home Equity, but Racial Gaps Persist," www.urban.org; Profiling Retirees Who Carry too Much Debt, www.crr.bc.edu.

Section 84: Navigating Sequence Risk—John Rekenthaler, "Sequence Risk During Retirement," *Morningstar* (February 15, 2024), www.morningstar.com.

Section 85: Time Segmentation— LIMRA, "More Than Half of All U.S. Workers Have Difficulty Understanding Retirement Savings in Terms of Future Monthly Income" (September 25, 2018), www.limra.com.

Section 86: Retirement Planning Checkups—FINRA, www.finra.org/investors/insights/annual-401k-checkup.

Chapter VII. Living In Retirement

Section 87: Retirement is Not Binary—Peter Halama et al., "Meaning making in retirement transition: a qualitative inquiry into Slovak retirees," *International Journal of Qualitative Studies on Health and Well-being* (2021).

ENDNOTES

Section 88: Stop Saving Right Before Retirement—www.nber.org/digest/may18/working-longer-can-sharply-raise-retirement-income.

Section 89: Retirement Housing—Business Wire, "Older Homeowners Least Likely Cohort to Consider Tapping into Home Equity Despite Record Property Values, According to New Research from FAR," (July 26, 2022).

Section 90: Downsizing in Retirement—www.seniorliving.org/housing/downsizing/.

Section 91: Managing Debt in Retirement—NWM Planning and Progress Study 2024, www.news.northwesternmutual.com/planning-and-progress-study-2024.

Section 92: Continuing Care Retirement Communities—www.mylifesite.net/blog/post/2019-mylifesite-consumer-survey-report/.

Section 93: Inflation—Pew Research Center, "Public's Positive Economic Ratings Slip; Inflation Still Widely Viewed as Major Problem" (May 23, 2024), www.pewresearch.org.

Section 94: The Four Percent Finding—Christine Benz, Amy C. Arnott, Jason Kephart, "Morningstar's Retirement Income Research: Reevaluating the 4% Withdrawal Rule," *Morningstar* (March 3, 2025).

Section 97: Silver Divorce—Sharon Jayson, "Divorce Skyrocketing Among Aging Boomers," www.aarp.org.

Section 98: Social Network in Retirement—Social Relationships and Epigenetic Aging in Older Adulthood: Results from the Health and Retirement Study (2023), www.sciencedirect.com.

Section 99: Changing Interest Rates—Donna Fuscaldo and Daniel Bortz, "Retired? Winners and Losers of the Fed's Latest Rate Cut," AARP (September 1, 2024), www.aarp.org.

Section 100: Refilling Buckets—Morningstar Research 2023: A Comparative Study of Retirement-Income Bucket Strategies (June 22, 2023), www.morningstar.com.

Section 101: Medicare—Andrew Marden, "Americans Don't Know Much About Medicare, Survey Finds," nerdwallet (October 10, 2023), www.nerdwallet.com.

Section 102: Aging in Place—AARP Home and Community Preferences Survey, www.aarp.org.

Section 103: Aging and Frailty—National Institute of Health. Physical Frailty: ICFSR International Clinical Practice Guidelines for Identification and Management.

Section 104: Health is Wealth—www.massmutual.com/about-us/news-and-press-releases/press-releases/2024/03/massmutual-research-most-retirees-are-happier-in-retirement.

Section 105: Long-term Caregivers—The Long-Term Care Poll, www.longtermcarepoll.org/report-long-term-care-in-america-expectations-and-reality.

Section 106: Cognitive Decline and Financial Decision Making—Alzheimer's Organization, Mild Cognitive Impairment, www.alzheimers.gov/alzheimers-dementias/mild-cognitive-impairment.

Section 107: Pet Care and Planning in Retirement—Nancy Walecki, "Animal companions help their owners live longer, happier lives," *Harvard Magazine* (April 11, 2023), www.harvardmagazine.com.

Section 108: Second Careers—Pew Research Center, www.pewresearch.org/social-trends/2023/12/14/the-growth-of-the-older-workforce/.

Section 109: Finding Meaning in Retirement—10 Facts About the Financial Fragility of Retirees in the Post-Pandemic Economy (November 2024), www.transamericainstitute.org/research/publications/details/retirees-personal-finance-research-press-release-2024.

Chapter VIII. When Finality Becomes Reality

Section 110: Estate Planning Basics—Jamie Hopkins, "Americans Value Digital Assets at $191,516, But Awareness Still Lags," *Forbes* (December 17, 2024), www.forbes.com.

Section 112: Digital Estate Planning Process—Bryn Mawr Trust 2024 Digital Estate Survey, www.bmt.com/news-insights-events/bryn-mawr-trust-survey/.

Section 113: Inherited Accounts—IRS, www.irs.gov/retirement-plans/plan-participant-employee/retirement-topics-beneficiary.

Section 114: Trusts: Revocable versus Irrevocable—Sarah Jones, "Estate Planning Statistics to Read before Writing Your Will," LegalZoom www.legalzoom.com/articles/estate-planning-statistics.

Section 115: Prepare for a Good End of Life—Ryan Sutherland, "Dying Well-Informed: The Need for Better Clinical Education Surrounding Facilitating End-of-Life Conversations," *The Yale Journal of Biology and Medicine* (December, 2019).

Section 116: Medicaid Spend Down—American Academy of Actuaries, "Medicaid and Long-Term Care Insurance" (February 25, 2019), www.actuary.org.

Section 117: Long-Term Care Delivery—Administration for Community Living, "How much care will you need?" (February 18, 2020), www.acl.gov.

Section 118: Longevity—Rob Williams, "Guide on Taking Social Security: 62 vs. 67 vs. 70," www.schwab.com/learn/story/guide-on-taking-social-security.

Section 119: Elder Abuse—Get the Facts on Elder Abuse, NCO (July 8, 2024), www.ncoa.org/article/get-the-facts-on-elder-abuse/.

Section 120: Medicaid—Preeti Vankar, "Total Medicaid Enrollment from 1966 to 2023," Statista (July 3, 2025), www.statista.com.

Section 121: Leaving a Legacy—www.askalicetang.com/womens-million-dollar-conversations/.

Section 122: Giving Back: Charitable Giving—Joseph F. Coughlin, PhD, "8,000 Days," Hartford Funds (March, 2025), www.hartfordfunds.com.

Section 123: Qualified Charitable Distributions—IRS, www.irs.gov/newsroom/qualified-charitable-distributions-allow-eligible-ira-owners-up-to-100000-in-tax-free-gifts-to-charity.

Section 124: Giving to Grandchildren—Amie Clark, "Grandparents Spend an Average of $4,000 a Year on Grandkids," The Senior List (November 20, 2024), www.theseniorlist.com.

Section 125: The G3 Summit—Maureen Salamon, "Gratitude enhances health, brings happiness—and may even lengthen lives," *Harvard Health Publishing* (September 11, 2024), www.health.harvard.edu.

ACKNOWLEDGMENTS

Creating *Your Retirement Sketchbook* has been a journey filled with learning, laughter, late nights, and a lot of love. I'm grateful to every person who helped bring this book to life.

First, to my family—the foundation under every step I take. Specifically, thanks to my mom Jane, dad Eric, my sisters, my wife Kathy, and our kids—thank you for your love, patience, and constant support. You are the reason behind everything I do.

A heartfelt thanks to the teams at WSFS and Bryn Mawr Trust for your leadership and inspiration, and to the FinServ Foundation community—mentors, volunteers, and Fellows—for the work you do to shape the next generation of leaders.

—Jamie

Writing *Your Retirement Sketchbook* has been an incredible experience. As my first book, it has challenged me, inspired me, and reminded me of the power of collaboration. I am deeply grateful to everyone who played a role in bringing this book to life.

To my parents and family: thank you for your unwavering support and encouragement.

To my work family, including the Endeavor Law team, Endeavor Retirement team, partners and clients: thank you for teaching me that simplicity is an essential ingredient to any good recipe. Your support, partnership, friendship and feedback—even when critical—is always valued and appreciated.

To my co-author, Jamie Hopkins: thank you for your creativity and dedication to this project. This book is a testament to what can happen when ideas and passion come together.

Finally, to every reader who picks up this book—thank you for trusting us to be part of your retirement journey. My hope is that these pages empower you to design a life you love.

And, of course, to Sunny and Sadie: Those extra paws on the keyboard helped bring these pages to life!

—**Bonnie**

A heartfelt thank you to Grace for infusing creativity into this project and bringing each concept to life with such artistry. Your patience, collaboration, and imaginative spirit made this book possible.

ABOUT THE AUTHORS

Jamie Hopkins is a best-selling author, solutions builder, runner and financial professional. Jamie is the Chief Wealth Officer, WSFS Bank, CEO of Bryn Mawr Trust Advisors, and president of FinServ Foundation. He is a professor at Creighton University and an adjunct professor of retirement planning at The American College of Financial Services where he helped co-create the RICP designation. He is a contributor to *Forbes* and has been elected to the Fellows of the American Bar Foundation. He also was selected as one of the top 40 financial service professionals under the age of 40 by *InvestmentNews* and one of the top 40 young attorneys by The American Bar Association. Jamie was also named as the RIA thought leader of the year by WealthManagement.com.

Bonnie Treichel, Esq. is the Founder of Endeavor Law and the Founder and Chief Solutions Officer of Endeavor Retirement, a consulting firm dedicated to solving problems for plan sponsors, advisors, and service providers in the retirement plan industry. She is a nationally recognized speaker and thought leader on retirement plan governance and best practices. Bonnie serves on the Board of the FinServ Foundation and has been honored with several national awards, including *InvestmentNews* 40 Under 40 (2023) and the ABA's On the Rise—Top 40 Young Lawyers Award (2022). Outside of work, Bonnie enjoys traveling, running, cycling, volunteering with Make-A-Wish, and spending time with her golden retrievers, Sadie and Sunny.